"This is a superbly edited volume which breaks new ground in a significant area that has gone largely overlooked for far too long. Each [chapter] makes an interesting and useful contribution; they all add up to stimulating and insightful reading. The quality of scholarship is excellent and represents varying methodologies and paradigms so much a part of today's study of complex interpersonal and mediated communication processes. The treatment of the subject is comprehensive—all important topics are discussed with ample examples and recent evidence. This book raises key issues that should generate considerable attention and discussion."
Timothy P. Meyer, PhD, Professor, Department of Communication and the Arts, University of Wisconsin at Green Bay

"A worthy collection covering many important bases. This anthology should be in the hands of anyone concerned with the interaction between subcultural and mainstream interests."
Sari Thomas, PhD, Director, Institute of Culture and Communication, Department of Radio-Television-Film, Temple University, Philadelphia, Pennsylvania

"This volume calls attention to the fact that we know little about mass media's role in the construction of sexual identities. Traditional mass media research has neglected this important issue particularly where lesbians and gay men are concerned. These [chapters] successfully whet our appetites and will hopefully stimulate others to explore the many questions that remain unanswered."
R. Jeffrey Ringer, PhD, Chair of the Caucus on Gay and Lesbian Concerns of the Speech Communication Association; Co-founder and Chair, Central Minnesota AIDS Project, St. Cloud, Minnesota

Gay People, Sex, and the Media

Gay People, Sex, and the Media

Michelle A. Wolf, PhD
Alfred P. Kielwasser, MA
Editors

Gay People, Sex, and the Media, edited by Michelle A. Wolf and Alfred P. Kielwasser, was simultaneously issued by The Haworth Press, Inc., under the same title, as a special issue of *Journal of Homosexuality*, Volume 21, Numbers 1/2 1991, John De Cecco, Editor.

Harrington Park Press
New York • London

ISBN 0-918393-77-9

Published by

Harrington Park Press, 10 Alice Street, Binghamton, NY 13904-1580
EUROSPAN/Harrington, 3 Henrietta Street, London WC2E 8LU England

Harrington Park Press is a subsidiary of The Haworth Press, Inc., 10 Alice Street, Binghamton, NY 13904-1580.

Gay People, Sex, and the Media was originally published as *Journal of Homosexuality*, Volume 21, Numbers 1/2 1991.

Cover design by Marshall Andrews.

Library of Congress Cataloging-in-Publication Data

Gay people, sex, and the media / Michelle A. Wolf, Alfred P. Kielwasser, editors.
  p. cm.
  Includes bibliographical references.
  ISBN 0-918393-77-9 (alk. paper)
  1. Mass media and sex. 2. Gays. I. Kielwasser, Alfred P.
P96.S45G3 1991
302.23′08′664 — dc20

91-380
CIP

CONTENTS

Preface   1
       James Lull, PhD

Acknowledgments   5

Introduction: The Body Electric — Human Sexuality
  and Mass Media   7
       Michelle A. Wolf, PhD
       Alfred P. Kielwasser, MA

GAYS, LESBIANS, AND POPULAR CULTURE

Out of the Mainstream: Sexual Minorities and the Mass
  Media   19
       Larry Gross, PhD

AIDS AND THE MASS MEDIA

Sensationalism or Sensitivity: Use of Words in Stories
  on Acquired Immune Deficiency Syndrome (AIDS)
  by Associated Press Videotext   47
       Bruce E. Drushel

The Important Role of Mass Media in the Diffusion
  of Accurate Information About AIDS   63
       Kathleen K. Reardon, PhD
       Jean L. Richardson, PhD

RESEARCH ON ADOLESCENT SEXUAL
  SOCIALIZATION

Television Viewing and Adolescents' Sexual Behavior   77
       Jane D. Brown, PhD
       Susan F. Newcomer, PhD

Television Viewing and Early Initiation of Sexual
Intercourse: Is There a Link?   93
          James L. Peterson, PhD
          Kristin A. Moore, PhD
          Frank F. Furstenberg, Jr., PhD

INTERPRETING CONTENT/CONSTRUCTING
MEANING

Sex and Genre on Prime Time   119
          Corless Smith, PhD

Dr. Ruth Westheimer: Upsetting the Normalcy
of the Late-Night Talk Show   139
          Rodney A. Buxton, MA

Of Mice and Men: An Introduction to Mouseology Or, Anal
Eroticism and Disney   155
          Arthur Asa Berger, PhD

The Magazine of a Sadomasochism Club: The Tie That
Binds   167
          Rick Houlberg, PhD

The Gay Voice in Popular Music: A Social Value Model
Analysis of "Don't Leave Me This Way"   185
          R. Brian Attig, MA

SEXUAL MINORITIES AND COMMUNICATION LAW

Lesbian and Gay Rights as a Free Speech Issue: A Review
of Relevant Caselaw   203
          Paul Siegel, PhD

BIBLIOGRAPHY

Gays, Lesbians, and the Media: A Selected Bibliography   261
          Fred Fejes, PhD

ILLUSTRATIONS

Fear — Deception — Irrationality (mixed media photographic
   print with oils) *and*

We Watch Television (multiple negative silver print)   279
   Gary Burgstedt, MFA

Self-Fusion (photograph)   283
   Robin Parker Garcia

ABOUT THE EDITORS

Michelle A. Wolf, PhD, is Associate Professor of Broadcast Communication Arts at San Francisco State University. She has also taught at the University of Texas at Austin and the University of Massachusetts, Amherst. Her classroom teaching experiences include instruction in interpersonal, public, and mass communication. Dr. Wolf continues to write about various aspects of her more primary research interest in relationships between theory and method in the study of human communication processes, particularly in the context of mediated communication. She is currently studying the intrapersonal functions of popular music and is conducting field work to document the complex tactics involved in audience usage of popular television texts.

Alfred P. Kielwasser, MA, currently an instructor at the University of San Francisco, San Francisco, California, has taught a wide range of courses on interpersonal and mass communication at San Francisco State University and the University of San Francisco. He has written about media uses and gratifications, children and television, social cognition, and naturalistic inquiry. His current research interests include the many issues that evolve out of exploring gay and lesbian culture from a communication perspective. He is also researching the intrapersonal dynamics of human communication and is conducting field research designed to integrate critical and empirical lines of inquiry. He continues his ongoing search for greater understanding of the complex relationships, unique to communication research, between theory and method.

The publisher notes thanks and appreciation for Rick X and the cable show "The Closet Case Show" (CCTV) of New York City for his inspiring and responsible leadership in the gay media.

Gay People, Sex,
and the Media

Preface

In my neighborhood, the feared sexual disease of the 1980s is SIDA (Sindroma Inmune Deficiencia Adquirida), known to non-Spanish speakers as AIDS. Describing the disease with a different language is but one discursive element that separates the Hispanic community from the rest of San Francisco. The lead article in this month's issue of *El Tecolote*, one of San Francisco's Spanish-language newspapers, calls attention not only to the medical devastations of the disease, but to the intercultural battle that is waged in the struggle for prevention and treatment of SIDA. The article points out that medical services and information campaigns designed to deal with SIDA appeal primarily to members of the City's *Anglo* gay community, a well-organized, vocal, politically-potent group—a dominant subculture. Peculiarities of Latino culture, including especially the inestimable impact of Catholicism and *machismo* on the creation and intensification of guilt feelings around gayness, limit the willingness of many SIDA sufferers to seek treatment even as they continue to take sexual risks. These factors require a culturally-specific response from the medical community and from programmers of the mass media.

Splashed across the pages of the *San Francisco Examiner* and *Chronicle* at the same time is a story about a related local struggle. This one developed between the gay community in San Francisco and the NBC television network. Gay activists protested the filming of an episode of a new drama series, Midnight Caller, a story that was based on the behavior of a bisexual man with AIDS who willfully sought to infect his sexual partners. Protestors said that by airing the program, NBC was promoting a "false and vicious image of people living with AIDS."

These cases reflect the very issues that concern the contributors to this volume—images, the role of technology in the distribution of images, and the psychological, sociological, and cultural disposi-

1

tion of mediated imagery—the invisible places where images and audiences meet. The mass media regularly gush images of sexuality, sex, sexiness, of romance and relationships, of pleasures, of SIDA and AIDS—imagery that is created for popular consumption and sold for profit. Imagery that promotes formation of what the editors call a "sexual culture." Mediated imagery that defines sex and prescribes preferred sexual behavior while at the same time serves it up as a resource to be put to use by media consumers— audience members—in ways that satisfy their needs and interests.

We are concerned here with dimensions of a controversial content area that is embedded within a social process commonly known as "mass communication"—a descriptor that names an academic field as well. Even in its young age, scholarship in mass communication is today undergoing serious reconsideration that focuses largely on the adequacy of research methodology. At the heart of the dispute is the problem of coming to terms with "audience"— viewers, listeners, readers—the most evasive component of any mass communication system. In the examples I used at the beginning of this brief piece, for instance, the most compelling issues ultimately revolve around consideration of the force of media texts *as they interact with audiences.* How do Latinos cope with Anglo-oriented messages? How would the general public react to a portrayal of an AIDS victim as a murderer where the weapon is the disease itself? These are concrete empirical questions that require imaginative research strategies and acceptance of diverse methodological contributions.

The aforementioned cases help illustrate the fact that the limitations of traditional approaches to doing research in mass communication may indeed be most apparent when we study how sexual identities are formed and how sexual activity is carried out. There may exist no more fundamental yet complex social processes. And while we *know* that the mass media somehow play a central role in the way societies develop sexual awareness and cultivate particular lifestyles, we are far less certain of *how* social actors actually construct their own sexual identities and come to perceive the sexual lives of others.

These social processes operate within a matrix of interdependent influences. The symbolic agenda of the mass media, the subtleties and nuances of interpersonal networks, the impact of policy priorities of social institutions, and the specific requirements of cultural groups in their roles as media audience members all intermesh to form fragile sexual (and all other) identities. This blending of influences promotes patterns of thinking and acting that coalesce in ways that characterize not only mainstream culture, but subcultures too. The opaque, hegemonic, and dynamic character of these considerations is so empirically elusive that we mislead ourselves by relying on the practices of traditional social science to somehow reveal the statuses and processes that influence sexual identities and behavior. The reasonable call now is for theoretical and methodological diversity, integration, and appreciation.

The collection of studies and essays that follows, therefore, can be seen as part of a larger debate now going on in the field of "media studies" or "mass communication," exacerbated here by the importance of the topic. Relevant research issues addressed in the following pages run the gamut of methodological possibilities — from textual and discourse analyses of sexually-oriented material to empirical studies of the diffusion of sex information and processes of socialization to sexual identities and roles, together with historical and critical evaluations and recommendations regarding legal and policy implications. The dialogue that these analyses will stimulate through distribution of this volume (a mass communication process itself!) is more than worthy.

Methodological and theoretical advances and integrations aside, however, the mysteries that are contained within the themes featured in the pages that follow will persist. We can readily observe, for instance, that the ideological hegemony of mass media-reinforced mainstream values pertaining to the formation of sexual identity often clashes head on with the emotional and physical priorities and the behavioral agenda of audience members. Men and women construct their sexual identities in ways that are far more diverse than the range of prescriptions that are presented on the popular media would predict. Development of one's sexual identity is an utterly personal matter, but one that is inherently social and, as my description of the frustrations of the Latino community indicates, is furthermore characterized and differentiated by emotionally-charged cultural values and practices. Now, in the era of electronic media, theoretical relationships that stand among processes of sexual identity formation, consciousness formation generally, and patterns of everyday life are sufficiently intriguing to have encouraged a number of scholars from diverse disciplines, representing a variety of methodological orientations and theoretical positions, to produce the work that appears herein. I trust that the reader will benefit greatly from this thoughtful collection of essays, a compilation that is especially powerful because of its synthesis of territories that are rarely combined.

James Lull, PhD
San Jose, CA

Acknowledgments

We would like to extend special thanks to the following individuals who offered their time and expertise as manuscript submission reviewers: Alison Alexander, Department of Communication Studies, University of Massachusetts (Amherst); Ann Auleb, Department of Biology, San Francisco State University; Herb Kaplan, Department of Broadcast Communication Arts, San Francisco State University; Gregory Kendrick, Department of History, University of California (Los Angeles); Maia Krache, KQED, Incorporated, San Francisco; Dafna Lemish, Institute for the Study of Media and Family, Israel; James Lull, Department of Radio-TV-Film, San Jose State University; Timothy P. Meyer, College of Communication, University of Wisconsin at Green Bay; Deanna Morris, Department of Broadcast Communication Arts, San Francisco State University; Susan Douglas Ryan, Department of Broadcast Communication Arts, San Francisco State University; Janellen Smith, Department of Mass Communication, Menlo College; and Jeff Weintraub.

In addition to the indispensable advice of our reviewers, we have also enjoyed the assistance of many other colleagues and friends. Two administrators in particular provided supportive, stimulating environments for our research and teaching. Their often invisible hard work helped to make our own work possible. We extend our appreciation to Ronald J. Compesi, Chair, Department of Broadcast Communication Arts, San Francisco State University, and Steven C. Runyon, Director, Mass Media Studies Program, University of San Francisco.

This project would not exist except for the interest and commitment of John P. De Cecco, Director, Center for Research and Education in Sexuality, San Francisco State University. We continually benefited from his gentle guidance as we struggled through editorial

5

tasks that were new to us and that, just as he predicted, took more time than we ever anticipated.

We would also like to thank Gary Borgstedt for contributing his mixed-media illustrations toward the enhancement of this collection; Robin Parker Garcia for her photograph; James Lull, for adding our Preface to his many writing commitments; and, of course, our contributing authors, for the most obvious reasons of all.

Finally, to our families and friends, we owe recognition and gratitude for more than just their input into this project. These individuals continue to stand with us through so many academic expeditions, supporting whatever happens to be "the new thing that Al and Michelle are working on." In particular, our deepest thanks and love belong to Jacqueline I. Kielwasser, Mark J. Theis, Patricia J. Paige, Patricia Aguilera, Michelle Ryan, Robin Scammell, Paul Glancy, Sharyn Wolf, Debbie Wolf, and David J. Searles.

Introduction:
The Body Electric —
Human Sexuality and Mass Media

Michelle A. Wolf, PhD

San Francisco State University

Alfred P. Kielwasser, MA

San Francisco, CA

I sing the body electric,
The armies of those I love engirth me and I engirth them,
They will not let me off till I go with them, respond to them,
And discorrupt them, and charge them full with the charge
of the soul.

— Walt Whitman, *Leaves of Grass*

Writing the introduction to a recent anthology covering the rather broad area of human communication, James Anderson reflects on the principles guiding his editorial work:

Michelle A. Wolf is Professor of Broadcast Communication Arts at San Francisco State University.

Correspondence may be directed to Professor Wolf at the Broadcast Communication Arts Department, 1600 Holloway Avenue, San Francisco State University, San Francisco, CA 94132.

Alfred P. Kielwasser has taught a wide variety of courses on interpersonal and mass communication at San Francisco State University and at The University of San Francisco.

Correspondence may be directed to Mr. Kielwasser at 163 Park Street, San Francisco, CA 94110-5835.

There has been much criticism, some of it justified, of professional academics writing only to other professional academics and then only to those of their own kind. There has developed in communication and other disciplines a "boutiques of inquiry" mentality. Articles are written in coded language about issues empowered by members with the righteousness of incised perspectives. In spite of my frank language, there is clear value in such articles for some of the work that must be done in this and every other field of inquiry. There is other work to be done, however. (1988, p. 11)

That other work to which Anderson refers involved bringing together diverse papers and attempting to make them accessible to a wider, interested audience. In many ways, the editorial tasks associated with creating our collection were guided by a similar principle. Yet Anderson's audience remained, in the end, a relatively homogeneous one, that of communication scholars. And while the contributors to our own collection of articles are also scholars, we envision that their work will be read — and found useful — by a truly diverse range of readers.

Both mass communication and human sexuality are enormously complex and pervasive processes; both are relentlessly influential in the life cycle of the individual. Ironically, understanding the interactions of these processes is not facilitated by their ubiquity. One-time media guru Marshall McLuhan likened this situation to that of a fish in water (McLuhan & Fiore, 1968). The fish, he explained, will be the last creature to discover water. In fact, water is an invisible environment for the fish precisely because of its obvious ubiquity. We also tend to remain unaware of (or perhaps ignore) the more routine and commonplace features of our daily lives. We continuously immerse ourselves in television, radio, films, newspapers, magazines, and recorded music, but rarely pause to consider the implications of these ongoing media activities.

The mass media are indeed everywhere. They form a unique electrified environment that many of us — much like McLuhan's fish — have yet to truly discover. Our title for this introduction, borrowed from Walt Whitman's poem, "I Sing the Body Electric," underscores this observation. Our sexual selves — in body and mind — have taken on fantastically new (and often disturbing) configurations through the complicated influences of the electronic media that we so avidly consume. To sample the contours of this electric ecology, consider a few simple facts:

- In the United States, more households have television sets than have refrigerators or indoor plumbing (National Institute of Mental Health, 1983, p. 23). *Excluding* Alaska and Hawaii, the number of U.S. households with television is estimated to be 88,600,000 (Woodhead, 1988, p. 13).
- A greater percentage of the U.S. Gross National Product comes from activities involving the creation and exchange of information than from manufacturing products (Berger, 1988, p. 319).
- About 99% of U. S. homes have radios (Jamieson & Campbell, 1988, p. 4).
- Roughly 60% of all households in the U.S. have at least one videocassette recorder; only 4% of these households contained a videocassette recorder six years ago (Nielsen Media Research, 1988, p. 2).
- Over 55% of the U.S. households with television have subscribed to cable television services; that's about 50,241,840 households (Nielsen Media Research, 1989, p. 4).
- Television is similarly popular around the world. For example, 90 to 99% of all homes in the following countries have television sets: Belgium, Luxembourg, Canada, France, Ireland, Italy, Japan, Sweden, Switzerland, United Kingdom and West Germany (Liebert & Sprafkin, 1988, p. 3).
- It is estimated that by the time a child born today reaches 18 years of age, she or he will have spent more time watching television than engaging in any other single activity besides sleep (Liebert & Sprafkin, 1988, p. ix).
- *Playboy* and *Penthouse* are the most widely-read magazines on American college campuses (Hiebert & Ruess, 1988, p. 162).
- Sexually-explicit videocassettes account for at least 15% to 25% of total videocassette sales. Only one of every four videocassette distributors does not carry X-Rated videotapes (Brown, 1988/1986, pp. 168-169).

- In a 1986 Harris survey of 1,000 adolescents, television was ranked fourth as a source of sex information, followed only by friends, parents, and courses at school (Liebert & Sprafkin, 1988, p. 203).
- The late 1980s have been marked by press references to a current frenzy in the film industry to engage homosexual issues and themes, intensifying public concern over the implications of gay and lesbian media portrayals (Weiss, 1986, p. 4; cf. Dyer, 1984; Lippe, 1986; Russo, 1988).
- Supermarkets around the country remain well-stocked with a variety of tabloids catering to a presumed interest in the sexually sensational. Articles report such diverse "news" as "Radio Fans Turned Off by Macho Dad's Sex Swap: Deejay Who Charmed the Ladies Becomes One!" (*Weekly World News*, 1988), "Gay Bigfoot Molesting Little Boys" (*National Examiner*, 1985) and "Gay Hooker Ring Tours White House" (*The Sun*, 1989).

Clearly, this list could go on. But the point here, however obvious, resonates for all of us: It is not possible for the forces and processes of mass communication to have *no* effect on our lives. Naturally, then, it is not possible for these same processes to have *no* effect on the sexual aspects of our lives. The question is not *whether* mass communication and human sexuality processes interact, but, more properly, how and why such interactions occur. The issues addressed in the series of articles that follows concern how and why the mass media and mass communication are used to construct mediated sexual realities and help to inform our sexual identities.

Because this collection was largely stimulated by our perceived demand for a group of papers that cuts across many of the boundaries found in more traditional publications on sexuality and mass communication, the articles cover a broad range of sexual identity, socialization, and mass communication issues and represent a variety of theoretical and methodological orientations. As such, they cannot be neatly grouped into discrete and conceptually-consistent or convenient categories. This special issue begins with a discussion and analysis of several concerns regarding minority perspectives in the context of the study of mass media content and effects.

Larry Gross proposes that the world is becoming a Leviathan, a huge monster with telecommunications as its nervous system. After discussing how television cultivates mainstream cultural values, Gross argues that minority images are, at best, poorly represented, and laments the fact that television maintains a presumably "normal" gender system in which lesbians and gays are belittled, subverted and ignored. To deal with this offensive situation, he calls for alternative mass media channels and continued demand for more equitable mediated images.

While Gross believes that the AIDS epidemic has expanded the array of negative mediated images of lesbians and gays, Bruce Drushell found little evidence for this claim in his study of the content of Associated Press Videotext reports on the disease. Although Drushell's analysis of words used in AIDS reports by Associated Press journalists did not reveal unusual distortion or overemphasis of homosexuals as perpetrators of the disease, he does not suggest that such distortion is nonexistent. Apparently, if it does occur, such bias is probably the result of more subtle factors than the simple choice of words (for example, decisions by mass media gatekeepers to use sensational story headlines and photographs, and to perpetuate the popular view of AIDS as a decontextualized collection of tragic deaths).

In another analysis of mediated information about AIDS, Kathleen Reardon and Jean Richardson studied individuals with an elevated risk of AIDS-related symptoms and doctors who treat AIDS patients. The two researchers focused on how members of these different populations perceived the gravity of the AIDS threat, took measures to protect themselves and others against AIDS, and evaluated the adequacy of media coverage of the disease. Finding little consensus between subject groups in these three areas, the authors claim that the AIDS epidemic poses a massive challenge for the mass media to disseminate more accurate information.

The next two articles address relationships between mass media content (primarily television) and sexual socialization. The research report of Jane Brown and Susan Newcomer, as well as the article by James Peterson, Kristen Moore, and Frank Furstenberg, Jr., are both quantitative studies of relationships between television usage and the initiation of adolescent heterosexual intercourse. Though the data that they analyzed did reveal a link between television usage and sexual intercourse, Brown and Newcomer's ambitious desire to establish directional causality was not realized. Still, the authors legitimately challenge television creators to offer more realistic and socially responsible portrayals of heterosexual practices, including the use of contraceptive devices and the integration of educational messages about pregnancy. Peterson, Moore, and Furstenberg explore the same variables by using data from a longitudinal study of the well-being of children in the United States, but find no support for any significant relationships between the quality and quantity of sexually-oriented television content and early initiation of sexual intercourse. These data, which indirectly call into question the findings of Brown and Newcomer, are explored in the context of methodological and theoretical issues.

Several of the authors in this issue directly explore and deconstruct the content of mass media. Five such papers were accepted, in part, because of their unique approaches to mass media texts. Corless Smith argues that while sexual activity is not explicitly represented on prime time network television, it is *suggested* in distinctly different forms that vary according to program genre (e.g., situation comedies explore the realm of taboo, while detective shows display the sexual underworld). According to Smith, images that transcend the constraints of genre are more useful objects for critical analysis. Further exploring televised content, Rodney Buxton uses the concepts of dialogue and celebrity discourse to examine the ideological complexity of a particular genre, late-night talk/variety programs. Using as examples selections from some recent television programs that address the relatively new media celebrity Dr. Ruth Westheimer, Buxton argues that his ideological analysis makes a significant contribution that goes beyond the more predominant, traditional studies of this genre as an economic vehicle for the promotion of popular culture.

Based on a very different (and slightly off-beat) critical framework, Arthur Asa Berger offers his contribution to the study of popular culture mice, or "mouse-ology" according to his neologism. Comparing Disney's Mickey Mouse (who, according to the author, extends to the American psyche) to Herriman's Krazy Kat, Berger considers the sexual-symbolic significance of the two comic characters and their creators. An equally singular study of mediated content is Rick Houlberg's report on the monthly magazine of a sadomasochism club. Based on his descriptive analysis of 47 issues of the magazine, a review of the results of a readership survey, and data from non-participant observation of some of the club's activities, Houlberg explores a number of issues confronted by individuals whose sexual orientations are generally perceived as falling out of the mainstream. This area of research, one that has been largely neglected by mass media researchers, offers unique opportunities to explore sexual identity and the creation of alternative forms of social reality and shared meaning through mass communication.

In the fifth and final critical analysis of mass communication content, R. Brian Attig considers the gay voice in popular music as a vehicle for affecting social values associated with homosexuality. Considering an exemplary song that makes a statement about gay experience from a gay perspective, Attig argues that this message had to be conveyed in subtle ways in order to receive commercial airplay. This analysis of the popular song "Don't Leave Me This Way" deals with value opposition and symbolic content, narrative content, lyrical content, and other overt and covert analytical criteria.

We have also included one detailed, descriptive review of some of the struggles confronted by lesbian and gay litigants. Paul Siegel explains that in many of these legal cases, lesbians and gays encounter what Dressler (1979) refers to as "judicial homophobia" as a result of their self-identification as a sexual minority. This analysis of sexual/legal issues is not limited to their existence solely in the context of mass communication. Rather, as Siegel notes, his review is an examination of free speech caselaw involving the gay civil rights movement. Considering the communication process in a broad sense, special attention is paid to First Amendment issues in lesbian and gay litigation.

Finally, our collection concludes with a selective bibliography of print, aural, and visual resources on gays, lesbians, and the mass media. As Fred Fejes points out, his task of compiling these references, and of locating and including both popular and scholarly listings, was constrained not only because much of this material is not broadly indexed, but also because few libraries subscribe to many of the more popular gay publications.

You will notice that we resisted writing a traditionally-evaluative introduction; we purposely chose not to review these articles from our own critical vantage point. We believe that each selection speaks best for itself, and have positioned our role as compilers of, rather than commentators on, this material. This has not been easy, since we certainly do have our own theoretical outlooks on many of these issues, and our own political and research agendas as well. Quite frankly, some of the studies included here do not reflect the sort of methodological pluralism that we have argued for elsewhere (Kielwasser & Wolf, 1989; Kielwasser & Wolf, 1988; Wolf, 1987; Wolf & Kielwasser, 1989). In lieu of considering *only* those studies with which we could agree, we chose to accept contributions that address important, interdisciplinary themes in interesting or provocative ways. Thus, we leave the site of evaluation where, ultimately, it should be—with the reader.

At a most general level, however, George Gerbner, Professor at the Annenberg School of Communication, University of Pennsylvania, offers a useful context for evaluating the cumulative importance of the studies included here: "All animals react to things, but humans act in a world of towering symbolic constructions that we call culture." "Culture," he goes on to say,

> is that system of messages and images which regulates social relations; introduces us into roles of gender, age, class, and vocation; gives us models of conformity and targets for rebellion; provides the range of personalities, temperaments, and mentalities said to be our "characteristics"; helps us rise to selfless acts of courage and sacrifice; and makes us accept (or even perpetuate) repression and slaughter of countless unknown people assigned to the appropriate categories of barbarians and other enemies. In other words, culture is that symbolic organization which socializes us and cultivates our fantasies about a world we do not experience directly. It is a system of stories and other artifacts, increasingly mass-produced, that mediates between existence and our consciousness of existence, and thereby helps shape both. (1988, p. 320)

Each of the contributors to this compilation has a number of intriguing insights to offer about the "system of stories" that constellates, if you will, our sexual culture, and forms the shape of our "body electric." They address many of the dynamics listed by Gerbner, and a diverse range of subject matter has been purposely selected for inclusion. All of the studies are united in diversity, though, by each author's implicit and perspicacious realization that the mass media — through a seemingly infinite supply of stories and the uses to which those stories are put — contribute significantly to the very definitions we form of ourselves and of each other. In this respect, Gerbner is right: our culture is indeed mass-mediated. And, by extension, *so are we.*

Acknowledging this fact places not only social scientific, but also political demands upon media scholars, consumers and creators. We must consider and reconsider the creation and consumption of our stories, enabling the sorts of postmodern strategies described by Hebdige (1988) as "the opening up to critical discourse of lines of enquiry which were formerly prohibited, of evidence which was previously inadmissible so that new and different questions can be asked and new and other voices can begin asking them . . . , the opening up of institutional and discursive spaces within which more fluid and plural social and sexual identities may develop," in which we might enhance "our collective (and democratic) sense of *possibility*" (p. 226). In short, we must all seek to discover the content of our electric environments, discern the functions of such content, *and* act upon this content in ethically defensible ways. A point made by the Executive Director of the Alliance for Gay and Lesbian Artists in the Entertainment Industry, Chris Uszler, is illustrative in that regard: "A recent *Los Angeles Times* poll found that 56% of those surveyed said they did not know anyone who was gay or lesbian . . . . So how do they form their opinions? Well, certainly through friends, through religion, through their upbringing — but also through the media. And, of all those, what do we [gays] have access to? It is the media" (Vandervelden, 1987, pp. 10-11). While Uszler's observation is somewhat naive, it is true that as gays and lesbians continue to battle discrimination, confronting entangled questions regarding their public and private identities, the mass media will continue to figure prominently in that process. Contributions of the mass media to the daily discourse about homosexuality can either exacerbate or attenuate phobic and heterosexist definitions of human sexuality, reinforcing the particular necessity for more programmatic research in this area.

In the broadest sense, we see the mass media as integral aspects of the processes by which sexual consciousness is formed and re-formed. We use the term "sexual consciousness" with a purposeful imprecision, including within it the full range of hopes, fears, and commitments, both public and private, that we all hold in regard to sexuality. Accordingly, there continues to be a need for research that is not limited by what human sexuality researchers have re-ferred to as the "genitalization" of sexual relationships (De Cecco, 1985, p. xi). Arguing that "genitality is *not* all of sexuality," Han-sen and Evans (1985, p. 2) have commented on the constraints that result from "the faulty placement of emphasis on genital sexual activity, rather than on the larger issues of loving." While mass communication studies remain largely focused upon the more easily operationalized aspects of human sexuality, it is clear that such re-search will benefit from less ruptured conceptions of sexual con-sciousness. Consideration of sexuality and mass communication in the larger context of love and affection makes good theoretical and practical sense. This context could lead to more sophisticated the-ory-building and, perhaps, stimulate research *results* that are more useful to research *subjects*.

We hope that the individual articles presented in *Human Sexual-ity and Mass Media* will inform and challenge your thinking about mass communication and human sexuality, encouraging not merely more research, but informed public action upon these pressing con-cerns. There are many significant ideas here that, while they do not always fully explain every relevant concern, do point to the best possibilities for explanation through exploration. Ultimately, we believe that the publication of any significant idea is not the end, but the means.

Thus reflection shows that the Realm of Introductions is incomparably more vast than the Realm of Literature, for what the latter endeavors to *realize*, Introductions merely announce from afar.

— Stanislaw Lem, *Imaginary Magnitude*

REFERENCES

Anderson, J. A. (Ed.). (1988). *Communication yearbook 11*. Newbury Park, CA: Sage.

Berger, A. A. (Ed.). (1988). *Media USA: Process and effect*. New York: Longman.

Brown, J. D. (1988). Sex in the media. In R. E. Hiebert, & C. Ruess (Eds.), *Impact of mass media* (2nd ed.) (pp. 167-171). New York: Longman.

Cross, D. W. (1983). *Mediaspeak*. New York: Mentor.

De Cecco, J. P. (1985). Preface. *Journal of Homosexuality, 11*(1/2), xi-xiii.

Dressler, J. (1979). Judicial homophobia: Gay rights' biggest roadblock. *Civil Liberties Review*, pp. 19-27.

Dyer, R. (1984). *Gays and film* (rev. ed.). New York: New York Zoetrope.

Gay bigfoot molesting little boys. (1985, July 16). *National Examiner*, p. 5.

Gay hooker ring tours White House. (1989, September 5). *The Sun*, p. 15.

Gerbner, G. (1988). Liberal education in the information age. In A. A. Berger (Ed.), *Media USA: Process and effect* (pp. 319-325). New York: Longman (original work published 1983/1984).

Hansen, C. E., & Evans, A. E. (1985). Bisexuality reconsidered: An idea in pursuit of a definition. *Journal of Homosexuality, 11*(1/2), 1-6.

Hebdige, D. (1988). *Hiding in the light: On images and things*. London: Comedia/Routledge.

Hiebert, R. E., & Ruess, C. (Eds.). (1988). *Impact of mass media* (2nd ed). New York: Longman.

Jamieson, K. H., & Campbell, K. K. (1988). *The interplay of influence: Mass media and their publics in news, advertising, politics* (2nd ed.). Belmont, CA: Wadsworth.

Kielwasser, A. P., & Wolf, M. A. (1988, May). *Thinking about television: Towards a social cognition theory of mass communication*. Paper presented at the Annual Meeting of the International Communication Association, New Orleans, LA.

Kielwasser, A. P., & Wolf, M. A. (1989). The appeal of soap opera: An analysis of process and quality in dramatic serial gratifications. *Journal of Popular Culture, 23*(1), 111-124.

Liebert, R. M., & Sprafkin, J. (1988). *The early window: Effects of television on children and youth* (3rd ed.). New York: Pergamon.

Lippe, R. (1986, December). Gay visibility: Contemporary images. *CineAction!: A magazine of radical film criticism and theory*, pp. 81-88.

McLuhan, M., & Fiore, Q. (1968). *War and peace in the global village*. New York: Bantam.

National Institute of Mental Health. (1983). Television and behavior: Ten years of scientific progress and implications for the Eighties. In E. Wartella, D. C. Whitney & S. Windahl (Eds.), *Mass communication review yearbook 4* (pp. 23-35). Beverly Hills: Sage.

Nielsen Media Research. (1988, Fall). Videocassette recorders in the 80's. *The Nielsen Report*, pp. 2-5.

Nielsen Media Research. (1989, June). Cable making good connections. *Media News*, p. 4.

Radio fans turned off by macho dad's sex swap: Deejay who charmed the ladies becomes one! (1988, November 22). *Weekly World News*, p. 6.

Russo, V. (1988, September 27). The temptation of acceptable lies: Why no protest of the whitewashing of gay lives on the American screen? *The Advocate*, p. 69.

Vandervelden, M. (1987, January 20). Changing gay images on the screen: Alliance for Gay and Lesbian Artists. *The Advocate*, pp. 10-11, 20.

Weiss, A. (1986). From the margins: New images of gays in the cinema. *Cineaste*, *15*(1), 4-8.

Wolf, M. A. (1987). How children negotiate television. In T. R. Lindlof (Ed.), *Natural audiences: Qualitative research of media uses and effects* (pp. 58-94). Norwood, NJ: Ablex.

Wolf, M. A., & Kielwasser, A. P. (1989, October). *Television fantasy and reality from a child's frame of reference*. Paper presented at the Seventh International Conference on Culture and Communication, Philadelphia, PA.

Woodhead, W. M. (1988, Fall). TV usage and the presence of children. *The Nielsen Report*, pp. 12-14.

GAYS, LESBIANS, AND POPULAR CULTURE

Out of the Mainstream: Sexual Minorities and the Mass Media

Larry Gross, PhD

University of Pennsylvania

SUMMARY. In a society dominated by centralized sources of information and imagery, in which economic imperatives and pervasive sources of values promote the search for large, common-denominator audiences, it is useful to look at the fate of those who, for one reason or another, find themselves outside of the mainstream. This paper addresses the general questions of minority perspectives in the context of the study of mass media content and effects. More specific attention is paid to the situation of lesbian women and gay men as members of the mass media audience.

In a society dominated by centralized sources of information and imagery, in which economic imperatives and pervasive values promote the search for large, common-denominator audiences, what is the fate of those groups who for one or another reason find themselves outside the mainstream? Briefly, and it is hardly a novel

Larry Gross is Professor of Communications at the Annenberg School, University of Pennsylvania, Philadelphia, PA 19104. He is Associate Editor of *The International Encyclopedia of Communications* (Oxford, 1989), Co-Convenor of the ICA Task Committee on Lesbian and Gay Concerns, and Co-Chair of the Philadelphia Lesbian and Gay Task Force. Dedicated to Vito Russo (1946-1990).

observation, such groups share a common fate of relative invisibility and demeaning stereotypes. But there are differences as well as similarities in the ways various minorities (racial, ethnic, sexual, religious, political) are treated by the mass media. And, given important differences in their life situations, members of such groups experience varying consequences of their mediated images.

In this paper I will discuss the general question of minority perspectives applied to the study of mass media content and effects, and I will elaborate in greater detail the situation of sexual minorities (lesbians and gay men) as members of the mass media audience.

Sexual minorities differ in important ways from the "traditional" racial and ethnic minorities; they are in an interesting sense, akin to political minorities (so-called radicals and "fringe" groups). In both cases their members typically are self-identified at some point in their lives, usually in adolescence or later, and they are not necessarily easily identifiable by others. These two groups also constitute by their very existence a presumed threat to the "natural" (sexual and/or political) order of things, and thus they are inherently problematic and controversial for the mass media. These characteristics can be seen to affect the way members of such groups are depicted in the media (when they do appear), and also suggest ways to think about the effects of such depictions on the images held by society at large and by members of these minority groups.

Before turning to the discussion of minority audience perspectives, it would be helpful to briefly characterize the role of the mass media, television in particular, in our society.

THE SYSTEM IS THE MESSAGE

First, the economic, political and social integration of modern industrial society allows few communities or individuals to maintain an independent integrity. The world is becoming a Leviathan, like it or not, and its nervous system is telecommunications. Our knowledge of the "wide world" is what this nervous system transmits to us. The mass media provide the chief common ground among the different groups that make up a heterogeneous national and international community. Never before have all classes and groups (as well as ages) shared so much of the same culture and the same perspectives while having so little to do with their creation.

Second, representation in the mediated "reality" of our mass culture is in itself power; certainly it is the case that non-representation maintains the powerless status of groups that do not possess significant material or political power bases. That is, while the holders of real power—the ruling class—do not require (or seek) mediated visibility, those who are at the bottom of the various power hierarchies will be kept in their places in part through their relative invisibility. This is a form of what Gerbner and I (1976) have termed symbolic annihilation. Not all interests or points of view are equal; judgements are made constantly about exclusions and inclusions and these judgements broaden or narrow (mostly narrow) the spectrum of views presented.

Third, when groups or perspectives do attain visibility, the manner of that representation will itself reflect the biases and interests of those elites who define the public agenda. And these elites are (mostly) white, (mostly) middle-aged, (mostly) male, (mostly) middle and upper-middle class, and entirely heterosexual (at least in public).

Fourth, we should not take too seriously the presumed differences between the various categories of media messages—particularly in the case of television. News, drama, quiz shows, sports and commercials share underlying similarities of theme, emphasis and value. Even the most widely accepted distinctions (i.e., news vs. fiction programs vs. commercials) are easily blurred. Decisions about which events are newsworthy and about how to present them are heavily influenced by considerations of dramatic form and content (e.g., conflict and resolution) that are drawn from fictional archetypes; and the polished mini-dramas of many commercials reveal a sophisticated mastery of fictional conventions, just as dramatic programs promote a style of consumption and living that is quite in tune with their neighboring commercial messages. More important, the blending of stylistic conventions allows for greater efficacy and mutual support in packaging and diffusing common values.

Fifth, the dominant conventions of our mass media are those of "realism" and psychologically-grounded naturalism. Despite a limited degree of reflexivity which occasionally crops up, mainstream film and television are nearly always presented as transparent mediators of reality which can and do show us how people and places look, how institutions operate; in short, the way it is. These depictions of the way things are, and why, are personified through dramatic plots and characterizations which take us behind the scenes to the otherwise inaccessible backstages of individual motivation, organizational performance, and subcultural life.

Normal adult viewers, to be sure, are aware of the fictiveness of media drama: no one calls the police when a character on TV is shot. But we may still wonder how often and to what extent viewers suspend their disbelief in the persuasive realism of the fictional worlds of television and film drama. Even the most sophisticated among us can find many components of our 'knowledge' of the real world which derive wholly or in part from fictional representations. And, in a society which spans a continent, in a cosmopolitan culture which spans much of the globe, the mass media provide the broadest common background of assumptions about what things are, how they work (or should work), and why.

Finally, the contributions of the mass media are likely to be especially powerful in cultivating images of groups and phenomena about which there is little first-hand opportunity for learning; particularly when such images are not contradicted by other established beliefs and ideologies. By definition, portrayals of minority groups and "deviants" will be relatively distant from the real lives of a large majority of viewers.

TELEVISION AS THE MAINSTREAM

The average American adult spends several hours each day in this television world, children spend even more of their lives immersed in its "fictional reality." As I have already suggested, the mass media, and television foremost among them, have become the primary sources of common information and images that create and maintain a world view and a value system. In a word, the mass media have become central agents of enculturation. In the Cultural Indicators Project (cf. Gerbner, Gross, Morgan and Signorielli, 1986) we have used the concept of "cultivation" to describe the influence of television on viewers' conceptions of social reality. On issue after issue we find that assumptions, beliefs and values of heavy viewers of television differ systematically from those of light viewers in the same demographic groups. Sometimes these differences appear as overall, main effects, whereby those who watch more television are more likely—in all groups—to give what we call "television answers" to our questions. But in many cases the patterns are more complex. We have found that television viewing, not surprisingly, serves as a stable factor differentially integrated into and interacting with different groups' life situations and world views. In our recent work we have isolated a consistent pattern which we have termed "mainstreaming" (Gerbner, Gross, Morgan and Signorielli, 1980, 1982, 1986). The mainstream can be thought of as a relative commonality of outlooks and values that television tends to cultivate in viewers. By mainstreaming we mean the sharing of that commonality among heavy viewers in those demographic groups whose light viewers hold divergent positions. In other words, differences deriving from other factors and social forces—differences that may appear in the responses of light viewers in various groups—may be diminished or even absent when the heavy viewers in these same groups are compared. Overall, TV viewing appears to signal a convergence of outlooks rather than absolute, across-the-board increments in all groups.

CHOICES OR ECHOES?

The mainstream which we have identified as the embodiment of a dominant ideology, cultivated through the repetition of stable patterns across the illusory boundaries of media and genre, and absorbed by otherwise diverse segments of the population, nevertheless has to contend with the possibility of oppositional perspectives and interpretations. What options and opportunities are available to those groups whose concerns, values and even very existence are belittled, subverted and denied by the mainstream? Can the power of the mass media's central tendencies be resisted; can one avoid being swept into the mainstream? The answers to such questions depend in large part on which group or segment we are discussing; while many minorities are similarly ignored or distorted by the mass media, not all have the same options for resistance and the development of alternative channels.

In general the opportunities for organized opposition are greatest when there is a visible and even organized group which can provide solidarity and institutional means for creating and disseminating alternative messages. There are numerous examples of groupings that have sprung up, as it were, along the right bank of the mainstream. Most organized and visible among these are the Christian fundamentalist syndicated television programs. These programs provide their (generally older and less educated) viewers with an array of programs, from news to talk shows to soap operas to church services and sermons, all reflecting perspectives and values that they quite correctly feel are not represented in mainstream, prime time television or in the movies (cf. Gerbner, Gross, Hoover, Morgan, Signorielli, Cotugno and Wuthnow, 1984; Hoover, 1985). As one of Hoover's conservative, religious respondents put it, in discussing network television,

> I think a good deal of it is written by very liberal, immoral people. . . . Some of the comedies, the weekly things that go on every week, they make extramarital affairs, and sex before marriage an everyday thing like everybody should accept it . . . and they present it in a comic situation, a situation that looks like it could be fun and a good deal of these weekly shows I don't like go for that. (Hoover, 1985, pp. 382-383)

The religious sponsoring and producing organizations are not merely engaged in meeting their audiences' previously unmet needs for a symbolic environment in which they feel at home; they are also attempting to translate the (usually exaggerated) numbers of their audiences and their (constantly solicited) financial contributions into a power base from which they can exert pressure to alter the channel of the mainstream and bring it even closer to where they now reside, up on the right bank.

At the moment, and for the foreseeable future in the United States, at least, there is no comparable settlement on the left bank of the mainstream. There are many reasons why the organized left has been unable to match the right's success in harnessing the available resources of media technology. It is not hard to see that some minority perspectives are in fact supportive of the dominant ideology, however much the media's need for massive audiences might sacrifice or offend their interests, while other minority values are truly incompatible with the basic power relationships embodied in that mainstream.

Minority positions and interests which present radical challenges to the established order will not only be ignored, they will be discredited. Those who benefit from the status quo present their position as the moderate center, balanced between equal and opposing "extremes"—thus the American news media's cult of "objectivity," achieved through a "balance" which reflects an invisible, taken-for-granted ideology. As a CBS spokesman explained it, when dismissing attempts by Jesse Helms and Ted Turner to take over the network:

> Anyone . . . who buys a media company for ideological reasons must be prepared to pay dearly for that conviction. The right-wingers and the left-wingers in this country are vociferous but small in number compared to the ordinary citizen, who, when it comes down to it, is a centrist. (Roth, 1985, p. 163)

The fatal flaw in the credo of centrism and moderation is that how one defines the "responsible" extremes will determine where the center will appear to be. In the United States the mass media grant legitimacy to positions a lot further to the right than to the left, which puts the "objectively balanced" mainstream clearly to the right of center. Jesse Helms can be elected and reelected to the Senate and can embark on a public campaign to take over CBS; his opposite number on the left, whoever that might be, couldn't conceivably claim or receive that degree of visibility, power and legitimacy.

Yet, in the final analysis, neither flank can avoid serving in one way or another to buttress the ramparts of the status quo, and to keep the truly oppositional from being taken seriously. American presidential politics recently sported a matched pair of Christian candidates, and neither the Minister of the Left, Jesse Jackson, nor the Minister of the Right, Pat Robertson, could hope to do more than exert some small pressure on their respective branches of the Property Party, whose two official divisions—the Democrats and the Republicans—offer an illusion of choice within the political mainstream.

HOMOSEXUALS AND TELEVISION: FEAR AND LOATHING

Close to the heart of our cultural and political system is the pattern of roles associated with sexual identity: our conceptions of masculinity and femininity, of the "normal" and "natural" attributes and responsibilities of men and women. And, as with other pillars of our moral order, these definitions of what is normal and natural serve to support the existing social power hierarchy. The maintenance of the "normal" gender role system requires that children be socialized—and adults retained—within a set of images and expectations which limit and channel their conceptions of what is possible and proper for men and for women. The gender system is supported by the mass media treatment of sexual minorities. Mostly, they are ignored or denied—symbolically annihilated; when they do appear they do so in order to play a supportive role for the natural order and are thus narrowly and negatively stereotyped. Sexual minorities are not, of course, unique in this regard (cf. Gross, 1984). However, lesbians and gay men are unusually vulnerable to mass media power; even more so than blacks, national minorities, and women. Of all social groups (except perhaps communists), we are probably the least permitted to speak for ourselves in the mass media. We are also the only group (again, except for communists and, currently, Arab "terrorists") whose enemies are generally uninhibited by the consensus of "good taste" which protects most minorities from the more public displays of bigotry. The reason for this vulnerability lies in large part in our initial isolation and invisibility. The process of identity formation for lesbian women and gay men requires the strength and determination to swim against the stream. A baby is born and immediately classified as male or female, white or black, and is treated as such from that moment, for better or worse. That baby is also defined as heterosexual and treated as such. It is made clear throughout the process of socialization — a process in which the mass media play a major role — that one will grow up, marry, have children and live in nuclear familial bliss, sanctified by religion and licensed by the state.

Women are surrounded by other women, people of color by other people of color, etc., and can observe the variety of choices and fates that befall those who are like them. Mass media stereotypes selectively feature and reinforce some of the available roles and images for women, national minorities, people of color, etc.; but they operate under constraints imposed by the audiences' immediate environment. Lesbians and gay men, conversely, are a self-identifying minority. We are assumed (with few exceptions, and these — the "obviously" effeminate man or masculine woman — may not even be homosexual) to be straight, and are treated as such, until we begin to recognize that we are not what we have been told we are, that we are different. But how are we to understand, define and deal with that difference? Here we generally have little to go on beyond very limited direct experience with those individuals who are sufficiently close to the accepted stereotypes that they are labelled publicly as queers, faggots, dykes, etc. And we have the mass media. The mass media play a major role in this process of social definition, and rarely a positive one. In the absence of adequate information in their immediate environment, most people, gay or straight, have little choice other than to accept the narrow and negative stereotypes they encounter as being representative of gay people. The mass media have rarely presented portrayals which counter or extend the prevalent images. On the contrary, they take advantage of them. Typically, media characterizations use popular stereotypes as a code which they know will be readily understood by the audience, thus further reinforcing the presumption of verisimilitude while remaining "officially" innocent of dealing with a sensitive subject. But there is more to it than stereotyping. For the most part gay people have been simply invisible in the media. The few exceptions were almost invariably either victims — of violence or ridicule — or villains. As Vito Russo noted recently, "It is not insignificant that out of 32 films with major homosexual characters from 1961 through 1976, 13 feature gays who commit suicide and 18 have the homosexual murdered by another character" (1986, p. 32). Even this minimal and slanted presence, however, seems to be threatening enough to the "industry" that gay characterizations and plot elements always come accompanied by pressbook qualifications and backpedaling. In his survey of the treatment of gay people in American film, Russo (1981) presents a sampling of the predictable distancing that gay themes evoke from directors (*"The Children's Hour* is not about lesbianism, it's about the power of lies to destroy people's lives," William Wyler, 1962; *"Sunday, Bloody Sunday* is not about the sexuality of these people, it's about human loneliness," John Schlesinger, 1972; *"Windows* is not about homosexuality, it's about insanity," Gordon Willis, 1979), and actors (*"The Sergeant* is not about homosexuality, it's about loneliness," Rod Steiger, 1968; *"Staircase* is not about homosexuality, it's about loneliness," Rex Harrison, 1971). It is easy to imagine how comforting these explanations must have been to lesbian and gay audience members looking for some reflection of their lives in the media. But it isn't only the audiences who appear to require protective distancing from gay characters and themes. We are frequently treated to show-biz gossip intended to convey the heterosexual bona fides of any actor cast in a gay role, as when the actor playing the swish drag queen Albin in the stage version of *La Cage Aux Folles* told several interviewers that he had consulted with his wife and children before accepting the role.

The gay liberation movement emerged in the late 1960s in the United States, spurred by the examples of the black, anti-war, and feminist movements. Consequently, media attention to gay people and gay issues increased in the early 1970s, much of it positive (at least in comparison with previous and continuing heterosexist depictions and discussions), culminating (in the sense of greater media attention — in the pre-AIDS era) in 1973, with the decision by the American Psychiatric Association to delete homosexuality from its "official" list of mental diseases. By the middle 1970s, however, a backlash against the successes of the gay movement began to be felt around the country, most visibly in Anita Bryant's successful campaign to repeal a gay rights ordinance in Dade County, Florida, in 1977. Since then the gay movement and its enemies, mostly among the "new right," have been constant antagonists (right wing fund-raisers acknowledge that anti-homosexual material is their best bet to get money from supporters), and television has often figured in the struggle. But, although the right wing has attacked the networks for what they consider to be overly favorable attention to gay people, in fact gay people are usually portrayed and used in news and dramatic media in ways that serve to reinforce rather than challenge the prevailing images.

Kathleen Montgomery (1981) observed the efforts of the organized gay movement to improve the ways network programmers handle gay characters and themes. In particular she describes the writing and production of a made-for-TV network movie that had a gay-related theme, and involved consultation with representatives of gay organizations. And the result?

> Throughout the process all the decisions affecting the portrayal of gay life were influenced by the constraints which commercial television as a mass medium imposes upon the creation of its content. The fundamental goal of garnering the largest possible audience necessitated that (a) the program be placed in a familiar and successful television genre – the crime-drama, (b) the story focus upon the heterosexual male lead character and his reactions to the gay characters rather than upon the homosexual characters themselves, and (c) the film avoid any overt display of affection which might be offensive to certain segments of the audience. These requirements served as a filter through which the issue of homosexuality was processed, resulting in a televised picture of gay life designed to be acceptable to the gay community and still palatable to a mass audience. (p. 56)

Acceptability to the gay community, in this case, means that the movie was not an attack on our character and a denial of our basic humanity; it could not be mistaken for an expression of our values or perspectives. But of course they weren't aiming at us, either;

they were merely trying to avoid arguing with us afterwards. In Vito Russo's (1986) words, "mainstream films about homosexuals are not for homosexuals. They address themselves exclusively to the majority" (p. 32). However, there will inevitably be a great many lesbians and gay men in the audience.

The rules of the mass media game have a double impact on gay people: not only do they mostly show us as weak and silly, or evil and corrupt, but they exclude and deny the existence of normal, unexceptional as well as exceptional lesbians and gay men. Hardly ever shown in the media are just play gay folks, used in roles which do not center on their deviance as a threat to the moral order which must be countered through ridicule or physical violence. Television drama in particular, reflects the deliberate use of clichéd casting strategies which preclude such daring innovations.

The stereotypic depiction of lesbians and gay men as abnormal, and the suppression of positive or even "unexceptional" portrayals serves to maintain and police the boundaries of the moral order. It encourages the majority to stay on their gender-defined reservation, and tries to keep the minority quietly hidden out of sight. For the visible presence of healthy, non-stereotypic lesbians and gay men does pose a serious threat: it undermines the unquestioned normalcy of the status quo, and it opens up the possibility of making choices to people who might never otherwise have considered or understood that such choices could be made.

The situation has only been worsened by the AIDS epidemic. By 1983 nearly all mass media attention to gay men was in the context of AIDS-related stories, and because this coverage seems to have exhausted the media's limited interest in gay people, lesbians became even less visible than before (if possible). AIDS reinvigorated the two major mass media "roles" for gay people: victim and villain. Already treated as an important medical topic, AIDS moved up to the status of "front page" news after Rock Hudson emerged as the most famous person with AIDS. At present AIDS stories appear daily in print and broadcast news—often with little or no new or important content—and the public image of gay men has been inescapably linked with the specter of plague. Television dramatists have presented the plight of (white, middle class) gay men with AIDS, but their particular concern is the agony of the families/friends who have to face the awful truth: their son (brother, boyfriend, husband, etc.) is, gasp, gay! But, even with AIDS, not too gay, mind you. In the major network made-for-TV movie on AIDS, NBC's *An Early Frost*, a young, rich, white, handsome lawyer is forced out of the closet by AIDS. "We know he is gay because he tells his disbelieving parents so, but his lack of a gay sensibility, politics and sense of community make him one of those homosexuals heterosexuals love" (Weiss, 1986).

An Early Frost is thus another example of the pattern discerned by Montgomery: altho this time the familiar and successful genre is family- not crime-drama, the focus is still on the heterosexual characters and their reactions. As William Henry (1987) notes in a recent overview of TV's treatment of gays (or lack of same) during the past 15 years,

> When TV does deal with gays it typically takes the point of view of straights struggling to understand. The central action is the progress of acceptance — not self-acceptance by the homosexual, but grief-stricken resignation to fate by his straight loved ones, who serve as surrogates for the audience. Homosexuality thus becomes not a fact of life, but a moral issue on which everyone in earshot is expected to voice some vehement opinion. Just as black characters were long expected to talk almost exclusively about being black, and handicapped characters (when seen at all) were expected to talk chiefly about their disabilities, so homosexual characters have been defined almost entirely by their "problem." (pp. 43-44)

Being defined by their "problem," it is no surprise therefore that gay characters have mostly been confined to television's favorite problem-of-the-week-genre, the made-for-TV movie, with a very occasional one-shot appearance of a gay character on a dramatic series (examples include episodes of "Lou Grant," "Medical Center" and "St. Elsewhere," among others). Continuing gay characters tend to be so subtle as to be readily misunderstood by the innocent (as in the case of Sidney in "Love, Sidney," whose homosexuality seemed to consist entirely of crying at the movies

and having a photo of his dead lover on the mantlepiece), or confused about their sexuality and never seen in an ongoing romantic
relationship (as in the case of the off-again-on-again Steven Carrington in "Dynasty," whose lovers had an unfortunate tendency to
get killed).

Despite their greater freedom from the competition for massive
mainstream audiences—or perhaps because of their need to com-
pete for the primary audience of teens and young adults—commercial films are no more welcoming to gay characters than television.
In fact, as Vito Russo shows in the revised edition of his 1981
study, *The Celluloid Closet* (1987), recent films are awash in gay
villains and victims once more.

> The use of the word faggot has become almost mandatory.
> Outright slurs that would never be tolerated in reference to any
> other group of people are commonly used onscreen against
> homosexuals. . . . [A]nti-gay dialogue is most often given to
> the very characters with whom the audience is supposed to
> identify. (p. 251)

Films offer their makers a degree of license which isn't available
to television producers—an opportunity to use language and depictions of sexuality that go far beyond the limits imposed on television—but as far as gay people are concerned, this mostly serves as a
hunting license.

COLONIZATION: THE STRAIGHT GAY

There are several categories of response to the mainstream media's treatment of minorities; among them are internalization, subversion, secession and resistance. To begin with, as we've already
noted, we are all colonized by the majority culture. Those of us who
belong to a minority group may nevertheless have absorbed the values of the dominant culture, even if these exclude or diminish us.
We are all aware of the privileging of male-identified attributes in
our patriarchal culture, and the dominance of the male perspective
in the construction of mass media realities. Similarly, the mass media in the United States offer a white-angled view of the world

which is shared with people of color around the world. In a study of Venezuelan children in which they were asked to describe their heroes, the child's hero was North American in 86% of the cases and Venezuelan in only 8%; English-speaking in 82% and Spanish-speaking in 15%; white heroes outnumbered black heroes 11 to 1; and heroes were wealthy in 72% of the cases (Pasquall, 1975).

Sexual minorities are among the most susceptible to internalizing the dominant culture's values because the process of labelling generally occurs in isolation and because:

> We learn to loathe homosexuality before it becomes necessary to acknowledge our own. . . . Never having been offered *positive* attitudes to homosexuality, we inevitably adopt *negative* ones, and it is from these that all our values flow. (Hodges & Hutter, 1977, p. 4)

Internalization and colonization can also result in the adoption of assimilationist strategies which promise upward (or centerward) mobility, although at the cost of cutting off one's "roots." Gay people by and large know how to "pass"; after all, it's what they've been doing most of their lives. But the security attained is fragile and often illusory, and certainly won't provide support in resisting the inferiorizing pressures of the straight culture they attempt to blend into. And all too often, there really isn't any resistance anyway, as the process of internalization has achieved the desired goal. The Zionist polemicist Ahad Ha-Am drew on a Biblical analogy to describe this phenomenon, in his essay on Moses: "Pharaoh is gone, but his work remains; the master has ceased to be master, but the slaves have not ceased to be slaves" (1904/1970, p. 320).

The supposedly liberal and tolerant domain of the media does not necessarily permit homosexuals (or other minorities) to overcome the burdens of self-oppression:

> When it comes to keeping minorities in their place, the entertainment industry continues to divide and conquer. For all the organizing that women have done, for instance, in their attempts to break down the barriers, well-placed women executives say they've received very little mutual support from

their equally well-placed peers. The old-boy network rules, and the individual women, gays, blacks, or hispanics who attain some degree of success usually have to camouflage themselves in the trappings of their masters. (Kilday, 1986, p. 40)

Similarly, gay writer Merle Miller recalled that, "as editor of a city newspaper, he indulged in 'queer-baiting' to conceal his own homosexuality" (Adam, 1978, p. 89). Openly gay actor Michael Kearns

speaks of a gay agent who makes it a habit to tell "fag jokes" at the close of interviews with new actors. "If an actor laughs, he's signed up; if he doesn't, he isn't." (Hachem, 1987, p. 48)

Working backstage, it would seem, does not exempt one from falling under the spell of the hegemonic values cultivated and reflected by the media. However, as Raymond Williams (1977) has suggested, hegemony "is never either total or exclusive. At any time, forms of alternative or directly oppositional politics and culture exist as significant elements in the society" (p. 111).

RESISTANCE AND OPPOSITION

The most obvious form of resistance, but possibly the most difficult, would be to simply ignore the mass media, and refuse to be insulted and injured by their derogation and denial of one's identity and integrity as a member of a minority group. Unfortunately, although some of us can personally secede from the mass mediated mainstream, or sample from it with great care and selectivity, we cannot thereby counter its effect on our fellow citizens. We cannot even prevent our fellow minority group members from attending to messages which we feel are hostile to their interests (this is, of course, a familiar dilemma for parents who feel that commercial TV is not in the best interests of their children). Given the generally high levels of TV viewing at the lower rungs of the socio-economic ladder, it can be expected that large segments of the population consume media fare that serves to maintain their subordinate status. In the United States, black households are disproportionately heavy TV consumers:

Black households, which represented about 9 percent of all television households surveyed, accounted for about 14 percent of all household viewing. According to the United States Census Bureau, blacks constituted 12 percent of the population last year. (Morgan, 1986)

We might expect self-identified ideological minorities to be better able to resist the siren's song of the mass media; and we've noted that the religious right has developed alternative channels to provide their adherents with a source of value congruent media fare. We've also noted the absence of equivalent programming on the left bank of the mainstream. Leftists, it seems, are faced with fewer choices, and they experience the ambivalence of being aware of the central role the media play in consensualizing a dominant ideology and yet not wanting (or being able) to pull completely out of the mainstream themselves. In an ongoing study of American leftists' relationships to the mass media, Eugene Michaud (1987) has encountered many expressions of such hostility and ambivalence, despite which the respondents interviewed continue to watch TV:

Frankly, I detest TV. It's the source of many family disputes. I really find TV obnoxious and really intrusive on whatever you're trying to do. . . . For most people, I think TV is a way of relaxing—it's a distraction . . . life is hard—so it's very easy to watch TV. (male, 36)

I have a lot of trouble with the TV news. I get upset and I want to run away. Or I get obnoxious and start sneering at it, and my wife gets upset because she's trying to listen. . . . I realize that there's this vast treasure trove of ideas and images from TV which most people are plugged into. . . . (male, 44)

I hate watching the TV news and having someone give me the straight administration line. . . . The way I watch TV is if I don't have anything else to do and I'm bored. (female, 32)

We watch network news sometimes, but I feel like its junkfood news. I find it very frustrating. They never analyze anything. . . . It's also so easy to turn on TV, and there's all this visual stuff. It's so effortless. (female, 32)

> I do watch Nightline, but it pisses me off to no end . . . the way they manipulate things to put forth a certain point-of-view. It's a total set-up. (male, 32)

Observers of the current television scene will not be surprised to learn that there are one or two shows that do manage to appeal to Michaud's leftist respondents. Most frequently praised is "Hill Street Blues," although it's generally judged to have declined after its first few seasons. Its spinoff, "St. Elsewhere," receives similar reviews. The decline is often interpreted in ideological terms:

> I used to watch "Hill Street Blues" regularly, but I mostly don't bother any more . . . it used to try to demonstrate the ambiguity people felt towards each other and towards their work. Now, it's just the traditional good guys against the bad guys. I think it's a reflection of the Reagan era. (female, 34)

The ratings smash hit "Cosby Show" is popular among some leftists, despite its up-scale values, because it features a black family and because "there's a lot of love, which is appealing, and it does capture the real dynamics of family life in a funny way." (male, 30)

Lesbian women and gay men do not constitute an ideological minority in the same way that American leftists do (although those gay people who are part of the "movement" certainly tend to be left-identified), and they are less likely to condemn the mass media ·in the way the left does. However, few lesbian women and gay men could remain unaware of how they are treated in the media—when their existence is even acknowledged—and their relationship to the media is likely to be colored by this awareness. Just as racial and ethnic minority groups pay close attention to programs which feature their members, so too gay people will tune in regularly to any program which promises an openly or explicitly lesbian or gay character (or even a favorite performer assumed to be gay). The images and messages they will encounter will not, as we've already noted, provide them with much comfort or support. More typically, they will again be marginalized, trivialized and insulted.

Yet, of course, the determination of a message's value and impact can never be made in the abstract. Just as for some heterosexists *any* mention of gay people is excessive, for many isolated gay people any recognizably gay character may provide some degree of solidarity. As Pete Freer notes,

> ... the notion of a "negative" representation is difficult precisely because the meanings are not fixed within the text but generated between text and audience. Hence my memories of certain films (e.g., *A Taste of Honey*) that I saw when young, in which the very existence of a gay character was a positive experience — I recognized myself. The same film, seen today, fills me with horror. Now I know I'm not alone; then I didn't. (1987, p. 62)

While working on this paper I went to see the latest film written and directed by Woody Allen, *Radio Days*, and was irritated, though not surprised by the inclusion of a gay character whose only function is to evoke a laugh at his own expense, and to further underline the hopelessness of a woman who would fall in love with him. My irritation was caused not only by Woody Allen's gratuitous insult — I've come to expect these from him — but also by the hilarity it produced among the audience. The experience of having one's status as "fair game" emphasized in this graphic fashion while sitting in a movie theatre is familiar to gay people, just as it is to people of color and to women. Even when a gay characterization is intended to be sympathetic (as in the wildly successful *La Cage Aux Folles*), the gay members of the audience may wince at the falsity of the image, and find themselves laughing at different times than the straight audience does. There can be a perverse pleasure in this perception — Elizabeth Ellsworth (1986) describes lesbian feminist reviewers of *Personal Best* (a film written and directed by a straight man, which includes a lesbian relationship as a central theme, despite the usual pressbook obfuscation) who, "expressed pleasure in watching the dominant media 'get it wrong,' in watching it attempt, but fail, to colonize 'real' lesbian space" (p. 54).

It can be argued that the best stance for gay people to adopt vis-à-vis the mass media would be to repay them with the same indifference and contempt they reveal towards us. Unfortunately, while this might be a gratifying and appropriate individual solution, it is not realistic as a general strategy. One may be able to reduce one's own irritation by ignoring the media, but their insidious impact is not so easily avoided. What can't be avoided, however, can be better understood, and studies of lesbian and gay audiences and their responses should be included in the emerging research agenda.

SUBVERSION

A second oppositional strategy is the subversion and appropriation of mainstream media, as well as the occasionally successful infiltration. The classic gay (male) strategy of subversion is camp — an ironic stance towards the straight world rooted in a gay sensibility:

> a creative energy reflecting a consciousness that is different from the mainstream; a heightened awareness of certain human complications of feeling that spring from the fact of social oppression; in short, a perception of the world which is coloured, shaped, directed and defined by the fact of one's gayness. (Babuscio, 1977, p. 40)

This characterization would, of course, also fit many other minorities who experience oppression, but the gay sensibility differs in that we encounter and develop it at a later stage in our lives; it is nobody's native tongue. Moreover, while sharing much with other minority perspectives, camp is notably marked by irony and a theatrical perspective on the world which can be traced to the particular realities of gay experience:

> The stigma of gayness is unique insofar as it is not immediately apparent either to ourselves or to others. Upon discovery of our gayness, however, we are confronted with the possibility of avoiding the negative sanctions attached to our supposed failing by concealing information (i.e., signs which other people take for gay) from the rest of the world. This crucial fact of our existence is called *passing for straight*, a phenomenon generally defined in the metaphor of theatre, that is, playing a role: pretending to be something one is not; or, to shift the

motive somewhat, to camouflage our gayness by withholding facts about ourselves which might lead others to the correct conclusion about our sexual orientation. (Babuscio, 1977, p. 45)

Camp offers a subversive response to mainstream culture, and provides both in-group solidarity and an opportunity to express distance from and disdain for the roles most gay people play most of the time. Exchanged in private settings, camp is a mechanism of oppositional solidarity which repairs the damage inflicted by the majority and prepares us for further onslaughts. As a restricted code used in public settings, camp can be a way to identify and communicate with other "club members" under the unknowing eyes of the straight world — in itself an act of subversive solidarity (as well as self-protection). Camp can also be a form of public defiance and a risky expression of a difference which dares to show its face.

Camp is also the quintessentially gay strategy for undermining the hegemonic power of media images (cf. Babuscio, 1977; Dyer, 1986). The sting can be taken out of oppressive characterizations and the hot air balloons of official morality can be burst with the ironic weapon of camp humor. Most importantly, by self-consciously taking up a position outside the mainstream, if only in order to look back at it, camp cultivates a sense of detachment from the dominant ideology.

> The sense of being different . . . made me feel myself as "outside" the mainstream in fundamental ways — and this does give you a kind of knowledge of the mainstream you cannot have if you are immersed in it. I do not necessarily mean a truer perspective, so much as an awareness of the mainstream as a mainstream, and not just the way everything and everybody inevitably are; in other words, it denaturalizes normality. This knowledge is the foundation of camp. (Cohen and Dyer, 1980, pp. 177-178)

Camp can also be seen in the appropriation of mainstream figures and products when they are adopted as "cult" objects by marginal groups. Camp cult favorites are often women film stars who can be seen as standing up to the pressures of a male-dominated movie industry and despite all travails remaining in command of their careers (Bette Davis, Joan Crawford, Mae West), or at least struggling back from defeat (Judy Garland; cf. Dyer, 1986). Cult movies like *The Rocky Horror Picture Show* provide occasions for meeting others who share a common perspective, and turning a media product into the pretext for communal interaction. In a study of patrons waiting to see *Rocky Horror* outside a Rochester, NY, movie theatre, it was learned that, excluding the first-timers, the mean number of times the movie had been seen was eleven (Austin, 1981, p. 47). The audience members are there to participate in a ritual and a social event which creates and reinforces a solidarity of non-mainstream identification. The *Rocky Horror* cult has served all over the United States as an opportunity for lesbian and gay teenagers to meet and support each other in the coming out process.

IN OUR OWN VOICE

The most effective form of resistance to the hegemonic force of the dominant media is to speak for oneself. At one level this means attempting to be included in the category of recognized positions and groupings acknowledged by the mass media. Achieving this degree of legitimation is not a negligible accomplishment, and it is not to be despised or rejected as an important minority goal. The success of various minorities in exerting pressure on the media can be seen in the care with which images of these groups is balanced and presented. In fact, the television networks have taken to complaining about the difficulties they face in finding acceptable villains.

> "In their desire to avoid stereotyping, I think broadcast standards and practices sometimes go to an absurd extreme," said Bruce J. Sallan, ABC's vice president in charge of motion pictures on television. "There are almost no ethnic villains on television. We can't do a Mafia picture at ABC, because broadcast standards won't let us deal with Italians involved in organized crime." (Farber, 1986)

A recent ABC-TV film, *The Children Of Times Square*, was allowed to have a black villain after he was balanced by sympathetic black characters: "We had instructions from the network that if a black is shown in a bad light, we must also show a black in a good light" (Farber, 1986).

Gay people have not yet achieved the degree of social power and legitimacy which would permit them to demand the same self-censorship on the part of the media, and consequently we are still treated to gay villains and victims unbalanced by gay heroes or even just plain gay folks. As we've seen from Kathleen Montgomery's research, gay pressure can hope at most for a limited success: a story which offends neither minority nor mainstream sensibilities too much. Could we hope for much more? Probably not, since the numbers simply aren't there to put sufficient pressure on the media — and numbers are the bottom line. We might exact concessions along the way, forcing some respect for our humanity, but we cannot expect the media to tell our stories for us, nor allow us to do so through their channels.

The ultimate expression of independence for a minority audience struggling to free itself from the dominant culture's hegemony is to become the creators and not merely the consumers of media images. In recent years lesbian women and gay men have begun — although with difficulty — to gather the necessary resources with which to tell our own stories.

There have always been minority media in the United States; various immigrant groups supported newspapers, books, theatre and occasionally movies in their native languages. But these immigrant voices were stilled as succeeding generations were assimilated into mainstream culture, losing touch with the language and culture of their grandparents. The black press has survived and occasionally flourished alongside the mainstream media, and black culture (music and dance in particular) has been the source of much inspiration and talent which have crossed over into the mainstream (sometimes in whiteface).

Since the 1970s a lesbian and gay alternative culture has offered a range of media sources and products — press, music, theatre, pornography — which are unmistakably the product of gay people's sensibility. Here, too, there is the occasional cross-over, as when Harvey Fierstein's *Torch Song Trilogy* wound its way from off-off-Broadway to a Tony Award for best play on Broadway. But cross-ing-over is no guarantee of protection from the dominant culture. Even speaking in his own voice — quite literally, as Fierstein starred in his play — the gay author may find that straight audiences do not see beyond their preconceptions. *Torch Song Trilogy* was reviewed in *The New York Times* by Walter Kerr (1982), the "dean" of Broadway theatre critics, and the review is both patronizing and simply wrong. Much of the action in the third act centers around the fact that Arnold, the protagonist, has adopted a gay teenager, and around the "return" of his former lover who is in the process of leaving his wife. The play ends with clear intimations of an emerg-ing gay "nuclear family" — with Arnold as Mother, his returned lover as Daddy, and their adopted gay son. What does Walter Kerr do with this? He misunderstands — or at least misrepresents — it so badly that I must assume bigotry blinded him to plot details so obvi-ous no tyro critic could miss them. He implies that the adopted son is a "kept" boy Arnold has picked up. The former lover is de-scribed as "also sharing the flat, though not yet the boy." When the boy tells the former lover, "I'd be proud to call you daddy," Kerr detects "possible betrayal, sensual shiftings" — that is, he thinks the boy is seducing the man!

One clue to Kerr's stupidity — astounding in so veteran a critic — may be found in his comment about "this rambling and, because it can only move in circles, repetitive plot." Why, we might ask, can it only move in circles? The answer is not to be found in the theory of drama, but in the tired homophobic clichés of psychiatric theo-ries about gay people. Kerr "knows" that we are all caught up in narcissistic repetition compulsibns. The truth is, of course, that Kerr is the one who is handicapped by a repetition compulsion, sitting there on the aisle wrapped in the old miasmal mist.

When mainstream critics do not blame gay artists for things which they have themselves misread into the works they are review-ing, they may still find fault with them for not rising above their parochial concerns, that is, for addressing themselves to the concerns of their fellow gay people. In a letter to the *New York Times Book Review* justifying his negative review of Edmund White's *States Of Desire: Travels In Gay America*, Paul Cowan (1980) assures us that, "it's crucial to communicate across tribal lines. Good literature has always done that — it has transformed a particular subject into something universal. Mr. White didn't do that: in my opinion it's one of the reasons he failed to write a good book." I'm tempted to say, aha, the old universalism ploy! Perhaps good literature *has* always transformed a particular subject into something universal. But, of course, there's always a double standard in the application of the universalism criterion.

In an essay entitled "Colonialist criticism," the Nigerian writer Chinua Achebe (1976) decries those Western critics who evaluate African literature on the basis of whether it overcomes "parochialism" and "achieves universality":

> It would never occur to them to doubt the universality of their own literature. In the nature of things, the work of a Western writer is automatically informed by universality. It is only others who must strive to achieve it. (p. 11)

In the past decade lesbian and gay filmmakers have been able, with difficulty, to raise the money needed to produce independent documentaries and fictional films which have inaugurated a true alternative channel in the crucial media of movies and television. The pioneering documentary *Word Is Out* (1977), and the more recent Oscar-winning *Life And Times Of Harvey Milk*, among others, represent authentic examples of gay people speaking for ourselves, in our own words; although even here there have been compromises in order to meet the demands of the Public Broadcasting System — the only viable channel for independent documentaries in the United States (cf. Waugh, 1988). And, even more recently, and tentatively, there are the stirrings of lesbian and gay fiction films exhibited through mainstream (art) theatres and becoming accessible to a nationwide gay audience.

There is, alternatively, a homosexual cinema. It neither concerns itself overtly with issues of gay politics nor does it present gay sexuality as society's perennial dirty secret. The key to gay films, whether they are made by heterosexuals or homosexuals, is that they do not view the existence of gay people as controversial. . . . These films may reflect the fear, agitation, and bigotry of a society confronted with such truth, but it is not their view that such emotions are rational or even important to explore. (Russo, 1986, p. 43)

The products of the nascent lesbian/gay cinema find a powerful response among their primary audience, and can easily become cult films of a different sort than the midnight orphans of the main-stream industry. *Desert Hearts* is such a film. Made on a small budget, raised in two and a half years of arduous grass-roots fund raising, and based on a novel by lesbian author Jane Rule, *Desert Hearts* achieved both cross-over box office success and a cult following among lesbians.

"I've waited 25 years for this movie," says Pat, a 47-year-old secretary in San Francisco, California. "I'm sick of seeing only heterosexual love stories. *Desert Hearts* is a movie I can finally identify with. It's like when I was little, we only had 'white dolls' to play with, as if all babies were white. Movie makers have done the same thing; they've generally ignored gays until the last few years. This movie is a positive step in making lesbian movies more acceptable to the general public. I've seen it 22 times and am still not tired of it." . . . "I think that women are drawn to it, lesbians are drawn to it in the same way that black people were drawn to *Superfly*. It isn't so much the content. It's a matter of the identification with it and way it's been presented," says screenplay writer Natalie Cooper. "I'm glad that it served — for anyone — no matter how small, something that could make people feel okay, instead of feeling peripheral or put down. Just to say, 'Hey, I dig it and I love it; I do that, too.' They can say, 'This is our movie, this is our thing.' It makes them feel, dare I say maybe, not proud but viable." (Husten, 1987, p. 8)

Finally, then, the answer to the plight of the marginalized minority audience would seem to lie in the cultivation of alternative channels, even while we continue to press upon the media our claims for equitable and respectful treatment. But neither goal can be easily achieved, and each will require overcoming formidable obstacles.

REFERENCES

Achebe, C. (1976). Colonialist criticism. In *Morning yet on creation day*. NY: Anchor Books.

Adam, B. (1978). *The survival of domination: Inferiorization and everyday life*. NY: Elsevier.

Austin, B. (1981). Portrait of a cult film audience: *The Rocky Horror Picture Show*. *Journal of Communication, 31(2)*, 43-54.

Babuscio, J. (1977). Camp and the gay sensibility. In R. Dyer (Ed.), *Gays and Film* (pp. 40-57). London: British Film Institute.

Cohen, D. & Dyer, R. (1980). The politics of gay culture. In Gay Left Collective (Eds.), *Homosexuality: Power and politics* (pp. 172-186). London: Allison & Busby.

Cowan, P. (1980, March 9). [Letter to the editor]. *New York Times Book Review*.

Dyer, R. (1986). *Heavenly bodies: Film stars and society*. NY: St. Martin's Press.

Ellsworth, E. (1986). Illicit pleasures: Feminist spectators and *Personal Best*. *Wide Angle, 8(2)*, 45-56.

Farber, S. (1986, March 1). Minority villains are touchy network topic. *The New York Times*, p. 50.

Freer, P. (1987). "AIDS and . . ." In G. Hanscombe & M. Humphries (Eds.), *Heterosexuality* (pp. 52-70). London: GMP.

Gerbner, G., & Gross, L. (1976). Living with television. *Journal of Communication, 26(2)*, 172-199.

Gerbner, G., Gross, L., Morgan, M., & Signorielli, N. (1980). The 'mainstreaming' of America. *Journal of Communication, 30(3)*, 10-29.

Gerbner, G., Gross, L., Morgan, M., & Signorielli, N. (1982). Charting the mainstream: Television's contributions to political orientations. *Journal of Communication, 32(2)*, p. 100-127.

Gerbner, G., Gross, L., Morgan, M., & Signorielli, N. (1986). Living with television: The dynamics of the cultivation process. In J. Bryant & D. Zillmann (Eds.), *Perspectives on media effects* (pp. 17-40). Hillsdale, NJ: Lawrence Erlbaum Associates.

Gerbner, G., Gross, L., Hoover, S., Morgan, M., Signorielli, N., Cotugno, H. & Wuthnow, R. (1984). *Religion and television*. The Annenberg School of Communications, University of Pennsylvania.

Gross, L. (1984). The cultivation of intolerance. In G. Melischek, K. Rosengren

& J. Stappers (Eds.), *Cultural indicators: An international symposium* (pp. 345-364). Vienna: Austrian Academy of Sciences.

Ha-'Am, Ahad (Asher Ginzberg). (1970). Moses. In L. Simon (Ed.), *Selected essays of Ahad Ha-am*. NY: Atheneum.

Hachem, S. (1987, March 17). Inside the tinseled closet. *The Advocate*, pp. 42-48.

Henry, W. (1987, April). That certain subject. *Channels*, pp. 43-45.

Hodges, A., & Hutter, D. (1977). *With downcast gays: Aspects of homosexual self-oppression*. Toronto: Pink Triangle Press.

Hoover, S. (1985). *The 700 Club as religion and as television*. Unpublished PhD dissertation, University of Pennsylvania.

Huston, J. (1987, January 25). Fans make *Desert Hearts* a cult classic. *Gay Community News*, pp. 7-8.

Kerr, W. (1982, June 27). *Torch Song Trilogy* — Self mockery as a shield. *The New York Times*, p. II:3.

Kilday, G. (1986, April). Hollywood's homosexuals. *Film Comment*, pp. 40-43.

Michaud, E. (1987). *The whole left is watching*. PhD dissertation in progress (personal communication).

Montgomery, K. (1981). Gay activists and the networks. *Journal of Communication, 31(3)*, pp. 49-57.

Morgan, T. (1986, December 1). The black viewers' new allure for the networks. *The New York Times*, p. III:20.

Pasquali, A. (1975). Latin America: Our image or theirs? In *Getting the message across* (No editor listed). Paris: The *Unesco* Press.

Roth, M. (1985, April 24). CBS evaluates Turner takeover: 'Not a snowball's chance. . . . ' *Variety*, p. 163.

Russo, V. (1981, 1987 [rev. ed.]). *The celluloid closet: Homosexuality in the movies*. New York: Harper & Row.

Russo, V. (1986, April). When the gaze is gay: A state of being. *Film Comment*, pp. 32-34.

Waugh, T. (1988). Minority self-imaging in oppositional film practice: Lesbian and gay documentary. In L. Gross, J. Katz, & J. Ruby (Eds.), *Image ethics: The moral rights of subjects in photography, film and television* (pp. 248-272). New York: Oxford University Press.

Weiss, A. (1986). From the margins: New images of gays in the cinema. *Cineaste, 15(1)*, 4-8.

Williams, R. (1977). *Marxism and literature*. Oxford: Oxford University Press.

Sensationalism or Sensitivity: Use of Words in Stories on Acquired Immune Deficiency Syndrome (AIDS) by Associated Press Videotext

Bruce E. Drushel

Miami University, Oxford, Ohio

SUMMARY. Although it appeared initially reluctant to cover the story at all, the mainstream press in the United States has supplied almost daily reports on AIDS since the mid-1980s. The author examined four weeks of stories on the Associated Press Videotext service in early 1986 in an effort to evaluate the validity of critics' charges that journalists were over-emphasizing the role of homosexuals in the progress of the disease, and that their stories were laden with negative or sensationalistic terms. The author found little evidence from the words used in the stories of distortion in telling the AIDS story, but speculated that such distortion might be found in selection, editing, and presentation decisions made by gatekeepers.

Bruce E. Drushel is Instructor of Mass Communication in the Communication Department at Miami University in Oxford, OH. He is also a doctoral candidate at Ohio University. His dissertation topic is job satisfaction in the broadcasting industry. His other research interests include bias in press coverage and media policy and regulation.

Correspondence should be addressed to Bruce E. Drushel, 151 Williams Hall, Miami University, Oxford OH 45056.

47

Accusations of media distortion and bias in coverage of a broad range of social and political issues have been common over the years. But one area of press reporting, that of health and science stories, has come under particular scrutiny from media critics. The complexity of health and science events and issues may make them difficult for the average news consumer to interpret. While the same may be said of most technical or highly specialized topics, health stories in particular have the potential for greater impact on the individual. They may hold clues, for instance, to ways of prolonging life, enhancing its quality, and avoiding disease and death.

The public does rely to a great extent on the press for information on health care issues. One survey found 89 percent of its sample had read at least one article on health in magazines. Slightly smaller percentages had read an article in the newspaper or had seen a health story on television. But less than 14 percent of those surveyed found the material very helpful (Wright, 1975).

In his examination of writing on health and science subjects, Tannenbaum (1963) found evidence of reporter bias toward the more unusual aspects of stories as opposed to those directly related to the issue under study. Likewise, Glyn and Tims (1982) stopped short of calling coverage of the Tellico Dam controversy of the 1970s sensational, but did conclude that, "peripheral issues did seem to be treated with undue emphasis" (p. 130).

Besides giving the audience inaccurate or misleading information, distorted or sensationalistic stories and headlines can also drive its members away. In his study of reactions to articles about cancer, Bishop (1974) found the one with a more encouraging headline was read by a far greater percentage of his subjects than was the one with the more frightening headline. He concluded that reinforcing, supporting messages may be more effective vehicles of information transmission than those employing "shock techniques" (p. 47).

Just how commonplace this alleged distortion in reporting which favors bizarre and frivolous elements in stories is has also been the subject of some disagreement between reporters and members of the community who serve as their sources of information. In one survey, science writers said they believed those in their profession rarely sensationalized. Scientists disagreed (Ryan, 1979).

Nevertheless, the charges persist, reaching even to the coverage of death. Combs and Slovic (1979) found that deaths due to disease were underreported in newspapers in favor of those due to homicide, natural disasters, and accidents. Death by disease, they concluded, was a private matter as far as the press was concerned, unless that disease threatened to become an epidemic. Coincidentally, Acquired Immune Deficiency Syndrome (AIDS), was first reported in the United States the same year this study was published.

Even in a century that has seen so much destruction from warfare, disease, and assaults to the environment, it would be difficult to imagine a more fearsome potential threat to the health and survival of the human race than AIDS. Because of its capacity not only to take large numbers of human lives, usually by a prolonged and painful process, but also to affect discussions of public policy and issues well-removed from it, one author (Patton, 1985) has gone so far as to place AIDS alongside the bomb as the primary metaphor of our time.

Within 18 months of its discovery in the United States, more than a thousand cases of the disease had been reported among male homosexuals, Haitians, drug addicts, and those intravenously receiving blood (Cahill, 1983). By 1983, some 1,300 cases had been reported in this country, with homosexuals and bisexuals accounting for 71.8 percent. Those using or abusing injectable drugs comprise the second largest group at risk of contracting the disease, with 24.5 percent of the cases. Hemophiliacs, at risk because of their reliance on periodic blood transfusions, are just less than one percent of the cases. Another 5.8 percent are infected from a variety of other means (Foege, 1983).

Haitian immigrants to the United States accounted for 5.5 percent of the cases as of April, 1983 (Foege, 1983), and were at one time listed as one of the top three AIDS risk groups. But because researchers could discover no racial or ethnic predisposition to the disease, the Centers for Disease Control in Atlanta (CDC) no longer considers them a risk group (Vieira, 1986).[1]

AIDS cases reported in the United States as of April of 1983 occurred primarily in larger urban areas on the east and west coasts. New York City had 66.1 cases per million residents; nearby Newark had 16.2 per million. Miami had 30.8 cases per million. On the west coast, San Francisco had 50.5 cases per million residents. Los Angeles had 12.4 (Foege, 1983).

It is now believed hundreds of thousands have at least been exposed to the virus, an increasing number of heterosexuals among them. More than 25,000 have been diagnosed as having AIDS itself, with well over half that number having already died. And AIDS is no longer confined to large coastal cities. Towns, small and large, midwest, south, and north, all have reported cases of the disease.

The media, while slow to cover early reports of the disease, soon reported AIDS stories almost daily. This was perhaps inevitable, since, according to Altman (1986), the story of the disease had all the necessary qualifications to warrant major attention:

1. It appeared to have deadly consequences.
2. There had been a dramatic increase in the number of cases.
3. Its scope was both national and international.
4. It appealed to voyeurism and fear.

Some observers, (e.g., NBC News Science Correspondent Robert Bazell), have attributed the early lag in coverage to a reluctance by the media to air or publish stories about homosexuals. They maintain that it was only after the disease was reported among other segments of the population that a vigorous reporting effort began (Altman, 1986).

But it has been the quality, not the quantity, of press coverage of AIDS that has been most on the minds of media critics. Among the charges levelled against press accounts of the disease are: (a) that they have emphasized negative and discouraging events and that they have hindered rather than aided efforts to educate the public (Stein, 1985); (b) that they induced unnecessary panic early on because reporters failed to understand the difference between the meanings attached to the word "epidemic" by those in the medical profession on the one hand and laymen on the other (Burkett, 1986); (c) that they have been sensationalistic and cynical, have blamed the AIDS victim for his or her own plight, and have overemphasized the role of the homosexual in the spread of the disease

(Altman, 1986); (d) that competition among the various media has resulted in a dearth of coverage of less-interesting elements of the AIDS story which might nevertheless be more closely-tied to solutions to the problem (Patton, 1985); and (e) that the press has been less zealous in responding to AIDS than it had been for such other health threats as toxic shock syndrome and Legionnaires' disease (Weiss, 1983).

RESEARCH PROBLEM

Assuming for a moment that media reporting about AIDS does contain distortions, and that these distortions hold the potential to alter the salience of the story or any of its elements for public officials or their constituents, then the coverage of the disease by the press has broad social and policy implications.

The purpose of this study was to examine national press coverage of the AIDS story. The following questions were addressed:

1. Does coverage of AIDS by the national press tend to more closely link the disease with homosexuality than is warranted by risk group percentages?
2. Because of its large and well-known homosexual community, is San Francisco the locus of a disproportionate number of AIDS stories?
3. Is the national press using words with negative connotations in stories about the disease, its transmission, and those who have contracted it?

METHOD

Collecting a sample of national stories on any topic is problematic. First, the newspaper industry in the United States is dominated by a large number of regional and local dailies which rely on wire services for the majority of their national stories. Second, not all wire service stories are available to readers throughout the country. Rather than rely on a collection of locally edited wire stories from randomly selected dailies, or base his research on stories in a national paper such as *USA Today*, which was designed as a supplementary, not primary, source of information for its readers (Whetmore, 1985), the author collected his sample from the Associated Press's videotext service. Since AP Videotext stories are taken from the print versions available to member newspapers and are not subject to local gatekeeping decisions, the author believed they would serve as reasonably faithful renderings of the stories available.

Each story dealing with Acquired Immune Deficiency Syndrome carried by AP Videotext over a four-week period from January 22, 1986, to February 16, 1986, was collected. A computer then scanned the stories, and created an alphabetical listing of each word, together with the words and phrases surrounding it each time it was used. From this master word listing, the author prepared sublists of words referring to AIDS, those with the disease, how it was transmitted, those in AIDS risk groups, and cities where AIDS cases had been reported.

Value Rankings

To arrive at a measure of the positive or negative connotations the public attaches to the words in the sublists, two hundred communications undergraduate students from Ohio University were asked to rank the elements of three of the sublists: words referring to AIDS, words referring to those with AIDS, and words referring to methods of transmission. Because of errors in carrying out the instructions, just 166, or 83%, of the rankings were used. The author then computed the mean ranking for each word.

Tests for Relationship

Pearson's *r* correlation coefficients, which test the strength of relationships between pairs of variables, were calculated for each sublist. In those sublists with value-ranked elements, the correlation measured the relationship between the frequency of the word in the text sample and its mean ranking. In the case of the sublist containing the names of cities where AIDS had been reported, the relationship measured was that between the frequency of the city name in the sample and the number of AIDS cases reported in that metropolitan area. And in the sublist of words referring to AIDS risk groups, the correlation measured the relationship between the frequency of the words in each risk group category in the sample and the percentage of reported cases from each category.

RESULTS

The collection phase of the study netted 47 stories about AIDS with a total word count of 20,108. Ten words which, in context, referred to Acquired Immune Deficiency Syndrome, were located in the sample: affliction, ailment, condition, contagion, disease, disorder, epidemic, illness, infection, and scourge (see Table 1). Four words made up the sublist referring to those with AIDS: carrier, patient, sufferer, and victim (see Table 2). The sublist of words referring to how those with AIDS got the disease contained seven words: catch, contact, develop, exposed, infect, spread, and transmit (see Table 3).

A fourth sublist contained four categories of words referring to those at risk of getting AIDS. The words homosexual, bisexual, and gay made up the first category; intravenous drug users, abusers, and addicts were in the second; the words children, child, infant, girl, boy, and youth made up the third category; and hemophiliac was in the fourth.

The final sublist was of cities which reported more than ten cases per million residents: Los Angeles, Miami, Newark, New York, and San Francisco.

Value Rankings and Frequencies

In each of the sublists in which words were value-ranked, mean-rankings discriminated clearly among the words. Rankings of higher value indicate words the subjects perceived as having more negative connotations; rankings of lower value, less negative connotations.

Relationships between the sublists of value-ranked words and the frequency of the words in the sample were low-to-moderate and were not statistically significant. The highest association appeared to exist for words referring to the transmission of AIDS, $r = .47$, $p < .28$ (see Table 3). The next highest association was for words referring to AIDS itself, $r = .31, p < .38$ (see Table 1). The corre-

TABLE 1. Correlation between value rankings of words referring to AIDS and their sample frequency

Word Referring to AIDS	Mean Ranking	Text Frequency
epidemic	8.60	3
scourge	8.13	1
disease	7.51	141
contagion	6.20	2
infection	5.96	23
disorder	4.92	1
affliction	4.42	5
illness	3.96	11
ailment	3.07	1
condition	2.21	6

Pearson's r = .31, p < .38

TABLE 2. Correlation between value rankings of words referring to those with AIDS and their sample frequency

Word Referring to those with AIDS	Mean Ranking	Text Frequency
victim	3.45	43
sufferer	3.06	3
carrier	2.21	8
patient	1.19	31

Pearson's r = .03, p < .97

TABLE 3. Correlation between value rankings of words referring to transmission of AIDS and their sample frequency

Word Referring to AIDS Transmission	Mean Ranking	Text Frequency
infect	6.18	26
spread	5.02	24
transmit	4.72	43
contract	4.01	24
exposed to/exposure to	3.14	34
catch	2.70	2
develop	2.21	16

Pearson's r = .47, p < .28

lation coefficient for the sublist of words referring to those with AIDS was the lowest of the three, $r = .03, p < .97$ (see Table 2).

Risk Group, Story Location, and Frequency

The AP Videotext sample likewise offered little evidence of a relationship between the frequency of occurrence of words referring to risk group members and the percentage of known cases reported in each risk group, $r = .09, p < .91$ (see Table 4).

There did appear, however, to be evidence of a relationship between the number of cases of AIDS diagnosed from the five cities in the sublist and their frequency of mention in the text sample. When the text frequency was correlated with reported cases per million residents, the correlation was high, but not statistically significant, $r = .82, p < .09$ (see Table 5). But when the text frequency was compared with the raw total of diagnosed cases reported in each of the cities, the correlation was both high and significant, $r = .98, p < .003$ (see Table 6).

TABLE 4. Correlation between frequency of reported cases from AIDS risk groups and risk group frequency of mention in sample

AIDS Risk Groups	Percentage of Reported Cases [a]	Frequency in AP Videotext
homosexuals/bisexuals	71.8	44
intravenous drug users	24.5	43
children [b]	1.4	72
hemophiliacs	0.9	24

Pearson's $\underline{r}$ = .09, $\underline{p}$ < .91
[a] Percentages reflect overlap among groups
[b] Various explanations for having contracted AIDS

DISCUSSION

Value-Ranking and Frequency

Even though, as indicated above, there is little evidence that AP Videotext journalists systematically used words with either a negative or a positive connotation when writing about AIDS, those with AIDS, or how it was contracted, the relatively frequent use of certain words from each of the sublists is nevertheless worthy of note.

In the sublist of words referring to AIDS itself, for instance, "disease" was far and away the most frequently used. It was also thought to have a relatively negative connotation, compared with the other words on the sublist. This should not come as a surprise for two reasons. First, considering the relatively pessimistic current outlook for those with AIDS, it is appropriate that a moderately negative term be the one most used, if for no other reason than to convey the seriousness of the situation in a way that "illness," "disorder," and "ailment" cannot. Second, despite its perceived negativeness, "disease" is also generic and applied to a wide range of serious medical states—so much so that the federal agency in

TABLE 5. Correlation between reported cases per million of AIDS from American cities with most reported cases and their sample frequency

Cities Where AIDS Reported	Reported AIDS Cases (per million residents)	Frequency in AP Videotext
New York	66.1	14
San Francisco	50.5	7
Los Angeles	30.8	5
Miami	16.2	1
Newark	12.4	1

Pearson's r = .82, p < .09

charge of gathering and disseminating information about these states is called the Centers for Disease Control.

Likewise, "transmit," the word used most frequently to refer to the passage of AIDS from one person to another, while not as innocuous-sounding as "catch," fails to induce in the average person the sorts of fearsome images "infect" does. "Transmit," in its common usage, seems to be associated more with the fact of the passage of something than with any sort of assignment of cause, blame, or guilt.

Text frequencies in the sublist of words referring to those with AIDS were of a somewhat different pattern. While "victim," judged the most negative word in the sublist, was the most-used, the next most-frequent was "patient," which was assigned the least-negative ranking. This finding becomes less paradoxical when one considers that "victim" is used widely by the press to refer to those who find themselves, not usually of their own volition, in unfortunate circumstances. Hence, there are "accident victims," "shooting victims," "mugging victims," and even "victims of a hoax." The average person may perceive "victim" as carrying with it a relatively negative connotation, but its use in newswriting seems almost sympathetic.

TABLE 6. Correlation between frequency of reported cases of AIDS from American cities with most reported cases and their sample frequency

Cities Where AIDS Reported	Reported AIDS Cases	Frequency in AP Videotext
New York	4923	14
San Francisco	1730	7
Los Angeles	1306	5
Miami	475	1
Newark	373	1

Pearson's r = .98, p < .003

Risk Group and Frequency

There was evidence of some distortion in AP Videotext's representation of AIDS risk groups, although it was not directed toward disproportionately linking homosexuals with the disease. While figures cited earlier have homosexuals and bisexuals accounting for 71.8 percent of reported AIDS cases, their frequency of mention in the sample was just 24.0 percent of all risk group mentions. Abusers of intravenous drugs, who comprise the second-largest risk group, were also underrepresented in the sample, but to a far lesser extent. While they accounted for 24.5 percent of reported cases of the disease, they represented just 23.5 percent of risk group mentions in the sample.

Children and those with hemophilia were greatly overrepresented in the sample, largely because of the press attention to Ryan White, the young hemophiliac from Indiana, who was barred from public school after he contracted AIDS from a blood transfusion. Although the two risk groups combined make up just more than two percent of the known cases, they accounted for more than half of the mentions in the text sample.

Aside from the effects on the sample of the media's preoccupation with the Ryan White story, the underrepresentation of drug users and, particularly, of homosexuals and bisexuals, may have been less a conscious effort by journalists not to link them to AIDS and more an effort to avoid their mention entirely. It is quite possible that, while the press became increasingly more willing to report on the disease as its seriousness became more evident, its hesitance to mention its most significant risk group did not.

Another possible explanation is that AP Videotext journalists were either consciously or subconsciously tailoring their coverage towards the heterosexual majority rather than towards the homosexual minority, even though the latter group has had a much higher instance of the disease. The justification could have been that the majority might be less likely to be aware of AIDS and how it is transmitted than would a tightly-knit minority community, and that this ignorance actually would put heterosexuals at greatly increased risk of getting the disease through blood transfusions, sexual contact with a carrier, or through dirty syringes.

Location of Stories and Frequency

The relationship between reported cases of AIDS in the five cities examined and the cities' frequency of mention in the sample was very high. New York, which surpassed San Francisco both in total reported cases of the disease and in cases per million residents, was mentioned in that context in the sample nearly twice as often as San Francisco. What is remarkable is that, even assuming no systematic effort by journalists to link San Francisco with AIDS, the visibility and activist nature of the city's homosexual community would have led one to expect more stories about AIDS to have been generated there during its mobilization against the disease.

CONCLUSIONS

It thus appears that if the national press in the United States is presenting a distorted view of the unfolding AIDS story, that distortion is not reflected by and large in the words journalists use to tell that story. Little evidence was found of a systematic use of sensationalistic language in referring either to those with AIDS or at risk of getting it, the transmission of the disease, or the disease itself. Further, little support was found for claims of an over-emphasis on the role of homosexuality in the spread of the disease.

None of the foregoing by any means rules out the existence of pervasive distortion in reporting on AIDS. It merely indicates that distortion, if it is occurring, does so in much more subtle ways than in language, such as editing and presentation decisions which are made in preparing AIDS stories. Sensational headlines, photographs, and other visuals can alter the news consumer's perceptions. Omission of facts, especially background information that is key to accurate framing of the story, may result in the popular view of the AIDS story as merely a collection of tragic deaths, conflicting opinions on the relevance of social taboos, and dire yet vague predictions about the survival of our race, instead of as a health issue which has broad implications for society and which demands responses which are reasonable, well thought-out, and yet timely.

Another possible source of distortion and sensationalism in AIDS coverage may be found in the choices journalists make of which aspects of the story to emphasize. Believing they are actually boosting audience comprehension of the story, reporters may direct their writing towards the tangible: case studies, symbols, and events. Or, hoping to boost reader interest, they may focus on elements of the AIDS story with high conflict levels. In doing either, they may actually be trivializing the story and reducing long-term interest in it by relegating the issues to a secondary role.

NOTE

1. The percentages fail to total 100 percent because of some overlap among the risk groups, e.g., a bisexual intravenous drug user.

REFERENCES

Altman, D. (1986). *AIDS in the minds of America*. Garden City, NJ: Doubleday.
Bishop, R. L. (1974). Anxiety and readership of health information. *Journalism Quarterly, 51*(1), 40-46.
Burkett, W. (1986). *News reporting: Science, medicine, and high technology*. Ames, IA: The Iowa State University Press.

Cahill, K. M. (1983). Preface: The evolution of an epidemic. In K. M. Cahill (Ed.), *The AIDS epidemic* (pp. 1-6). New York: St. Martin's Press.

Combs, B., & Slovic, P. (1979). Newspaper coverage of causes of death. *Journalism Quarterly, 56*(4), 837-843, 849.

Foege, W. (1983). The national pattern of AIDS. In K. M. Cahill (Ed.), *The AIDS epidemic* (pp. 7-17). New York: St. Martin's Press.

Glyn, C. J., & Tims, A. R. (1982). Sensationalism in science issues: A case study. *Journalism Quarterly, 59*(2), 126-131.

Patton, C. (1985). *Sex and germs: The politics of AIDS.* Boston: South End Press.

Ryan, M. (1979). Attitudes of scientists and journalists toward media coverage of science news. *Journalism Quarterly, 56*(1), 26, 53.

Stein, M. L. (1985, November 2). AIDS: Getting the facts. *Editor & Publisher,* pp. 16-17.

Tannenbaum, P. H. (1963). Communication of science information. *Science, 140,* 579-87.

Vieira, J. (1986). The Haitian link. In V. Gong & N. Rudnick (Eds.), *AIDS facts and issues* (pp. 117-135). New Brunswick, NJ: Rutgers University Press.

Weiss, T. (1983). The public response. In K. M. Cahill (Ed.), *The AIDS epidemic* (pp. 157-161). New York: St. Martin's Press.

Whetmore, E. J. (1985). *Mediamerica.* Belmont, CA: Wadsworth Publishing Company.

Wright, W. R. (1975). Mass media as sources of medical information. *Journal of Communication 25*(3), 171-73.

The Important Role of Mass Media in the Diffusion of Accurate Information About AIDS

Kathleen K. Reardon, PhD
University of Southern California

Jean L. Richardson, PhD
University of Southern California

SUMMARY. This paper explores the vital role of mass media in diminishing the lack of consensus among those at risk for AIDS and those who treat them. It examines the perceptions of these groups with regard to the seriousness of the AIDS threat, what people at risk are really doing to protect themselves and others, and the accuracy and objectivity of media reports about AIDS. Results indicate that there is a disarming lack of consensus among those people who can do the most to influence the spread of AIDS. Results also indicate that those people at greatest risk for AIDS and for spreading the disease distrust the accuracy and objectivity of the media. The authors argue that consensus is required for a concerted fight on AIDS and that the mass media offer an effective avenue for encouraging it. They also explore methods for regaining media respect among high risk groups with regard to AIDS reporting.

According to results of two 1985 Gallup polls conducted for the New York City Department of Health (Clarke & Sencer, 1985),

Kathleen K. Reardon, University of Massachusetts, 1978, is Associate Professor of Business Communication and Preventive Medicine at the University of Southern California. Jean L. Richardson, UCLA, 1980, is Associate Professor of Preventive Medicine at the University of Southern California.

Correspondence may be addressed to Kathleen K. Reardon at ACC. 400C, University of Southern California, Los Angeles, CA 90089-1421, and to Jean L. Richardson at IPR, 35 North Lake Ave., Pasadena, CA 91101.

ninety-five percent of the United States population has heard of AIDS. Eighty percent realize that most AIDS patients are homosexuals and eighty-four percent know that intravenous drug (IV) users who share needles are at high risk for AIDS. These polls suggest that communication methods have succeeded in making the public aware of AIDS. The question remains, however, whether mass media are communicating messages to the public that are helping to decrease the spread of AIDS without creating panic and prejudicial responses.

For millions of people infected with the HIV, for the "worried well" in high risk groups, and for the heterosexual population, mass media can play a vital role in persuading people to use precautions against AIDS infection. Decades of research on the influence of opinion leaders, the agenda setting function of the mass media, the role of mass media in the diffusion of health information, and recent work on media dependency suggest that the mass media are in a unique position to respond to the need for reliable information about AIDS both in terms of its biological nature and the precise manner of its transmission. Unfortunately chronic health problems like AIDS typically become part of the news when they can be encapsulated into short-term, life-or-death drama (Turoe & Coe, 1985). Stories about actor Rock Hudson, who hid his homosexuality until he was dying from AIDS, and Fabian Bridges, a male prostitute in Texas who continued prostitution after he was diagnosed with AIDS, may have raised public awareness of AIDS but did little to convince people that this is a disease that may infect them if proper precautions are not taken immediately.

Mass media have likely contributed to the reported decreases in high risk behavior among homosexual men. In San Francisco, the proportion of homosexual and bisexual males who reported that they were monogamous, celibate, or practiced "unsafe" sex only with their steady partner increased from 69 percent in 1984 to 81 percent in 1985 (Puckett & Bart, 1985). In spite of these changes, among a cohort of homosexual men in San Francisco city clinics, the prevalence of serum antibodies to HIV increased from 4.5 percent in 1978 to 73.1 percent in 1985. The pace of contagion has far exceeded the pace of behavioral change. Additional measures may need to be taken by individuals to stop the spread of AIDS. Substantial reduction in the spread of AIDS will require substantial reduction in high-risk sexual practices (Puckett & Bart, 1985). Modifications in risk behaviors are also important for heterosexuals. Contrary to common belief, sexual preference is not always an either-or matter. According to the Kinsey report (Kinsey, Pomeroy, & Martin, 1948), 37 percent of the total while male population of the United States has at least some overt homosexual experience between adolescence and old age and most of these males do not consider themselves homosexuals.

Mass media can assist in dispelling the common belief that AIDS is a homosexual disease. In parts of Africa, AIDS affects men and women equally. In the United States, 7 percent of AIDS patients have contracted the disease through heterosexual sexual contact. This can occur through sexual relations with IV drug users who have been infected, from prostitutes who are viral positive, or through sexual relations with infected bisexual partners. It has been estimated that by 1991, 9 percent, or 7,000 people, will have contracted AIDS by heterosexual contact.

One major obstacle in the path of persuading both heterosexuals and homosexuals to take precautions against AIDS is that its onset may be delayed for years following HIV exposure (*Facts about AIDS*, 1985). Because the immediate consequences of sexual activity are highly reinforcing and because the potential negative consequences of certain sexual activities are distant and uncertain, knowledge of or fear of AIDS may fail to alter behavior (Kelly & St. Lawrence, 1986). Furthermore, those who test positive for HIV but are not diagnosed as having AIDS may respond to the threat with denial. Such people are a threat to themselves and those with whom they have intimate relations.

The mass media are in the unique position to respond to the need for reliable information that will motivate both homosexuals and heterosexuals to reduce their high risk behaviors. Yet, as Jonsen, Cooke, and Koenig (1986) note, "The turmoil of emotion stirred by the horror of the disease, its menace to the health of the society, and its association with sexuality make almost impossible a dispassionate analysis that sorts out principle from prejudice and basic values from expedient policies" (p. 64). Here again the media can play an important public service by restraining sensationalistic reporting that might foster prejudicial responses.

Whether it occurs through homosexual contact, heterosexual contact or sharing of IV needles, by 1991 over 270,000 people will have contracted AIDS and 179,000 will have died. This threat can only be blocked if a unified front exists in the attack on AIDS. There can be little dispute among those at high risk and the medical people treating them concerning the extent of the threat and how it may be reduced and ultimately destroyed.

THE STUDY

As part of a larger study, we investigated the extent of consensus among samples of people at elevated risk for AIDS, those with AIDS related symptoms and doctors of AIDS patients. While research has demonstrated that people are aware of AIDS, we were interested in whether people at risk for AIDS and physicians agree on the extent of risk and measures being taken to reduce it. We were also interested in their perceptions of the role mass media have played in conveying information about AIDS to the public.

Subjects

Four hundred and eighteen subjects participated in this study: 183 heterosexual physicians, 112 homosexual physicians, 30 homosexual men with symptoms associated with AIDS, and 93 healthy homosexual males. These four groups of people are immediately or indirectly affected by the AIDS epidemic.

Healthy homosexual men were contacted through two Los Angeles County campus homosexual support groups. Homosexual subjects who had symptoms associated with AIDS (persistent generalized lymphadenopathy or PGL) were patients at three Los Angeles County AIDS clinics.

Heterosexual physicians were all members of the Los Angeles County Medical Association (LACMA) and homosexual physicians were members of Southern California Physicians for Human Rights (SCPHR), an association of primarily gay males. Sixty-eight percent of the SCPHR physicians were exclusively homosexual and ninety-eight percent of the LACMA respondents were exclusively heterosexual. There were no significant differences between the two samples regarding the size of their practice or the number of AIDS patients they had. On a percentage basis, AIDS patients and those with related symptoms constituted 3.3 percent of the SCPHR and 1.8 percent of the LACMA patient load.

Procedures and Results

Members of the four groups were asked a series of questions pertaining to (a) the adoption of safe sexual practices by high risk groups, (b) belief in the efficacy of safe practices, (c) satisfaction with research efforts focused on AIDS, and (d) perspectives on the accuracy and objectivity of media reports about AIDS.

Questions were constructed as four-point scales anchored by strongly agree and strongly disagree. Comparisons of means (Scheffe's Test) were conducted between each pair of sample populations. Results are presented in Table 1. The significant differences in group means suggest the groups represented in this study often disagree on matters important to curbing the AIDS epidemic. Two items assessed the extent to which conservative sexual practices are being adopted by high risk groups. We asked subjects (Item 1) whether men with AIDS would continue to have sexual relations and (Item 2) whether the AIDS scare has caused more gay males to establish stable sexual relationships. Heterosexual doctors' responses to the first item differed significantly from the other three groups. As indicated in Table 1, 73% of the heterosexual doctors believed that most gay men with AIDS continue to have sexual relations. By contrast, seventy-seven percent of PGL patients reported disagreement with the assertion that AIDS patients would continue to have sexual relations. The responses of all three gay groups were significantly different from the responses of heterosexual doctors.

A second statement about stable sexual practices led to a somewhat different pattern of results. In response to the statement, "The AIDS scare has caused more gay males to establish stable sexual relationships," homosexual and heterosexual doctors were in agreement. Over eighty-five percent of each group agreed with the statement. Healthy gay men and PGL patients were somewhat less

TABLE 1
COMPARISONS OF RESPONSES AMONG GROUPS

Group   Percent Distribution

ITEM 1: Most gay men with AIDS related conditions would continue
         to have sexual relations.

	SA	MA	MD	SD	
Healthy Gay Men	4.3	31.2	34.4	30.1	(a)
PGL	10.0	13.3	26.7	50.0	(a)
Homosexual MDs	8.0	36.6	33.9	21.4	(a)
Heterosexual MDs	21.3	51.9	18.0	8.8	(b)*

ITEM 2: The AIDS scare has caused more gay males to establish
         stable sexual relationships.

	SA	MA	MD	SD	
Healthy Gay Men	14.7	62.1	15.8	7.4	(a)
PGL	33.3	40.0	20.0	6.7	(a,b)
Homosexual MDs	27.7	61.6	9.8	1.0	(b)
Heterosexual MDs	26.4	59.2	12.1	2.3	(b)

ITEM 3: There is nothing a person can do to protect himself from
         getting AIDS.

	SA	MA	MD	SD	
Healthy Gay Men	0.0	4.3	19.2	77.6	(a)
PGL	0.0	10.0	13.3	76.7	(a)
Homosexual MDs	1.0	0.0	8.0	91.2	(a)
Heterosexual MDs	.5	5.3	15.3	78.8	(a)

ITEM 4: The amount of money being spent on AIDS research is about right.

Healthy Gay Men	4.3	14.0	18.3	63.4	(a
PGL	3.3	16.7	13.3	66.7	(a
Homosexual MDs	1.8	7.1	8.9	82.1	(a
Heterosexual MDs	9.2	31.0	27.7	32.1	(b

ITEM 5: The reports of AIDS have been exaggerated.

Healthy Gay Men	7.5	24.5	29.8	38.3	(a)
PGL	13.8	34.5	17.2	34.5	(a)
Homosexual MDs	2.7	4.5	15.2	77.7	(b)
Heterosexual MDs	4.8	14.3	24.9	56.1	(c)

ITEM 6: Media reports have been intentionally biased to prejudice the straight community against the gay community.

Healthy Gay Men	8.7	41.3	35.9	14.1	(a)
PGL	13.3	33.3	40.0	13.3	(a)
Homosexual MDs	9.8	33.9	42.0	14.3	(a)
Heterosexual MDs	2.7	13.5	48.7	35.1	(b)

*a,b designate significant differences between groups at .05 level using Scheffe's Test for group mean differences.

convinced that gay males have been motivated by the AIDS epidemic to establish stable sexual relationships.

Although the sample size of PGL patients warrants conservatism in interpreting these results, it appears that the people involved with AIDS are not of one mind concerning the sexual practices of high risk groups. Gay men, whether doctors, healthy college students or PGL patients, generally believe that men with AIDS do not continue to have sexual relations. Heterosexual doctors, who may represent the conservative heterosexual community in the United States, believe that men with AIDS continue to have sexual relations. It is difficult to determine which group has a more accurate perspective. One might make the case that gay men should know what is actually going on. Alternatively, one might argue that they lack the objectivity of the heterosexual doctors. The most interesting finding here may be that none of the four groups is totally convinced that men with AIDS cease their sexual relations. Nor are they totally convinced that the threat of AIDS has motivated gay males to establish stable relationships. The implications of these findings are clear. The AIDS epidemic can only be curbed by widespread changes in sexual behavior. In the absence of such changes, AIDS will infect an increasingly larger portion of the gay population. Given that a fair percentage of homosexual males are not exclusively homosexual (32% of the homosexual doctors who participated in this study), the spread to the heterosexual community will also accelerate.

The second issue addressed in this study was belief in the efficacy of safe practices. When presented with the statement, "There is nothing a person can do to protect himself from getting AIDS," all four groups reported disagreement. This finding is somewhat reassuring, but it does not tell us the extent of behavioral change people at risk for AIDS are willing to make. Responses to the earlier item on the adoption of safe sexual practices suggests that monogamy is perceived by many gay men as a greater change than they care to make.

To assess satisfaction with efforts to fight AIDS, we asked subjects to tell us whether enough money is being spent on AIDS research. As Table 1 indicates, the heterosexual doctors' responses differed significantly from the other three groups. Forty percent of the heterosexual doctors agreed with the statement, "The amount of money being spent on AIDS research is about right." The other three groups tended to disagree with this statement. It is not surprising that gay men believe that more money should be spent on AIDS research. In the United States, they are the ones most threatened by the disease. Heterosexual doctors may feel less personal threat from AIDS and may reason that there are many diseases that are equally deserving of research money.

The last issue of interest to us pertained to the accuracy and objectivity of the information about AIDS available to the public. We asked subjects whether they thought reports about AIDS were exaggerated. Mean comparisons of their responses indicate that homosexual doctors are more convinced than any other group that the reports are not exaggerated, while heterosexual doctors are more convinced than healthy gay men and PGL patients. While over fifty percent of both healthy gay men and PGL patients agree with the doctors, a significant percentage of those two groups consider AIDS reports exaggerated.

While this finding does not tell us the nature of the exaggeration observed or not observed, it may help to explain why healthy gay men and PGL patients responded as they did to the item concerning the effects of the AIDS scare on the establishment of stable relationships. If a significant portion of the nonmedical gay community believes that reports of AIDS contagion have been exaggerated, it should come as no surprise to find they also believe that a significant number of gay men have not taken the major step of establishing stable sexual relationships to reduce the chances of contracting AIDS.

One plausible explanation for nonmedical gay men believing that reports of AIDS are exaggerated is that accurate reports are simply not reaching them sufficiently often for them to know the facts. According to Cronholm and Sandell (1981) scientific information, such as that about AIDS, primarily reaches those who already have some knowledge on the topic or those who are educated to value it. Doctors are more likely than the nonmedical community to be familiar with recent AIDS statistics and projections for spread of the disease. It may be that nonmedical gay men are also less likely than homosexual doctors to receive constant disconfirmation of their belief that AIDS is not a serious epidemic. In persuasion theory terms, unlike homosexual doctors, many nonmedical gay men may be reducing the dissonance that comes from engaging in behaviors that may lead to AIDS by avoiding information that disconfirms the belief that it won't happen to them. By assuming that reports about AIDS are exaggerated, nonmedical gay men further reduce the dissonance they feel when engaging in unsafe sexual practices.

A second information item concerned media bias. As indicated in Table 1, all three groups of gay men differ from heterosexual doctors in their assessment of media bias. Heterosexual doctors do not believe that media reports have been intentionally biased to prejudice the straight community against the gay community. Gay men are significantly less convinced of media objectivity in this regard.

It appears that a significant portion of the gay community perceives some degree of intentionality among the media to foster prejudice against gay people. It may be that such intentions exist and that they are malicious in intent. Perhaps the undertone of fear that accompanies any threat has, in this case, fostered attempts to locate and isolate a target of blame. An equally plausible explanation is that the mass media are having difficulty maintaining objectivity on this issue. It is difficult to be objective about a disease that we are as yet unable to control. Moreover, many people are uncomfortable with or offended by the association of AIDS with sexuality and are incapable of a dispassionate analysis of the problem.

It may also be the case, that the media are not attempting to prejudice straights against gays, but that the limited amount of time and space given to any story leads them to rely on outmoded stereotypes and dramatic cases for story lines. Photos and film coverage of AIDS often focus on men cuddling and kissing each other in public, behaviors not characteristic of most gay men. In this way the mass media contribute to the same type of "symbolic annihilation" of the gay population as they did when feminists were portrayed as bra burning, unattractive, hostile women (Gerbner, 1978). In their reliance on stereotypes, the media undercut, discredit, and isolate gay men. Our results suggest that this leads gay men to assume that the media is intentionally fostering antagonism among straight people toward the gay community.

A third explanation of the findings pertaining to media bias is implied in the responses of gay men to the earlier question concerning the extent of exaggeration in AIDS reports. It is possible that nonmedical gay men consider exaggerated reports as evidence of the mass media's intention to prejudice the straight community against the gay community. A typical reaction to prejudice is reciprocated antagonism. Should this occur, gay men may resist information campaigns designed to save their lives.

DISCUSSION

According to the San Francisco AIDS Foundation and the Centers for Disease Control, the best defense against AIDS is information. A vaccine for AIDS is not likely to be discovered, tested, and made available within the next decade (Osborn, 1986). It has been estimated that within the next ten years, AIDS will take the lives of hundreds of thousands of people unless safe sexual practices are adopted.

Our preliminary investigation into the perceptions and attitudes of people at risk for AIDS, those with AIDS symptoms, and doctors who treat AIDS patients indicates that there is little consensus concerning the extent of threat, measures being taken to curb the epidemic, and the credibility of media reports about AIDS.

While it is important to avoid panic, the seriousness of the AIDS threat must be conveyed to the public, especially to those who are at high risk of infection. It must become impossible for people to deny that AIDS is a threat to the entire society. The time between infection and manifestation of AIDS symptoms is often several years. During those years, people unaware of their infectious state spread the virus to others. To curb the AIDS epidemic, people who would rather not think about AIDS and those who reduce their dissonance over high-risk behaviors by derogating information sources or refusing to learn about AIDS must be persuaded to eliminate high-risk behaviors.

To accomplish the goal of persuading people to engage in safe sexual practices, more than hit or miss media campaigns will be needed. This investigation demonstrates that many gay men currently believe that the media are intentionally creating antagonism between heterosexuals and homosexuals. Moreover, mass media that do objectively and thoroughly report the facts on AIDS may not be reaching the people in need of the information. It may be useful to couple mass media campaigns with interpersonal campaigns. As Cronholm and Sandell (1985) explained, with particularly complex scientific topics personal communication may be suited to accessing otherwise inaccessible groups and to both clearly explaining and emphasizing the need for behavioral changes. Health researchers have found joint mass media and interpersonal campaigns effective in changing bad health habits such as smoking, drug abuse, and alcoholism (Maccoby & Farquhar, 1975; Best, 1980; Flay & Sobel, 1983).

The AIDS epidemic poses a massive diffusion and persuasion challenge. To the extent that mass media gain the respect of high risk groups, they may play a vital role in staying the tide of AIDS infection. This will require serious conversations by knowledgeable parties to uncover values, reveal prejudices, and formulate reasons and arguments based on epidemiological facts. In this way the media may serve a fundamental role in curbing the spread of a disease that, directly or indirectly, threatens all of us.

REFERENCES

Best, J.A. (1980). Mass media, self management and smoking modification. In P.O. Davidson & S.M. Davidson (Eds.), *Behavioral medicine: Changing health life-styles*. New York: Bruner/Mazel.

Clarke, P.D., & Sencer, J. (1985). Results of a Gallop poll on Acquired Immuno-deficiency Syndrome—New York City, United States. *Morbidity and Mortality Weekly Report, 34*, 513-514.

Cronholm, M., & Sandell, R. (1981). Scientific information: A review of research. *Journal of Communication, 31*(1), 85-96.

Facts about AIDS (pamphlet). (1985, August). U.S. Department of Health and Human Services. Public Health Services.

Flay, B.R., & Sobel, J.L. (1983). The role of mass media in preventing adolescent drug abuse. In T.J. Glynn, C.G. Leukefeld, and J.P. Ludford (Eds.), *Preventing adolescent drug abuse*. Rockville, Maryland: National Institute of Drug Abuse.

Gerbner, G. (1978). The dynamics of cultural resistance. In G. Tuchman et al. (Eds.), *Hearth and home: Images of women in the mass media*. New York: Oxford University Press.

Jonsen, A.R., Cooke, M., & Koenig, B.A. (1986). Aids and ethics. *Issues in Science and Technology, 2*, 56-65.

Kelly, J.A., & St. Lawrence, J.S. (1986). Behavioral intervention and AIDS. *Behavior Therapist, 9*, 121-125.

Kinsey, A.C., Pomeroy, W., & Martin, C. (1948). *Sexual behavior in the human male*. Philadelphia: W. B. Saunders.

Maccoby, N., & Farquhar, J.W. (1975). Communication for health: Unselling heart disease. *Journal of Communication, 25*, 114-126.

Osborn, J.E. (1986). The AIDS epidemic: An overview of the science, *Issues in Science and Technology, 2*, 40-55.

Puckett, S.B., & Bart, M. (1985, November 8). Self-reported behavioral changes among homosexual and bisexual men—San Francisco. *Morbidity and Mortality Weekly Report*, p. 2537.

Turoe, J., & Coe, L. (1985). Curing television ills: The portrayal of health care. *Journal of Communication, 35*, 36-51.

RESEARCH ON ADOLESCENT SEXUAL SOCIALIZATION

Television Viewing and Adolescents' Sexual Behavior

Jane D. Brown, PhD

University of North Carolina-Chapel Hill

Susan F. Newcomer, PhD

National Institute of Child Health and Human Development

SUMMARY. Over the past two decades the sexual content on television has increased in frequency and explicitness but has seldom included depiction of the use of contraceptives. Concurrently, the

Jane D. Brown is Professor of Journalism at the University of North Carolina at Chapel Hill. Susan F. Newcomer received her doctorate in sociology at the University of North Carolina at Chapel Hill. She is an expert consultant with the Demographic and Behavioral Sciences Branch of NICHHD in Washington, DC.

This research was supported by a grant from the Office of Population Affairs, Department of Health and Human Services, Grant #APR-000914A.

An earlier version of this article was presented to the American Psychological Association in Toronto, August 1984.

The authors wish to thank Richard Udry, director of the Carolina Population Center, for his helpful suggestions and access to the data set, and Gary Gaddy for analysis assistance.

Requests for reprints should be addressed to Jane D. Brown at: 204B Howell Hall CB #3365, University of North Carolina-Chapel Hill, Chapel Hill, NC 27599-3365.

77

age of initiation of heterosexual intercourse has decreased and the number of teenaged pregnancies has remained high. Are these trends related? This survey of 391 adolescents found that those who chose heavier diets of sexy television shows were more likely than those who viewed a smaller proportion of sexual content on television to have had sexual intercourse. This relationship held regardless of perceived peer encouragement to engage in sex and across race and gender groups. While causal direction is not clear from these data, the relationship suggests that either sexual activity results in increased interest in sexual content in the media and/or that viewing such content leads to sexual activity. In either case, the finding points to the need for further research and increased discussion and portrayal of the use of contraceptives on television.

In the past two decades the sexual content of the mass media has become increasingly frequent and explicit. On television, the most ubiquitous of the mass media, the frequency of references to and depictions of sexual activity has increased dramatically since the days of the twin bed and the good night peck of "Ozzie and Harriet" and "Father Knows Best." Greenberg and his colleagues documented an increase in rates of sexual content of 103 percent in the five years since 1980 in soap operas popular with adolescents. They estimated that the average adolescent viewer in 1985 was exposed to between 1,900 and 2,400 sexual references on television, depending on his or her viewing patterns (Greenberg, Stanley, Siemicki, Heeter, Soderman, & Linsangan, 1986; Greenberg, Linsangan, Soderman, Heeter, Lin, & Stanley, 1987).

In the same period, the rate of teen pregnancy in the United States was higher than any other industrialized country in the world. Between 1971 and 1986 the number of 15-year-old girls who had had intercourse increased from one in seven to one in four (Kantner & Zelnick, 1972; Planned Parenthood Federation of America, 1987). One in ten teenaged girls in the United States gets pregnant each year because few regularly use any method of contraception (Jones, Forrest, & Goldman, 1987).

Content analyses consistently have shown that unmarried heterosexual couples on television engage in sexual intercourse from four to eight times more frequently than married men and women. Contraceptives are rarely referred to or used, but women seldom get pregnant; men and women rarely contract sexually transmitted diseases unless they are prostitutes or homosexuals (Fernandez-Collado, Greenberg, Korzenny, & Atkin, 1978; Greenberg, Graef, Fernandez-Collado, Korzenny, & Atkin, 1980; Greenberg, Abelman, & Neuendorf, 1981; Lowry, Love, & Kirby, 1981). A content analysis of network programming in the fall of 1987 showed that the average program hour contained one to two references to sexual intercourse and no references to birth control; sexually transmitted diseases were mentioned only about once in every ten program hours (Harris, 1987).

While the mass media often are criticized for showing sex as glamorous, exciting and risk-free (Furstenberg & Brooks-Gunn, 1985) and are cited as one of the causes of increased risky sexual activity among the young (Hayes, 1987), surprisingly little research has been done on what effect this content has on viewers, especially younger adolescents who are perhaps most susceptible to the sexual images and values presented in the media (Brown, Childers, & Waszak).

In this study correlational data were used as an initial step in addressing the question of whether the frequency of viewing sexual content on television is related to the initiation of sexual intercourse. This research question is to some extent the most basic concern of critics of sexual content in the media. The suggestion is that somehow television content causes adolescents to engage in sexual intercourse earlier than they might otherwise. Such a phenomenon might be explained by a variety of models of media effects, including social learning theory (Bandura, 1977): adolescents see other unmarried teens or young adults enjoying going off to bed together on television, so they engage in similar behavior; and cultivation theory (Gerbner, Gross, Morgan, & Signorielli, 1986): heavy television viewers consistently see unmarried couples having sex and thus come to believe that such is the cultural norm.

At this point neither of these theoretical explanations has received much empirical study in regard to the media's effects on adolescent sexuality. In one of the only relevant studies, Baran and Courtright, in line with both the social learning and cultivation models, did find that television use correlated with adolescents' dissatisfaction with virginity and that high school students who thought that television accurately portrayed sexual behavior were more likely to be dissatisfied with their first experience of intercourse (Baran, 1976a,b; Courtright & Baran, 1980). We took a similar approach in this study as we looked at both how the frequency of viewing sexual content on television and the adolescent's perception of that content are related to sexual activity.

The mass media, of course, are not the only source of sexual socialization in this culture. Adolescent viewers compare the sexual picture they get from the mass media with other information, values and norms coming from parents, schools and friends. Since adolescents often cite peers as one of the most important sources of information about sex (Strouse & Fabes, 1985), we included measures of how much male and female friends were seen to be encouraging the adolescent to learn more about or engage in sex. Other factors also have been found to affect initiation of sexual intercourse (Hayes, 1987). We included some of the most important of these (gender, race, class and pubertal development) in our analyses as well.

METHOD

Sample

The population for the study was the entire student body of a junior high school in an urban area in North Carolina. In order to obtain data with the highest possible reliability from a normally unreliable population on a sensitive subject, questionnaires were filled out by individual students in their own homes in the presence of a trained interviewer. Parental and respondent permission was obtained beforehand and parents agreed that the adolescent's answers would remain confidential. In general, parents and teenagers were cooperative. Of 639 eligible students in the school, 504 participated in the first wave of the study in fall 1978 for a 79 percent response rate. Each student completed a set of questions about sexual attitudes and behaviors in 1978, fall 1979 and again in spring 1981. As part of the third wave of the study, the 391 students who were still in the region and agreed to participate (78 percent retention rate) completed a set of media use questions as well. Respondents ranged from 13 to 18 years old, with an average of just over 15 years old at the third wave of interviews.

In the second interview, more than half (52%) of the respondents reported having had heterosexual intercourse.[1] Consistent with national figures (Zelnik & Shah, 1983), black males were the most likely and white females the least likely to have experienced coitus.[2] In some of the analyses reported here, only the 190 adolescents who remained virgins through the first two interviews were included. This allowed us to examine the relationship of transition to intercourse and television viewing in the same time period.

Measures

In order to measure perceived peer and media encouragement for sexual activity, respondents were asked to "look at the sentences below and decide if *TV and Movies, Your best male friend, Your best female friend*, do that activity: (1) Encourage me to learn about sex. (2) Teach me things about sex. (3) Try to set sexual rules. (4) Encourage me to be more sexually active. (5) Encourage me to be less sexually active." Respondents could respond "yes" or "no" to each sentence. The measure was formed by summing across items that had been scored 1 if the response suggested perceived encouragement (e.g., "yes" to items 1, 2, and 4 and "no" to items 3 and 5) and 0 if the response suggested perceived discouragement (e.g., "no" to items 1, 2, and 4 and "yes" to items 3 and 5).

Three measures of television viewing were constructed. The *total television viewing* measure was formed by asking respondents to report, on a time line, the usual number of hours they spent viewing television on a "typical school day" and a "typical Saturday." The hours circled for the typical school day were multiplied by five and added to the hours specified for the typical Saturday. Average daily television viewing was computed by dividing the sum by six.[3]

The *sexy television viewing* measure was created by summing across viewing frequency for each of 67 current (1981) prime-time and afternoon television shows. Each show was weighted according to its length (in increments of 30 minutes), and the frequency with which the respondent reported viewing (0 = never; 1 = some weeks/days; 2 = most weeks/days; 3 = every week/day) and by a rating of the show's sexual content. The rating of sexual content was made by 34 independent judges (university students in a senior-level communications class), who rated each program with which they were familiar on a three-point scale (0 = not sexy; 1 = sometimes sexy; 2 = very sexy). The "sexiness" rating for each program consisted of the average score of all judges rating the program.[4]

The third measure, *proportion of sexy television viewing*, was created by dividing the respondent's score on sexy television viewing by the frequency of viewing the 67 listed shows (as weighted by length and frequency of presentation). This measure was conceptualized as assessing the extent to which an adolescent seeks out sexual content when watching television. It was expected that this measure of selective television viewing would be more highly related to sexual behavior since the adolescent apparently is viewing this kind of content for some reason and thus the content may have more effect. While not often measured, this motivation-effect connection is an underlying assumption of the uses and gratifications model of media effects (Rubin, 1986).

The adolescent's stage of *pubertal development* was measured by self-reports on eight different items which included breast or penis size, pubic hair development, menarche (for girls) and facial hair development (for boys).[5] The measures were combined into a factor score computed within gender and race subgroups.

The dependent variable, *sexual behavior*, was measured in two ways. The first was a Guttman scale assessing degrees of intimate experience (progressing from kissing to necking to petting to sexual intercourse). The second was a simple dichotomous measure of whether the adolescent reported having had heterosexual intercourse.

RESULTS

Summary statistics for the primary variables within gender and race groups are shown in Table 1 for the subsample of respondents who remained virgins in the first two interview rounds. By the third interview, one-third of these white females and more than 40 percent of the white males and black females in this subgroup reported

Table 1

Adolescent Sexual Behavior, Television Use and

Perceptions within Race/Sex Subgroups

	White Males	Black Males	White Females	Black Females
n	54	10	91	35
Percent Non-virgin	44	77	31	42
Television viewing				
Mean hrs./day	2.4	3.8	2.7	4.9
Sexy viewing[a]	129	222	180	279
Proportion sexy[b]	11.3	8.9	13.6	9.3
Perception of sexual encouragement by[c]:				
TV/Movies	2.4	1.6	2.7	2.4
Male friend	2.1	1.7	2.7	2.3
Female friend	1.8	2.0	1.9	2.3

Note. Table includes only those respondents still virgin in Wave 2 of the survey. These measures were taken in Wave 3. [a]Sexy viewing is a summed total of frequency of viewing 67 shows that had been weighted by a sexiness score and length and frequency of presentation. Overall Mean = 182, Sdv. = 85. [b]Proportion sexy viewing is a ratio score formed by dividing the sexy viewing score by the frequency of viewing 67 shows (weighted by length and frequency of presentation). Mean = 1.06, Sdv. = .134. [c]Each perception score was formed by summing across five items. Range = 0-5.

having had heterosexual intercourse. Black males were most likely to no longer be virgin by the third interview.

Consistent with other studies (Greenberg & Dervin, 1970), black teens reported higher levels of television viewing in general, with black females ranking highest among the four groups, at an average of almost five hours per day. White males reported the lowest levels (about two and one half hours per day). Blacks also averaged more frequent viewing of sexy programs than whites, but whites appeared to be more likely, on the average, to be seeking out such content.

When specific programs were ranked in terms of their average frequency of viewing (not shown in table), it was clear that adolescent viewing extended beyond the now defunct "family viewing hour." White males, especially, reported a high frequency of viewing late night movies and adult entertainment programs such as "Saturday Night Live." Adolescent girls, on the other hand, apparently were rushing home from school to catch the latest episode of "General Hospital," which was rated in one content analysis as the "sexiest" of the soaps (Lowry, Love, & Kirby, 1981). Other frequently viewed shows included "Dallas" and "The Love Boat."

In general, all but the black male adolescents reported in all three interviews that they found television equally or more encouraging about sex than either their best male or female friends. Female friends were seen as least encouraging about sex.

Television viewing patterns did differ by the sexual status of the adolescent. As can be seen in Table 2, non-virgins in all but the black male group were significantly more likely than virgins to be seeking sexy programming. There were no significant differences in the total frequency of viewing sexy content or the total number of hours per week. Thus, having had intercourse appeared to be related to seeking sexual content on television. Unfortunately, with these cross-sectional data we were unable to determine which came first—sexual intercourse or a proclivity for viewing sexual activity on television.

We were able, however, to test the robustness of this relationship with a multivariate model predicting the transition to intercourse while controlling for a number of other variables. Because the number of virgins in the third wave was relatively small, race and gen-

Table 2

Television Viewing[a] by Sexual Status

Television Viewing	White Males	Black Males	White Females	Black Females
Mean Hrs./day				
Virgins	15.4	22.6	16.0	31.0
n	(38)	(5)	(65)	(21)
Non-virgins	12.5	22.4	16.0	25.4
n	(21)	(5)	(65)	(22)
Sexy viewing				
Virgins	130	208	175	269
Non-virgins	128	236	196	310
Proportion sexy viewing				
Virgins	10.6	6.2	12.6	8.9
Non-virgins	12.5[b]	11.6	16.3[b]	10.5[b]

Note. Table includes all respondents from Wave 3 who provided complete data for these measures. [a] See Table 1 for an explanation of television viewing measures. [b] $p<.05$, one-tailed, between virgins and non-virgins.

der were entered as control variables in the equation rather than testing the model within race-gender subgroups. Mother's education was included as an indicator of social class. Level of pubertal development, previous non-coital sexual experience as well as perceptions of friends' and television's encouragement about sex as measured in the second wave of interviews also were included.

Logistic regression was used to test the model because the dependent variable was a simple dichotomy (virgin/non-virgin). This procedure fits a model with the selected independent variables to the data. If the model does not fit, the chi square value is low, suggesting that not enough information has been provided to predict whether the independent variables are related to the dependent variable. If the model fits, the chi square value is high and the p value is low. As can be seen by comparing Model 1 and Model 2 in Table 3, the only variable that significantly predicted to sexual intercourse in Model 1 is the teenager's prior non-coital sexual experience. The total model did not fit the data. When the ratio of sexy television viewing variable was added to the model, however, it fit, the chi square value was significant, and none of the other control variables were either increased or decreased significantly in value.

Table 3

Logistic Regression of Transition to Intercourse

	Model 1	Model 2
Mother's education	-.02	-.12
Pubertal development	.18	.22
Non-coital sex experience[a]	.32[b]	.34[b]
Male friend encourages sex[a]	.26	.23
Female friend encourages sex[a]	-.24	-.21
TV/Movies encourage sex[a]	-.11	-.08
Sex (1 = male)	.42	.78
Race (1 = white)	-.06	-.33
Proportion sexy viewing		.06[b]
Chi square	12.98	19.16
(df)	(8)	(9)
$\underline{p}$	.113	.024

Note. Table entries are unstandardized logistic regression coefficients. $\underline{N}$ = 190 (Virgins in Wave 1 and 2). [a]Measures from Wave 2 of the survey. [b] $\underline{p}$<.05.

This suggests that the relationship between viewing a high proportion of sexy television and engaging in sexual intercourse holds even after controlling for the perceived influence of male and female friends and previous non-coital sexual experience. Although this is not a conclusive test of the causal sequence between television viewing and adolescent sexual behavior, it does suggest that teenagers who selectively view sexy television are more likely to have had sexual intercourse, regardless of their friends' encouragement or discouragement to have sex and regardless of their previous sexual experience. The relationship is strongest for white females, but, insofar as they can be measured accurately due to small sample sizes, the relationship exists in the other race/gender groups as well.

We also tested a linear regression model predicting the proportion of sexy television viewing for all adolescents in Wave 3 using the same control variables as in Table 3 (mother's education, pubertal development, friend and television encouragement, race, and gender). These variables did not predict to the Wave 3 proportion of sexy television viewing. We reasoned that if sexual intercourse predisposes the adolescent to *then* choose more sexually-oriented television, adding previous sexual activity from Wave 2 to the model would result in a significant addition to variance explained in the proportion of sexy television viewed. Analyses showed, however, that adding either measure of Wave 2 sexual behavior to the model did not improve the amount of variance explained. This is an indication that the causal direction flows from a high proportion of sexy television viewing to sexual activity rather than vice versa. However, since the complete model could not be tested because television viewing data were available at only one timepoint, this must be seen as a tentative conclusion.

DISCUSSION

These analyses have shown that neither the total amount of television viewing nor quantities of sexually-oriented television viewing alone are related to the likelihood of adolescents having heterosexual intercourse. There is, however, evidence of a significant relationship between the *proportion* of sexy programming an adolescent watches on television and the adolescent's sexual activity status. Non-virgins are more likely than virgins to watch a high proportion of programs generally considered to contain sexual content. This relationship exists regardless of the adolescent's social class, pubertal development or friends' encouragement about sexual behavior.

These analyses also provide some support for the causal hypothesis that viewing a heavier concentration of sexual content on television leads to sexual activity rather than vice versa. The rival hypothesis, that sexual activity leads to the selection of sexy television programming, must not be discounted, however, since these are basically correlational data. It is probably most reasonable at this point to assume that both sequences are at work: as adolescents mature physically the sexual content on television becomes more relevant, such content is sought out, paid attention to, and subsequently modeled. Recent research on the active television audience (Rubin, 1986; Hodge & Tripp, 1986) certainly would predict this kind of pattern.

Regardless of the direction of influence, these findings clearly suggest the need for continued examination of the influence of media content on adolescent sexual socialization. While our data suggest that television content may have an independent effect in this process, we would predict that the effects of television will be modified not only by personal relevance (e.g., sexual maturity, peer pressure), but by alternative sources of sexual information (e.g., sex education in the schools, parental and peer discussion and example). These findings also point to the need to examine television programming policies. Analyses of content have shown consistently that sexual intercourse on television occurs most frequently among unmarried couples. The potentially harmful unintended consequences of unprotected sexual intercourse, such as pregnancy or disease, are rarely discussed or depicted. While the networks have responded recently in both entertainment programming and public service advertising campaigns to the threat of AIDS, they still refuse, at this writing, to allow advertising for contraceptives for the prevention of pregnancy. Adolescents tend to be poor contraceptors in the early stages of their sexual experience (Zelnik & Shah, 1983). If contraceptive advertising were included on television, especially in the adult-oriented shows sexually-active teens are most likely to watch, the use of contraceptives might become a more acceptable behavior sooner.

NOTES

1. Questionnaires were designed to address only heterosexual experience. Separate questionnaires were designed for males and females and questions about intercourse were phrased in terms of the other gender. Thus, these analyses do not represent adolescents' homosexual experience.

2. Most of the descriptive analyses discussed in this article were replicated with a larger longitudinal sample collected in a similar urban area in Florida in 1980 and 1982. A concern with both samples is that the proportions of black adolescents who stayed in the population and who were virgin in the first two waves of the studies is quite small. Analyses done on these subgroups are not likely to be statistically significant and interpretations must be made carefully.

3. The measure, therefore, does not include any estimate of viewing on Sundays.

4. A previous study suggested that such an approach could provide a meaningful measure of sexual content. Sprafkin, Silverman, and Rubinstein (1980) found in a study of reactions to sex on television that for a majority of intimate behaviors there was a high degree of correspondence between ratings provided by trained coders and untrained adult viewers. Further, in our study the composite reliability across raters (Holsti, 1969), even when computed using Scott's pi, (a conservative measure that assumes only nominal categories) was high, with a median reliability of .95.

5. These self reports have been shown to correlate well with physician's rankings of the adolescents' levels of pubertal development (Morris & Udry, 1980).

REFERENCES

Bandura, A. (1977). *Social learning theory.* Englewood Cliffs, NJ: Prentice-Hall.

Baran, S.J. (1976a). Sex on TV and adolescent sexual self-image. *Journal of Broadcasting, 20,* 61-68.

Baran, S.J. (1976b). How TV and film portrayals affect sexual satisfaction in college students. *Journalism Quarterly, 53,* 468-473.

Brown, J.D., Childers, K.W., & Waszak, C. (1990). Television and adolescent sexuality. *Journal of Adolescent Health Care, 11,* 62-70.

Courtright, J.A., & Baran, S.J. (1980). The acquisition of sexual information by young people. *Journalism Quarterly, 57,* 107-114.

Fernandez-Collado, C.F., Greenberg, B.S., Korzenny, F., & Atkin, C.K. (1978). Sexual intimacy and drug use in TV series. *Journal of Communication, 28*(3), 30-37.

Furstenberg, F.F., & Brooks-Gunn, J. (1985). Teenage child-bearing: Causes, consequences and remedies. In L.H. Aiken & D. Mechanic (Eds.), *Applications of social science to clinical medicine and health policy*. New Brunswick, NJ: Rutgers University.

Gerbner, G., Gross, L., Morgan, M., & Signorielli, N. (1986). Living with television: The dynamics of the cultivation process. In J. Bryant & D. Zillman (Eds.), *Perspectives on media effects* (pp. 17-40). Hillsdale, NJ: Lawrence Erlbaum Associates.

Greenberg, B.S., Abelman, R., & Neuendorf, K. (1981). Sex on the soap operas: Afternoon delight. *Journal of Communication, 31*(3), 83-89.

Greenberg, B.S., & Dervin, B. (1970). *Use of the mass media by the urban poor*. New York: Praeger.

Greenberg, B.S., Graef, D., Fernandez-Collado, C., Korzenny, F., & Atkin, C. (1980). Sexual intimacy on commercial TV during prime time. *Journalism Quarterly, 57*(2), 211-215.

Greenberg, B.S., Linsangan, R.L., Soderman, A., Heeter, C., Lin, C., & Stanley, C. (1987). *Adolescents and their exposure to television and movie sex* (Project CAST Report #4). East Lansing, MI: Michigan State University Department of Telecommunication.

Greenberg, B.S., Stanley, C., Siemicki, M., Heeter, C., Soderman, A., & Linsangan, R. (1986). *Sex content on soaps and primetime television series most viewed by adolescents* (Project CAST Report #2). East Lansing, MI: Michigan State University Department of Telecommunication.

Harris, L. (1987). *Sexual material on American network television during the 1987-88 season*. New York: Louis Harris and Associates, Inc.

Hayes, C.D. (Ed.). (1987). *Risking the future: Adolescent sexuality, pregnancy and childbearing* (Vol.1). Washington, DC: National Academy Press.

Hodge, B., & Tripp, D. (1986). *Children and television*. Palo Alto, CA: Stanford University Press.

Holsti, O.R. (1969). *Content analysis for the social sciences and humanities*. New York: Addison-Wesley.

Jones, E., Forrest, J., & Goldman, N. (1987). *Teenage pregnancy in industrialized countries*. New Haven: Yale University Press.

Kantner, J.F., & Zelnik, M. (1972). Sexual experience of young unmarried women in the United States. *Family Planning Perspectives, 4*, 9-18.

Lowry, D.T., Love, G., & Kirby, M. (1981). Sex on the soap operas: Patterns of intimacy. *Journal of Communication, 31*(3), 90-96.

Morris, N. & Udry, J.R. (1980). Validation of a self-administered instrument to assess stage of adolescent development. *Journal of Youth and Adolescence, 9*(3), 271-280.

Planned Parenthood Federation of America. (1987). *American teenagers speak: Sex, myths, TV and birth control*. New York: Author.

Rubin, A. M. (1986). Uses, gratifications, and media effects research. In J. Bryant & D. Zillman (Eds.), *Perspectives on media effects* (pp. 281-302). Hillsdale, NJ: Lawrence Erlbaum Associates.

Sprafkin, J.N., Silverman, L.T., & Rubinstein, E.A. (1980). Reactions to sex on television: An exploratory study. *Public Opinion Quarterly, 44*, 303-315.
Strouse, J., & Fabes, R.A. (1985). Formal versus informal sources of sex education: Competing forces in the sexual socialization of adolescents. *Adolescence, 20*(78), 251-263.
Zelnik, M., & Shah, F.K. (1983). First intercourse among young Americans. *Family Planning Perspectives, 15*, 64-70.

Television Viewing
and Early Initiation
of Sexual Intercourse:
Is There a Link?

James L. Peterson, PhD

Sociometrics Corporation, Los Altos, CA

Kristin A. Moore, PhD

Child Trends, Inc., Washington, DC

Frank F. Furstenberg, Jr., PhD

University of Pennsylvania, Philadelphia, PA

SUMMARY. Using data from the National Survey of Children, this paper examines the hypothesis that the amount of time children spend viewing television and the extent to which the content viewed is sexual in nature is related to the initiation of sexual activity. Several theories that would lead to this hypothesis are reviewed. The data do not provide any strong or consistent evidence for such links. However, some aspects of the context in which television is viewed are related to sexual activity. The authors suggest ways in which the design and measures could be strengthened to provide a more rigorous test of the hypothesis.

This article is a revised version of a paper presented at the 1984 Annual Meetings of the American Psychological Association in Toronto, Canada, August 1984. The research on which the article is based was funded under grant number APR 000916-01-0 from the Office of Adolescent Pregnancy Programs, Department of Health and Human Services. The views expressed herein are solely those of the authors.

Please direct all correspondence to James L. Peterson at Sociometrics Corporation, 170 State Street, Suite 260, Los Altos, CA 94022.

The incidence of pregnancy to teenagers has been a topic of considerable public and policy concern for several years. While the total number of births to teenagers has fallen in recent years, both the number of conceptions and the number of out-of-wedlock births has risen substantially (Moore & Burt, 1982). The proportion of births to teenagers that are out of wedlock has risen from less than one-third in 1970 to nearly one-half by 1979 (Baldwin, 1982), and to over three-fifths by 1986 (Moore, 1988).

The rise in out-of-wedlock births can be attributed primarily to the increase in premarital sexual activity among teenagers, rather than to less efficient use of contraception (Baldwin, 1982). Between 1971 and 1979 the proportion of never-married women 15-19 in U.S. metropolitan areas who had ever had intercourse rose from 28 percent to 46 percent. While comparable trend data are not available for men, the proportion of such males who were sexually experienced in 1979 was 69 percent (Zelnik & Kantner, 1980). We presume that this proportion also increased over the decade of the 1970s.

A number of factors have been found to be associated with the timing of initiation of sexual activity. For example, those starting early are more likely to be males and to be black (Zelnik & Kantner, 1980), to have reached physical maturity earlier (Billy & Udry, 1983), to place a greater value on independence and less on achievement, to be more tolerant of deviance, to be less religious, and to be more involved in problem behaviors (Jessor & Jessor, 1975; Jessor, Costa, Jessor, & Donovan, 1983), to have lower self-esteem (Micklin, 1981), to come from a single-parent family and to live in a poor neighborhood (Hogan & Kitagawa, 1983), and to have lower educational aspirations (Devaney, 1981; Furstenberg, 1976).

Television viewing has been thought by some to be another factor contributing to the high incidence of sexuality among teens. While a large body of research has examined the effects of television viewing on children, most of it has focused on the effects of exposure to violent television programming on children's aggression or antisocial behavior (Surgeon General's Scientific Advisory Committee, 1972; U.S. Department of Health and Human Services, 1982; Schramm, Lyle, & Parker, 1961). However, much less attention has been given to the effects of television viewing on children's sexual attitudes, beliefs, and behaviors. Ironically, as the public, researchers, and policymakers have focused a critical eye on violence in television programming, the producers of television fare have simultaneously lowered the level of violence but increased the sexual content of their programming (Franzblau, Sprafkin, & Rubinstein, 1977).

Sexuality on television is a broad topic which includes not only suggestive and erotic behavior, but gender roles, intimacy and affection, and marriage and family life as well (Roberts, 1982). As such, the picture of sexuality presented by television is often a distorted one (Greenberg, 1982; Roberts, 1982). For example, most references to sexual intercourse on television are to extramarital relationships, or to prostitution; sex and violence are commonly linked, and erotic relationships are seldom portrayed as warm (Fernandez-Collado, Greenberg, Korzenny, & Atkin, 1978).

Several reasons have been advanced as to why the sexual content of television programming should have an effect on children: the consistency of sexual messages projected by television programming; the adult nature of most of the programming children watch; children's limited access to countervailing views; and the realism of most television programming (Roberts, 1982). While several studies have examined the sexual content of television programming, little research to date has attempted to evaluate whether television viewing affects children's sexual attitudes, beliefs, or behaviors.

In the present paper we take up specific aspects of the hypothesized link between television and children's sexual activity: namely, does watching a lot of television or watching television with a high degree of sexual content contribute to the early initiation of sexual activity among adolescents?

Limitations in the data to be examined preclude the consideration of a broader range of consequences of television on children's learning about sexuality. For example, television might affect children's level of information about the risk of pregnancy, or about abortion, or it might affect their attitudes about the acceptability of premarital intercourse. We will be focusing on whether television is related to the occurrence of precocious sexual intercourse.

SPECIFIC HYPOTHESES

The specific mechanisms by which television might have an influence on sexual behavior correspond in large measure to the mechanisms by which violence on television is presumed to have an effect. Several theories have been proposed. The theory most commonly used in research on violence is social learning theory (Bandura, 1973). From this perspective, it is argued that children can learn behaviors by imitation, apart from actual performance or reinforcement. Television is seen as an increasingly influential agent of socialization that produces its effects through children's propensity to learn by imitation. A second mechanism that has been proposed operates by reducing inhibitions against existing behavioral tendencies (Berkowitz & Rawlings, 1963). Thus, the inhibitions of viewers who see actors engaging in desired but proscribed behaviors might be eroded.

A third line of reasoning focuses on the potential of media for arousing latent behavioral tendencies. Thus, television viewing may serve as a stimulus leading directly to psychological arousal that enhances whatever behavior may seem to be appropriate to the viewer. In this formulation, the content of the behavior may be primarily determined by other factors, but its expression at the time is a result of the arousal caused by exposure to television (Tannenbaum & Zillman, 1975). Finally, it has been argued that exposure to certain content on television may bring about a catharsis, or release in feeling or arousal. Thus viewing sexually oriented programming in this view would actually decrease the probability that the behavior will be imitated (Feshbach, 1961).

All of these formulations have been applied in studies of violence and media, primarily studies of the effects on children of viewing violence on television. But each model could be applied as well to the viewing of sexually oriented television material. The models overlap to some extent in their predictions, except for the last (catharsis model). In summarizing the various approaches which have been taken to the effects of television violence, Comstock (1978) extracts some general principles which he feels apply to the general behavioral effects of television viewing:

These findings lead us to advance some general principles regarding the influence of television portrayals on the behavior of young persons. They suggest that portrayals may influence behavior through the acquisition of new responses or through altering the likelihood of the performance of newly or previously acquired responses. Such alteration may occur through the changing of expectations regarding the outcome of behavior, through identification with the perpetrator of an act, by raising or lowering inhibitions, by changing the elicitory potential of environmental cues, and by assigning certain meanings to a class of behavior.

The various models mentioned above would all explain fairly direct and short-term effects of television viewing. This is especially the case with the arousal hypothesis. Among the models, social learning theory is the one most compatible with long-term effects. That is, television viewing may have more lasting effects through imparting information and ideas which serve to socialize children. Television programming may provide a context in which certain kinds of behavior are given meaning, and in which typical or expected sequences of behavior—with a beginning, development, and resolution—are presented to viewers. Children, with less experience than adults, are more likely to be influenced by such scripts (Withey, 1980).

When applied to the question of the initiation of sexual activity, most of these models lead us to hypothesize that there is at least a modest link between television viewing and sexual behavior. Given the pervasiveness of sexually oriented messages on television in general—advertising as well as programming—it can be argued that the greater the amount viewed, the more exposure to sexual content and the greater the probability of an effect on attitudes or behavior. On the basis of social learning theory, or the facilitation-disinhibition model, it can be argued that viewing programs with explicit sexual content will increase the probability of similar behaviors. Implicit sexual content (innuendo, double entendre, etc.), which is more common than explicit sexual content, might have a similar, though weaker effect. The arousal hypothesis suggests that any content that is highly stimulating (whether because of sex, violence, or something else) will increase the probability of sexual behavior, but only if such behavior were already a possibility within the immediate social context — a condition which is likely to be infrequent among young adolescents watching television. The socialization-scripting model also suggests that viewing will increase the probability of sexual behavior by defining contexts in which it might be appropriate and providing scripts for how it develops. Only the catharsis hypothesis would suggest that television viewing may lead to a reduction in the probability of sexual behavior.

DATA AND MEASURES

The data on which the analyses are based are from the first two waves of the National Surveys of Children, a longitudinal study of the well-being of U.S. children. The first wave, conducted in the fall and winter of 1976-77, was based on a probability sample of households in the continental United States containing at least one child aged seven through eleven. In cases where three or more children were eligible in one family, two were selected at random. Blacks were oversampled to yield at least 500 interviews with black children, thereby permitting more detailed analyses by race. Altogether, data were gathered on 2,301 children in 1,747 families. Weights have been developed to take account of oversampling by race, as well as the number of eligible children in the family and minor discrepancies between sample and census distributions on age, sex, race, and residence.

The second wave of the survey was conducted in the spring and summer of 1981. It was a follow-up of a subsample ($N = 1,423$) of the children, by then aged 11-16. The follow-up focused on marital disruption and its effects on children. For this purpose, the subsample was chosen to include all children in disrupted and high-conflict intact families and a subsample of those in low or moderate conflict families. Roughly half the children were in each of these broad groups. Additional weights were developed to take account of the subsampling procedures so that national estimates could again be made.

In each survey, interviews were conducted with the eligible child and the parent most capable of providing information about the child, usually the mother. A follow-up study of schools attended by the children in each survey was also carried out.

In the 1981 survey all of the respondents aged 15 and 16 were asked about the sexual experience of their friends and about their own sexual and pregnancy experience. One hundred and twenty of the 461 respondents in this age range indicated that they had had sexual intercourse.

One potential problem has been identified in the data; namely, there may be under-reporting of sexual activity on the part of 16-year-old females. Sixteen percent of the 15-year-old females and 20 percent of the 16-year-old females report having had sex, compared to 22 percent and 38 percent as reported by Zelnik and Kantner (1980). Two factors may partly account for the lower proportion. The timing of the 1981 follow-up was such that the bulk of the 16-year-olds are in the first half of their 16th year. In addition, Zelnik and Kantner's respondents represent urban residents, while the NSC respondents represent the entire United States. Studies of sensitive topics are often handicapped by data problems; thus it is important to bear in mind that the dependent variable is a measure of the proportion of youth who *report* having had sexual intercourse.

A number of measures relevant to television viewing were also included in the NSC. In the 1976 survey, when the oldest children were 10 and 11, parents were asked to estimate how much time on a usual weekday the child spent watching television. The children reported whether they had rules limiting the content or amount of television they could watch.

The 1981 survey contained more data about television viewing. Children provided their own estimates of viewing time, which averaged over an hour per day more than the parent estimates from 1976 (about four hours versus less than three). Three factors may account for the increase. First, other studies show that viewing increases sharply with age to an average of four hours at age 12, after which it declines slightly (Comstock, Chaffee, Katzman, McCombs, & Roberts, 1978). Second there has been a secular trend toward more television viewing, at least among adults and presumably among children as well (Bower, 1984). Third, parents may underestimate the viewing hours of their children.

Parents and children were also asked about rules regarding television in the 1981 survey, and children reported whether they discussed programs with their parents, indicated with whom they watched television, and listed their favorite programs.

From these data several measures of television viewing were constructed. Two basic measures were the amount of viewing in 1976 and in 1981. The data on favorite programs were used to construct a proxy measure of exposure to sexual content on television. Programs were classified into programs with a relatively high level of sexual content (e.g., "Dallas," soap operas), those with a moderate level (e.g., "Charlie's Angels"), those with a low level (e.g., "Dukes of Hazard"), and those with little or none (e.g., sports programs, news). A dichotomy combining content and amount was also constructed from the 1981 data, classifying in one category those whose favorite programs have a high level of sexual content *and* who are heavy viewers; all others were classified in the second category.

ANALYSIS AND FINDINGS

A previous analysis of these same data has shown that the antecedents of early sexual activity differ between males and females and between whites and blacks (Moore, Peterson, & Furstenberg, 1984). The earlier analysis estimated four separate models for the four race/sex groups. The data show differences not only in patterns of sexual activity between blacks and whites, but also differences in patterns of television viewing. Given these considerations and the small number of blacks available for analysis in this sample (about 50 males and 50 females age 15-16) we have chosen to restrict our attention to the white portion of the sample, and to conduct separate analyses by sex.

The first question we ask is whether there is any association between the total amount of television viewing (regardless of content) and whether the adolescent has ever had sexual intercourse. It should be noted that the data do not provide us with age at first intercourse, and that we know about television viewing only at two points in time — 1976 (before first intercourse for virtually the entire sample), and 1981 (after first intercourse for those who have become sexually active).

Bivariate Results

The data, shown in Table 1, indicate that there is no bivariate relationship between the amount of television viewing in 1976 and subsequent initiation of sexual activity. Fifteen percent of the females had had intercourse by the time of the 1981 survey, and this percentage varied little by average daily television viewing. For males, a curvilinear pattern appeared, but is not statistically significant given the relatively small samples involved ($X^2 = 4.46$, $df = 3$; $p > .2$). Heavy viewers (three hours per day or more) had the highest prevalence of sexual experience—35 percent. However, the lowest prevalence rate—12 percent—was found not among the lighter viewers, but among the moderate viewers—more than two to three hours per day. Though plausible *post hoc* explanations might be advanced for the higher sexual experience rate among boys who are light viewers, we do not place too much importance on this curvilinear pattern, given the lack of statistical significance. We only conclude at this point that the data, while not significant, are consistent with the hypothesis that heavy television viewing in preadolescence is related to a greater prevalence of sexual experience among early adolescent boys.

Table 1 also presents data on television viewing in 1981. In this case a positive relation between sexual experience and amount of viewing emerged for females across the lower end of the range of television viewing time. For males, the curvilinear pattern again appeared, although shifted up one hour on the scale. While neither pattern is statistically significant, the relationship for males approaches significance ($.05 < p < .10$).

The meaning of these relationships is unclear, however, since the ordering of events has been reversed. Television viewing is now the most recent event measured. This would make little difference if individuals' viewing habits remained quite constant over time. But the data show otherwise: nearly half the sample had shifted from the upper half of the scale to the lower half, or vice versa, between 1976 and 1981. Thus it could just as reasonably be argued for the 1981 viewing data that sexual experience influenced viewing patterns as the reverse.

Data on the content of television viewing are available in the

Table 1. Percentage of 15- and 16-Year-Old White Youth Who Have Ever Had Sexual Intercourse, by Amount of Television Viewing in 1976 and in 1981, for U.S. Males and Females, 1981

Percent Sexually Experienced, 1981[a]

Average Daily TV Viewing

	1 Hour or Less	More Than 1 to 2 Hours	More Than 2 to 3 Hours	More Than 3 to 4 Hours	More Than 4 to 5 Hours	More Than 5 Hours	Total
Viewing in 1976							
Females[c]	8%(34)	17%(78)	16%(40)	. . .	12%(20)[b]	. . .	15%(171)
Males[c]	24 (39)	21 (70)	12 (42)	. . .	35 (21)	. . .	21 (172)
Viewing in 1981							
Females[c]	5 (23)	7 (29)	20 (26)	17 (35)	20 (22)	18 (35)	15 (171)
Males[c]	44 (21)	23 (23)	23 (33)	11 (38)	15 (18)	20 (40)	21 (172)

a   Weighted Ns are given in parentheses. Both weights and percentages are rounded to nearest integer. Weights may not add to total due to rounding errors.

b   Due to an insufficient number of cases, data for the top three categories were combined for 1976.

c   The relationship between sexual experience and television viewing is not statistically significant for this row according to the chi-square test.

form of respondents' mentions of their favorite programs. Unfortunately, these data are from 1981 and thus subject to the ambiguities of interpretation just mentioned. Table 2 shows the bivariate relationship between television content and sexual experience. A mild positive association between the sexual content of the favorite program and sexual experience emerged for girls. For boys, however, the highest sexual experience rate is for those who name as their favorite program one with no sexual content. Neither of these results is statistically significant according to the X^2 measure. To check on the possible effects of a combination of heavy viewing and exposure to a high level of sexual content, the two measures were combined to produce a dichotomy that isolated this high exposure group. This dichotomy showed only a mild and statistically insignificant association with sexual experience — 17 percent of the high-exposure females, compared with 14 percent of other females, had been sexually active. The corresponding comparison for males was actually in the opposite direction: 19 percent versus 22 percent respectively.

Both the content measure and the combined measure are based on 1981 data, and therefore suffer from the same limitation as the 1981 measure of viewing time. That is, these television measures could just as easily — indeed more appropriately — be considered the dependent variables as the independent variables. From here on, therefore, we focus attention primarily on the 1976 measure of viewing time and its relation to sexual activity.

Moderator Variables

Before we accept the null hypothesis, a number of alternative hypotheses need to be considered to account for why there was not a stronger relationship between television viewing and sexual experience. An idea which has emerged from the television violence literature is that television is most influential when other influences are absent (Comstock, 1978). For example, the viewing of violent programming has a stronger influence on behavior when parents or other adults do not interpret the material for young viewers (Hicks, 1968). Alternatively, youth having particular characteristics might be more susceptible to the influence of television. These possibili-

Table 2. Percentage of 15- and 16-Year-Old White Youth Who Have Ever Had Sexual Intercourse by Sexual Content of Favorite Programs in 1981, for Males and Females, 1981

Percent Sexually Experienced, 1981[a]

Sex	High Sex Content	Moderate Sex Content	Low Sex Content	Little or No Sex Content	Total
Female[b]	16%(98)	14%(37)	12%(17)	11%(19)	15%(171)
Male[b]	22 (38)	20 (67)	17 (33)	28 (35)	21 (172)

a Weighted Ns are given in parentheses. Both weights and percentages are rounded to nearest integer. Weights may not add to total due to rounding errors.

b The relationship between sexual experience and television viewing is not statistically significant for this row according to the chi-square test.

104

ties make it necessary to consider several moderator variables which, when present, may mask or negate the influence of television. That is, it could be that television viewing has an effect only for certain subgroups or only under certain conditions.

Two classes of moderator variables would seem to be especially important. First we should consider characteristics of the child. Children with higher levels of intelligence may be better able to distinguish between reality and television fantasy, and thus be less susceptible to influence. We also expect that children with higher levels of educational aspirations would be more motivated to avoid sexual intercourse in order to prevent unintended pregnancies that might jeopardize their educational plans. Finally, children with higher levels of self-esteem might be better able to resist the influence of sexually oriented materials on television.

The second class of moderator variables includes measures describing relevant characteristics of the parent or parent/child relationships. Thus children whose parents co-view with them, or who discuss the content of television programs with them may be less influenced. Children whose parents have more liberal or permissive attitudes toward sexual behavior might be more influenced than those with more traditional attitudes. Parental rules about television viewing may also have a moderating effect, but one that is more complex. On the one hand it is to be expected that, other things being equal, stricter rules about what may be watched or how long television may be watched would lead to a diminution of effects. On the other hand, all things are not usually equal, and strict rules may be imposed only for children whose behavior shows a need for stricter supervision.

To check on all these possibilities, the bivariate association between television viewing in 1976 and sexual experience by 1981 was controlled by each of these moderator variables one at a time. The results were examined to see whether the relationship for boys was clarified and strengthened or whether a relationship emerged for girls within those categories of the moderator variables in which the television effect was expected to be strongest.

The measure of the average amount of daily television viewing was divided into four categories: one hour or less; more than one hour to two hours; more than two to three hours; and more than three hours. When this variable was further subdivided by the categories of the moderator variables, the cell sizes of some cells became quite small. In these cases adjacent categories of the television viewing variable were combined so that all cells had at least ten cases. The data are presented in Tables 3 and 4 in the form of sexual experience rates by amount of television viewing, subdivided by the categories of the moderator variables. The data are presented separately for females and for males.

Additional information is presented in the last two columns of Tables 3 and 4. The "Total" column presents sexual experience rates for the categories of the moderator variables without regard to the amount of television viewing. These figures show the main effects of the moderator variables on sexual experience. The last column presents correlations between amount of viewing and sexual experience. For these correlations, viewing was measured as a continuous variable in quarter hour increments, and sexual experience, as before, was measured as a dichotomy.

Females

Looking first at females (see Table 3), we note again the lack of an overall positive association between amount of viewing and sexual experience. While the experience rate is lowest for the lightest viewers, it is highest for the middle categories and drops for the heaviest viewers. The overall correlation is small and not statistically significant.

Significant correlations between television-viewing and sexual experience do not emerge for any of the subgroups defined by the several moderator variables. With regard to the child variables, we expected that higher viewing might produce higher rates of sexual experience for those low or moderate on the vocabulary test score, those with lower educational aspirations, and those with lower self-esteem. For none of these subgroups was there a significant correlation and, if anything, the differences are in the opposite direction.

Turning to the parent-child variables, we do find a modest positive correlation between viewing time and sexual experience for those who watch television apart from their parents. No association is found for those who watch with their parents. These results are

Table 3. Percent Sexually Experienced in 1981 by Amount of Television-Viewing in 1976: 15- and 16-Year-Old White Females

Moderator Variables	Percent Sexually Experienced in 1981					Correlation[c] of Amount of Viewing and Sexual Experience
	Average Daily Viewing				Total	
	One Hour or Less	Over 1 to 2 Hours	Over 2 to 3 Hours	Over 3 Hours		
All Females	8%(34)[a]	17%(78)	16%(40)	12%(20)	15%(171)	-.02
Child's Vocabulary Test Score[d]						
Low, Moderate	10 (24)	24 (43)	16 (27)	9 (15)[b]	17 (109)	-.05
High	5 (10)	9 (35)	20 (18)	----	11 (62)	.19
Educational Aspirations[e]						
High School or Less	18 (25)	----	08 (15)	----	15 (39)	-.07
Some College	26 (33)	----	24 (20)	----	25 (53)	-.09
College Graduate	10 (17)	5 (36)	21 (14)	0 (11)	8 (78)	-.04
Self-Esteem[d]						
Low, Moderate	13 (18)	18 (47)	19 (29)	10 (12)	16 (106)	-.04
High	4 (16)	17 (30)	13 (19)	----	12 (65)	.11
Child Watches TV With:[e]						
Parents	9 (13)	5 (33)	8 (27)	9 (15)	7 (88)	-.02
Others, or Alone	8 (21)	26 (44)	31 (18)	----	23 (83)	.15
Frequency Discusses TV With Parents[e]						
Often, Sometimes	8 (20)	9 (47)	20 (24)	9 (15)	11 (106)	.02
Hardly Ever; Never	9 (13)	32 (29)	14 (20)	----	21 (63)	.05
Parents' Sexual Attitudes[e]						
Traditional	9 (18)	16 (43)	7 (19)	11 (12)	12 (92)	-.07
Permissive	7 (16)	19 (33)	22 (28)	----	18 (77)	.12
Rules Regarding TV-Viewing[d]						
None	7 (16)	17 (48)	13 (30)	15 (16)	14 (111)	.02
Any	9 (17)	19 (30)	21 (13)	----	14 (60)	.04

Note: Footnotes to the table are found after Table 4.

Table 4. Percent Sexually Experienced in 1981 by Amount of Television-Viewing in 1976: 15- and 16-Year-Old White Males

Moderator Variables	Percent Sexually Experienced in 1981 Average Daily Viewing				Total	Correlation[c] of Amount of Viewing and Sexual Experience
	One Hour or Less	Over 1 to 2 Hours	Over 2 to 3 Hours	Over 3 Hours		
All Males	24%(39)[a]	21%(70)	12%(43)	35%(21)	21%(172)	.00
Child's Vocabulary Test Score[d]						
Low, Moderate	36 (14)	29 (26)	13 (30)	43 (12)	26 (81)	-.06
High	18 (25)	17 (44)	16 ——	(22)[b]	17 (91)	.01
Educational Aspirations[e]						
High School or Less	50 (10)	46 (10)	06 ——	(20)	27 (41)	-.34 p<.05
Some College	—— 20	(25) ——	40 ——	(17)	29 (43)	.35 p<.05
College Graduate	18 (20)	14 (43)	16 ——	(26)	15 (89)	-.02
Self-Esteem[d]						
Low, Moderate	20 (21)	15 (44)	10 (31)	36 (17)	18 (113)	-.08
High	29 (18)	32 (26)	23 ——	(15)	29 (59)	-.08
Child Watches TV With:[e]						
Parents	37 (20)	25 (30)	12 (31)	10 (10)	22 (91)	-.24 p<.05
Others, or Alone	10 (19)	18 (40)	14 (12)	57 (11)	21 (81)	.25 p<.05

Frequency Discusses TV With Parents[e]

Often, Sometimes	22 (14)	17 (35)	---- 06 (22)----	15 (70)	-.17
Hardly Ever; Never	24 (24)	24 (32)	14 (28) 52 (14)	25 (98)	.10

Parents' Sexual Attitudes[e]

Traditional	11 (22)	21 (39)	11 (21) 36 (16)	19 (57)	.13
Permissive	41 (17)	22 (31)	----15 (26)----	24 (5)	-.18

Rules Regarding TV-Viewing[d]

None	21 (23)	16 (48)	8 (31) 40 (18)	18 (120)	.07
Any	29 (16)	34 (22)	----20 (14)----	28 (52)	-.10

a The numbers in parentheses are weighted N's. While fractional weights were used, the numbers reported in the table, as well as the percentages have been rounded to the nearest integer.

b When the number of cases in a cell fell below 10, adjacent cells were combined to provide a larger base for percentages.

c The correlation is between a more detailed measure of average viewing -- coded in quarter hours -- and sexual experience -- a dichotomy. Correlations significantly different than zero (two-tailed test) are noted at the right. One-tailed tests of $r > 0$ yield no additional significant correlations.

d These variables were measured in 1976, the first wave of the survey.

e These variables were available only for the 1981 wave of the survey.

consistent with our expectations, but the results are not strong. The positive correlation — .15 — is not large and is not statistically significant.

Results somewhat consistent with our expectations are also found for the categories measuring parents' sexual attitudes. Among children whose parents hold more traditional attitudes, the pattern of sexual experience rates across the categories of television viewing shows only small and inconsistent variations. The correlation is small and actually negative. For those whose parents hold more permissive attitudes, there is a consistent positive trend and a modest positive correlation. However, the correlation is not statistically significant, and it is even smaller than that for children who watch television apart from their parents.

No consistent patterns of experience rates and no noteworthy correlations are found for the two remaining variables — the frequency of discussing television with parents, and the existence of rules regarding television viewing.

These data, then, provide no consistent evidence of a link for girls between the amount of television viewing in late childhood, and the subsequent early onset of sexual activity. This is the case for girls as a whole, and for several subgroups where such a relationship might be more likely to be found. In only two cases were there results consistent with our original expectations, and these results were weak.

On the other hand, there are fairly strong and interesting main effects among the moderator variables. Consistent with what we expected, sexual experience rates are higher for those who scored low or moderate (rather than high) on the vocabulary test score, those who had low or moderate (rather than high) self-esteem, those who watch television apart from their parents (rather than with them), those who hardly ever or never (rather than often or sometimes) discuss television with their parents, and those whose parents hold more permissive (rather than traditional) sexual attitudes. The differences are particularly striking for the two variables that have to do with parent-child interaction regarding television. Those who less frequently discuss television with their parents have nearly twice the sexual experience rate of those whose discussions are more frequent, and those who watch television apart from their parents have over three times the rate of those who watch with their parents.

No difference in sexual experience is found between those with or without rules regarding television. As for educational aspirations, the highest rate is found for those with intermediate levels — some college — with lower rates for those with both higher and lower aspirations. However, the rate is lowest for those who aspire to college graduation.

Males

The picture for boys is somewhat different. As noted before, there is a tendency for those boys who viewed the most to be more likely to be sexually experienced. This result is reprinted in the top row of Table 4. Thirty-five percent of those who had been heaviest viewers have had sexual intercourse compared with only 12 to 24 percent among those who had been lighter viewers. As noted before, however, the lowest rate of sexual experience is found not among the very lightest viewers, but among those whose average viewing is over two to three hours. As a consequence, the overall correlation between viewing time and sexual experience is zero.

When the sample of boys is partitioned into subgroups using the moderator variables, some significant results appear. However, they are only partly consistent with our original expectations.

There is a strong positive correlation ($r = .25, p < .05$) between viewing time and sexual experience among those who view television apart from their parents. For this group of boys, the experience rate for the heaviest viewers is nearly six times that of the lightest viewers. Interestingly, the correlation for the group that does view with their parents is not near zero, as we would expect, but is as negative and significant as the other correlation is positive. We speculate that parents may use the occasion of viewing television with their children to communicate their own values regarding the content being seen, so that with more viewing, this communication may be more frequent and effective.

The other significant correlations are found among categories of the variable measuring educational aspirations. These results give a mixed picture with regard to our expectations. As expected, the correlation for the boys with the highest aspirations — college graduation — is near zero and not significant. For those whose aspirations are somewhat lower — some college — a strong and significant positive correlation does emerge. Among this group heavier viewers are twice as likely to be sexually experienced as lighter viewers. However, contrary to our expectations, the correlation for those with the lowest aspirations — high school or less — is strongly negative, and significant. That is, the lighter the average viewing among this group, the higher the sexual experience rate.

None of the other correlations is statistically significant, and only some of them are even in the predicted direction. For example, modest positive correlations exist for those of low or moderate self-esteem, and for those who less frequently discuss television with their parents, consistent with expectations. But modest negative correlations exist for those of low or moderate vocabulary test scores, and for those whose parents have more permissive sexual attitudes, contrary to our hypotheses.

As was the case for females, the main effects of the moderator variables for males are strong and usually in the expected direction. Thus higher rates of sexual experience are found among males who have low to moderate vocabulary test scores, have lower educational aspirations, discuss television with their parents less frequently, and who have parents with more permissive sexual attitudes. For girls, no difference was found according to the presence or absence of rules regarding television. Among boys, on the other hand, those boys who report they have rules are half-again as likely to be sexually experienced as those who do not. This is consistent with the notion that parents explicitly impose rules — in a fashion that can be clearly recognized by the child — primarily in cases where the child's troublesome or difficult behavior warrants closer control.

No difference is found in the sexual experience rate of boys according to whether they view television with or apart from their parents. The only result which gives an opposite effect for boys in comparison with girls is for self-esteem: the higher sexual experience rate is for boys of high, rather than low or moderate self-esteem.

DISCUSSION

The findings presented above raise both substantive and methodological issues. On the substantive side, the results provide little support for an hypothesis linking the quantity or content of television viewing with the early onset of sexual activity. The content of favorite programs was neither consistently nor significantly related to sexual experience; and the amount of television viewing was related only occasionally and in weak or inconsistent ways. No overall association was found for females, and a positive correlation emerged for only two of several subgroups of females for which a correlation might have been expected. Even these correlations were small and not statistically significant.

For males, the association was more U-shaped than linear, resulting in a correlation near zero. Some positive correlations did emerge among subgroups for which such a correlation might be expected, and two of these were large and statistically significant. But others were in the opposite direction from that expected, and some large negative correlations emerged where they were not expected.

A number of factors may be involved in this pattern of results. Research on the link between television violence and aggression in children yielded inconsistent results when the child's favorite program was used as a proxy for the level of exposure to violent content. When content measures were based on diaries of programs actually watched, or on the content of special television or film segments shown to children in experiments, the results were much stronger and consistent. This suggests that the level of exposure to specific kinds of content is not well measured by the use of favorite programs.

Alternatively, it may be that sexual messages pervade television programming so thoroughly that the specific programs watched make little difference. Certainly, sexuality is used as an important element in much television advertising. It is not infrequently a topic of discussion in much news and public affairs programming. And such messages are not confined to television, but are found throughout other types of mass communication, especially magazines. Given the ubiquitous nature of this topic, the additional exposure implied by naming a soap opera, for example, as a favorite program may have little marginal effect.

Another aspect of the findings that deserves consideration is the fact that results are inconsistent between females and males. Here the answer may lie in closer examination of sex differences in the dependent variable – sexual experience. An unintended pregnancy tends to be considerably more consequential for teenage girls than for teenage boys. Whether a pregnant girl chooses to have an abortion, as many do, or to carry the pregnancy to term, the social, personal, and economic costs are very high. While the rates of sexual activity for younger teenage women are rising, they are still considerably below those for males of the same age. The costs of pregnancy are undoubtedly a factor in this difference. Also there are still normative differences in the acceptability of premarital sexual activity for males and females, and these differences lead to higher social costs for females. Given this situation, we would expect factors which in general have at most a modest influence on sexual activity to be more influential for boys than for girls. Looked at another way, premarital sexual activity is a more deviant behavior for teenage females than for teenage males. As such it is likely to be significantly influenced only by more powerful factors. Television viewing, therefore, may fall under the category of factors which at best have only a modest impact. This is entirely consistent with the finding that even among boys the impact emerges only for a couple of subgroups, and that these subgroups are those in which other more powerful influences (educational aspirations and parental involvement in viewing) are absent.

In the introduction we briefly mentioned several alternative and not entirely mutually exclusive models of the way in which television may influence behavior. These included modeling, disinhibition, arousal, catharsis, and socialization. Do the findings provide any help in choosing among these various models? Given the inconsistency and weakness of the results, it is hard to argue that the data lend support to any of the models, let alone allow us to choose among them. While more careful testing of the various models is needed before accepting the null hypotheses, there are some reasons to believe that a link between television viewing and sexual experience is less likely than one between viewing and aggressive or antisocial behavior.

The arousal, disinhibition, and to a lesser extent the modeling hypotheses all presume that the effects of viewing are fairly immediate. That is, viewing creates an impression, an emotional state or a social environment in which, as long as it lasts, the behavior in question is more likely to occur. While various forms of aggression among children are fairly common and could easily take place in the kinds of social contexts which might accompany or immediately follow the viewing of a television program, this situation does not apply to nearly the same extent to sexual behavior, especially intercourse. Thus, while an unmarried adolescent might conceivably be aroused by a television program to such an extent that he or she soon thereafter has sexual intercourse, this sequence of events seems highly unlikely.

Also, it should be borne in mind that the dependent variable we are dealing with is a status which, once entered, is not left. Thus, it might be more reasonable to expect a link between amount of viewing and frequency of sexual intercourse than a link between viewing and the crossing of the boundary between virginity and sexual experience by age 15 or 16.

Rather than acting in any immediate way, it seems much more likely that television viewing—if it has any effect at all on sexual activity—acts more indirectly by teaching, in the absence of other influences, certain values, language, and scripts that are consistent with and perhaps encourage sexual activity. Those who have learned such things from television, especially boys for whom the costs of unintended pregnancies are lower, may then be more likely to initiate or engage in sexual activity when an occasion arises. This may be in a social context much different than that in which the learning occurred. This interpretation is most consistent with a socialization model of television effects. Results indicating main effects for whether parents discuss television with the youth and whether they co-view programs also support the idea that socialization is involved in some way. In these cases, parents may use the stimulus of television as an opportunity to express their own values and expectations or to disapprove of behavior deemed inappropriate. The television viewing situation, therefore, may well be a context in which parents socialize their children.

Arriving at definitive conclusions on the basis of the current analyses is difficult because of several methodological limitations that stem mainly from the fact that the data were originally collected for a much different purpose. It is worth pointing out some of these limitations so that future research on this topic can minimize them. The most obvious are limitations in measurement. Exposure to specific content needs to be measured more precisely by recording actual programs viewed, and conducting a content analysis of those programs. The same raw data would also provide a more accurate measure of the amount of television viewed, rather than relying on parent or child estimates, as we have done. It may also be important to include television advertising in the content that is monitored and coded.

Another limitation is that our data contain only one measure of sexual activity, and a rather extreme one at that—the transition to sexual experience by 15 or 16. At a minimum, future analyses should obtain data on the age at which this transition occurred, as well as the circumstances in which it occurred and the level of sexual activity that has followed. In terms of the possible effects of television viewing it is also important to obtain information on attitudes about sexuality, and about behaviors that are more common than intercourse. With regard to attitudes, one of television's strongest influences may be in what children learn about sex roles and the ways in which men and women relate to each other in all spheres of behavior, not just erotic behavior. Sex role attitudes, in turn, ultimately do affect sexual activity and pregnancy and child-rearing as well.

It is also clear that a study design is needed that provides enough cases in relevant cells to conduct the multivariate analyses required to sort out the effects of television from those of the family and personal factors that may confound and mask these effects. In addition, studies are needed that can distinguish between short-term and long-term effects. Such studies would be helpful in evaluating the relative importance of several of the models of television effects that the present data could not do.

In summary, the data do not provide any strong or consistent evidence for a link between the quantity and content of television viewing and the initiation of sexual activity. Before a no-effects hypothesis is accepted, however, studies should be carried out that strengthen the design and measures in such a way that more rigorous testing can be conducted. In addition, since measures of whether the youth discusses television with his or her parents and whether the youth co-views with parents or other persons do seem related to sexual activity, future work should address the context in which adolescents receive media messages and the ways that other persons help adolescents interpret the messages they receive.

REFERENCES

Baldwin, W. (1982). Trends in adolescent contraception, pregnancy, and child-bearing. In E. R. McAnarney (Ed.), *Premature adolescent pregnancy and parenthood.* Grove & Stratton, Inc.

Bandura, A. (1973). *Aggression: A social learning analysis.* New Jersey: Prentice-Hall.

Berkowitz, L., & Rawlings, E. (1963). Effects of film violence on inhibitions against subsequent aggression. *Journal of Abnormal and Social Psychology, 60,* 405-412.

Billy, J., & Udry, J. R. (1983). The effects of age and pubertal development on adolescent sexual behavior. North Carolina: Carolina Population Center.

Bower, R. (1984). *Attitudes toward television: Changes over three decades.* Washington, DC: Bureau of Social Science Research.

Comstock, G. (1978, March). *Television and social values.* Paper prepared for National Institute of Mental Health planning project: Television as a teacher. Bethesda, MD.

Comstock, G., Chaffee, S., Katzman, N., McCombs, M., & Roberts, D. (1978). *Television and human behavior* (Chapter 5). New York: Columbia University Press.

Devaney, B. (1981). *An analysis of the determinants of adolescent pregnancy and childbearing* (Final Report to NICHD). Bethesda, MD.

Fernandez-Collado, C., Greenberg, B. S., Korzenny, F., & Atkin, C. K. (1978). Sexual intimacy and drug use in TV series. *Journal of Communication, 28*(3), 30-37.

Feshbach, S. (1961). The stimulating versus cathartic effects of a vicarious aggressive activity. *Journal of Abnormal and Social Psychology, 63,* 381-385.

Franzblau, S., Sprafkin, J. N., & Rubinstein, E. A. (1977). Sex on TV: A content analysis. *Journal of Communication,* 27(2), 164-170.

Furstenberg, F. F., Jr. (1976). The social consequences of teenage parenthood. *Family Planning Perspectives,* 8(July/August), 148-164.

Greenberg, B. S. (1982). Television and role socialization: An overview. In U.S. Department of Health and Human Services, *Television and behavior: Ten years of scientific progress and implications for the eighties,* Volume 2. Washington, DC: U.S. Government Printing Office.

Hicks, D. J. (1968). Effects of co-observer's sanctions and adult presence on imitative aggression. *Child Development, 38,* 303-309.

Hogan, D., & Kitagawa, E. (1983). *Family factors in the fertility of black adoles-*

cents. Paper presented at annual meetings of the Population Association of America.

Jessor, S., & Jessor, R. (1975). Transition from virginity to nonvirginity among youth. *Developmental Psychology, 11*(4), 473-484.

Jessor, R., Costa, F., Jessor, L., & Donovan, J. E. (1983). Timing of first intercourse: A prospective study. *Journal of Personality and Social Psychology, 44*(3), 608-626.

Micklin, M. (1981, June). *Adolescent socialization and heterosexual behavior.* Presentation at the NICHD Contractor/Grantee Workshop in Adolescent Pregnancy and Childbearing.

Moore, K. A. (1988). *Facts-At-A-Glance.* Washington, DC: Child Trends, Inc.

Moore, K. A., & Burt, M. R. (1982). *Private crisis, public cost: Policy perspectives on teenage childbearing.* Washington, DC: The Urban Institute Press.

Moore, K. A., Peterson, J. L., & Furstenberg, F. F., Jr. (1984, May). *Starting early: The antecedents of early premarital intercourse.* Paper presented at the annual meeting of the Population Association of America, Minneapolis, MN.

Roberts, E. J. (1982). Television and sexual learning in childhood. In U.S. Department of Health and Human Services, *Television and behavior: Ten years of scientific progress and implications for the eighties,* Volume 2. Washington, DC: U.S. Government Printing Office.

Schramm, W., Lyle, J., & Parker, E. B. (1961). *Television in the lives of our children.* Stanford, CA: Stanford University Press.

Surgeon General's Scientific Advisory Committee on Television and Social Behavior. (1972). *Television and growing up: The impact of televised violence.* Washington, DC: U.S. Government Printing Office.

Tannenbaum, P. H., & Zillman, E. (1975). Emotional arousal in the facilitation of aggression through communication. In L. Berkowitz (Ed.), *Advances in Experimental Social Psychology,* 8, 149-192.

U.S. Department of Health and Human Services. (1982). *Television and behavior: Ten years of scientific progress and implications for the eighties.* Washington, DC: U.S. Government Printing Office.

Withey, S. B. (1980). An ecological, cultural, and scripting view of television and social behavior. In S. B. Withey & R. P. Abeles (Eds.), *Television and social behavior: Beyond violence and children.* Hillsdale, NJ: Lawrence Erlbaum Associates.

Zelnik, M., & Kantner, J. (1980). Sexual activity, contraceptive use, and pregnancy among metropolitan-area teenagers: 1971-1979. *Family Planning Perspectives, 12*(5), 230-237.

INTERPRETING CONTENT/ CONSTRUCTING MEANING

Sex and Genre on Prime Time

Corless Smith, PhD

San Francisco State University

SUMMARY. Sexual activity is never explicitly represented on network television programs. Rather, realms of sexuality are suggested. These realms are represented differently according to the genre of the program; sitcoms explore the realm of the taboo, while nighttime soaps plumb the inevitable consequences of sexual activity. Detective shows display the sexual underworld. When a program shows sexuality from more than a generic perspective, it provides a more global representation and is also a more fruitful object of study.

In daily life most people do not experience sexuality as a single, unitary phenomenon. Instead, it is more accurate to conceive of a constellation of ways in which sexuality is experienced, thought about, displayed and expressed. The sexual world constellated through display and suggestion, convention and presentation, attitudes and acts is immense and pervasive—a virtual universe in

Corless Smith is Professor of Broadcast Communication Arts at San Francisco State University, 1600 Holloway Ave., San Francisco, CA 94132. She also produces documentaries and the continuing program "Radio Watches Television" for Pacifica station KPFA.

which each of us participates. Television programs are, generally, situated in a "real-seeming" world, and they want to participate in and reflect this constellation of sexuality as it is experienced in daily life, including fantasy-making, but television programs do so in highly limited ways.

In one large way, however, television's representation of sexuality is, in fact, an extraordinarily accurate counterpart to sex as it is experienced by most people in daily life. For most of us, intercourse is a private, unseen event, and this is precisely the way it is on prime time, where the closest we ever get to the act itself is a torrid preliminary, a blouse unbuttoning, soft focus over bedded bodies, or a sheet-clad aftermath. Here the social construction of daily reality corresponds to the social construction of television, the broadcasters' agreement with the audience about what is appropriately public. Yet on TV, as in real life, while the act of intercourse is hidden, its memory or expectation, the social context that creates it, frustrates it, or comments on it, and the vast realm of emotionality that accompanies it, is highly pervasive.

There must, of course, be profound differences between TV and everyday life in their presentations of sexuality. In daily life, for most of us, the act really does occur, no matter how seldom, and we experience it physically and emotionally rather than visually, as television leads us to experience it. The range of possibility in actual felt sexual experience is immense, and this vast range of unvisualized possibility is foreign, impenetrable territory for television. Sex on TV must be presented in speech or visuals; other components, such as touch, the most important aspect of physical sex, can only be suggested through these modes. Furthermore, television is a cynical medium; on it sex is often used despicably to sell something else. This is also true in daily life, but in a less concentrated form.

Rather than the act itself, TV presents the social context of sexuality. The biggest difference between how TV presents this social context and how we experience it in daily life is that on TV sex is presented through fictions, in the form of half-hour or hour-long stories with characters and plots. So, not only do TV programs participate in the constellation of sexuality, they also participate in the categories of fiction. As fictional creations, TV programs select settings, characters and plots from a range of possibilities. In the same way they must necessarily select from the set of all possible modes of sexual relationship, display, attitude, and expression. Such selections are predictable on contemporary prime time, however, not on the basis of the categories of life from which they are derived, but rather on fictional categories, in this case, on the basis of popular genres, those transformations of traditional genres first described in their televisual forms by Horace Newcomb (1974). Which sector of the sexual constellation a particular program foregrounds is a function of the genre to which the program belongs, or, conversely, any program's treatment of sexuality is an important indicator of its genre.

Adding the vocabulary of fictions to the vocabulary of sexuality on TV might be an expansive combination. In fact, the combination is limiting. Currently, about 30% of prime time television programming consists of the popular genre of situation comedies. Another 30% are nighttime soap operas, and yet another 30% are police-detective-crime shows, including those dealing with lawyers or those called action-adventure programs which may or may not focus on a crime. There are also several programs which utilize the supernatural as a key element in constructing their stories. The remainder of prime time consists of news programming such as "20-20," and movies whose membership in genres varies. Within each of these generic categories exists a spectrum of possibility and probability which can make similarly categorized programs quite different. For example, though we call both "Cagney and Lacey" and "Mike Hammer" police-detective-crime shows, clearly these are quite different sorts of programs, and their treatments of sexuality are, in fact, aspects that make them different. Furthermore, genres on TV are mixed through a process Mimi White (1985) has called intertextuality. Various functions appropriate to one genre can be transposed to another as a result of trying to enlarge the audience by enlarging the repertoire of appeal. In this way modes of sexuality most appropriate to the sitcom also turn up in the police drama, though the opposite is less often true, for reasons which will become apparent.

Intertextuality or the changing of genres towards each other is a function of historical change in marketing, but generic expression is also subject to social change. The social change most significant to the representation of sexuality has to do with changing definitions of gender and relationship. As sex roles have been changing, so have the behavior patterns of men and women in courtship and marriage and on the job. The process of progressive definition finds expression on contemporary television as it reflects and recreates its "real-seeming" world. A major cultural theme in contemporary relationships is that of the identity or antithesis of sex and intimacy; physical gratification may accompany emotional sharing or it may be quite separate. TV genres are positioned at various points along the axis of physicality and emotionality, and it is these locations which further assign them to one genre or another. There are also programs which take this dichotomy as their subject, exploring or illustrating it rather than assuming a generic posture towards it. Treatment of this strong polarity allows such programs to build strong dramatic tensions, and their more global orientation to sexuality offers not only more points of connection to the universe of sexuality in real life, but also more fertile ground for interpretation from the fictional point of view.

SITCOMS

The television galaxy is constructed so that two of the most popular types of programs participate in the set of possible modes of sexual display, action and attitude at opposite poles; those of the sitcom are most distant from those of the nighttime soap opera. This is true, for one reason, because humor, or the attempt at it, structures and fortifies the sitcosmos, as David Marc (1984) has called the world of the situation comedy; whereas, humor is almost anathema for the melodramatic universe of the soap. Laughter dispels tension and is therefore inimical to continuing stories whose appeal rests in renewing a tense suspense so that the viewer will return to watch again and again. Not for "Dynasty" or "Dallas" the broad bedroom jokes, the ironic posturings and snickers of "227" or "Growing Pains," slapstick and visual jokes that are signs of the sitcoms's roots in vaudeville. When Rose of "227" appears in a red sequined dress which reveals a broad wedge of cleavage, we are to read this as an affectation, as a "put on" for which the plot will probably offer a corrective "put down." When Alexis Carrington Colby appears in a similar dress, we read it entirely differently, as evidence of her sexual power and wealth. Lonnie Anderson's big bosom was a continuing joke on "WKRP"; on "Dallas" Pam's big bosom is an aspect of her "beauty."

When asked, most people say there is no sex on sitcoms. This is not true, but reflects the flavor of the truth. Sitcoms focus on families; children are frequently major characters, or else the cast is somehow in a familial relationship that is essentially wholesome. Sitcoms thus participate in that part of the constellation of real sexuality concerned with taboos—those things which are not supposed to be done or known, those things on the edge of the pubicly wholesome at which we peek. For the sitcom this is a restricted form of the taboo because something as serious as incest, for example, would be beyond the bounds of humor which demarcate the sitcom. In the sitcosmos taboo implies the hidden, not the forbidden, so that on sitcoms people are frequently discovered saying or doing things they ought not to do by someone else in the family.

In his seminal study of TV genres, Horace Newcomb (1974) pointed out that the sitcom depends upon a character whose failure to know certain social rules foments some kind of chaos which is rectified by the show's end. Frequently, the chaos so-fomented has to do with breaking socio-sexual rules, transgressing mild social taboos. On "Newhart," for example, Bob is removing something from the eye of an attractive woman when his wife walks in. It looks like the couple is kissing. Bob looks up anxiously, confused, "It's not what you think, honey." His wife rolls her eyes or storms out, and the remainder of the program constitutes the explanation.

The discovery of the transgression against the taboo prompts the most familiar gesture of the sitcosmos, rolling eyeballs, which, in turn, elicits the equally familiar ironic shrug. For example, when an officious grandma comes to visit on "Alf," Alf hides under the bed in the master bedroom unbeknownst to the married couple who are its occupants. The next evening at bedtime, when he makes his presence known and tells the couple he's been hiding there the night before, they look slightly aghast and roll their eyes. "You didn't hear anything, did you?" they ask, meaning "You didn't hear what you ought not to have heard, did you?" The viewers know he did. Ironic shrug from Alf.

In this way, the sitcom is rife with innuendo, one of the major modes of referring to the taboo. Another is ironic humor, a major device of the sitcom, naturally, since sitcoms are supposed to be funny. On "Golden Girls" Blanche's aunt chides her for asking for something in too abject a manner. "Don't beg," she says. "You sound like your Uncle Carmine when he'd been away on a goat drive." On the same episode Sophia relates an incident that took place at a party 40 years before. "Salvatore gives me a passionate kiss. Being a respectable married women, I copped a few feels." The humor arises because Sophia is a wizened old lady whose demeanor indicates neither the vocabulary nor the action of "copping a few feels." In this way sitcoms bring us a lot of broad jokes about sex, jokes that aren't sexy or provocative, and on television, as opposed to in the theater, jokes that don't too far exceed "good taste," jokes that are not too raunchy while still making reference to the unseen and the unspoken. Not just sexuality but all aspects of the body are treated in this way. Flatulence is another favorite.

A good deal of sexually-related laughter on sitcoms stems from reaction to what the program outlines implicitly as inappropriate sexual relations, among the elderly, for example; the "Golden Girls" are allowed romance but not sex. Or, laughter and ridicule result from a character's misunderstanding of what is sexy. Television is continuously at work developing the definition of what is and what is not sexy, especially in ads, but largely in programs as well, and it is a very narrow definition as one would expect. Sitcoms do not themselves play a large role in developing this definition; rather, they assume it and further ratify it as a background against which divergences can be ridiculed, as on "227" when Rose appears in her red dress and Tina Turner wig and her escort is revealed to be wearing elevator shoes.

While sitcoms are harsh because they enforce narrow sexual standards, their soft spot lies in a sexually related area. Because sitcoms are familial they promote intimacy as a norm and as a context for sexuality. Scenes wherein this is somehow explained to children are innumerable. The kids may roll their eyes when mom and dad say they want to go to bed early, but "they love each other," and sex between the parents, though hidden, is firmly placed within the context of familial relationship. Also, we never see much physical excitement. It may be referred to or acted out in caricature, but never actually seen in the ironic world of the sitcom where all is conversation or slapstick.

It was their intimacy that made Sam and Diane's relationship for the viewers of "Cheers," though we also imagine that they must be "doing it." Judge Harry figures out that he loves the public defender when he has to get her out of jail on "Night Court." On "Who's the Boss" there is continual intimacy between the main characters, but sex is withheld from them and the audience. Their obvious sexual attraction and suitability (they're both sexy according to TV's definition) keeps viewers tuned in to this show, just as it kept them tuned in to the prolonged foreplay on "Moonlighting," which was not, however, a sitcom, for one reason because it lacked a full-blown familial context, and for another because eventually Maddie and David "did it."

Despite the emotional intimacy of the main characters on "Who's the Boss," however, if one of them sees the other emerging from the shower, he or she will cover the eyes, make a big deal, be embarrassed, and the laugh track will be activated. No matter how intimate its emotional world, and even that is circumscribed, in the sitcosmos sexuality is the field of the taboo. This side of life makes us blush, but none of these minor infractions of the taboo will get members of the sitcosmos expelled from the happy world of the laugh track, and chances are very good that whatever the transgression was, it will be forgotten by next week.

NIGHTTIME SOAP OPERAS

Not so on the nighttime soap opera where transgressions are never forgotten and sex always has consequences. Never has sexual activity or display been so heavily meaningful as on these ponderous dramas. Almost all the characters on nighttime soaps have been romantically involved with each of the other characters at some time, and for the faithful viewer who follows these characters through their many convolutions, each of them looms large with the ghosts of past lovers and relationships which they take with them like contrails into every new encounter. For example, on "Knots Landing" Gary Ewing has been married to both Valine and Abby, and both still feel attracted to him, while he is in the process of marrying yet another woman. When "Dallas"'s J.R., with his wife Suellen on his arm, confronts his chief rival, Cliff Barnes, at the annual Oil Baron's Ball, the viewer knows that at one time Suellen and Cliff had an affair, as have Cliff and J.R.'s current mistress, Mandy, who is also in attendance at the ball.

This is one way in which sex is never without consequences in the nighttime soap, and these consequences are almost always problematic in an ongoing fashion as mandated by the programs' format. Citizens' groups often complain that television glamorizes sex without showing the consequences that can result from it. This criticism is inappropriate to the world of the nighttime soap opera wherein pregnancies frequently result and wherein they are almost always problematic, exaggerating the problematic aspects they can assume in daily life. Valine's twins are really Gary's children, not her husband Ben's. Donna is pregnant on "Dallas," but she is divorcing her husband Ray, who is becoming involved with Jenna, who is carrying Bobby Ewing's baby. Bobby, meanwhile, is married to Pam. On "Dynasty" Sammy Jo's hot sex with Clay Fallmont makes her an expectant mother who wants the reluctant Clay to marry her.

Considerations of plot particular to the nighttime soap opera further emphasize the relentless consequences of sexual activity. Soaps need to maintain a steady stable of characters while continuously varying the stable slightly, introducing new characters who can interact with the permanent ones and help to create new plot movements. To accomplish this, lost or hitherto unrecognized children turn up often. Blake Carrington's son Adam appears from Montana; a daughter arrives from London. Ray Krebs on "Dallas" is introduced as the illegitimate son of Jock Ewing. A bombshell of a girl arrives at Mack's door on "Knots Landing" announcing that she is the daughter he never knew he conceived with his college sweetheart who was spirited away because Mack wasn't "good enough for her." These examples of the labyrinthine results of sexual relations point out a way in which the nighttime soaps participate in an old-fashioned view of sexual congress as constituent in creating lineage and dynastic lines—who will inherit what descends from sexuality.

This, in turn, points to the major import of sexuality on the nighttime soaps—sex is closely linked with power. It can be a commodity to be traded for power, as April on "Dallas" uses it. If a character has what is "sexy" then he or she can trade it for money or influence. On "Knots Landing" Paige gets into Peter Hollister's apartment and fixes him a meal of which she is the main course; she's just trying to get ahead. "Dynasty"'s Alexis bestows her sexuality on the deserving, and her very real attraction to Dex is often shown as a weakness in her otherwise invincible egomania and pursuit of total power.

Nighttime soaps are certainly the sites of some of the most explicit sexual scenes on primetime television. There are lots of scenes of nude male torsos shot from the front and nude female torsos shot from the back. Sheet-wrapped preludes and aftermaths are also common. Sex is made very hot, too hot in many cases, but irresistible, so the characters seem to fall into sexual relations almost against their wills, as well they might given the way nighttime soaps construct the unrelenting effects of sex. Yet, paradoxically, the characters also flee to sexual interludes as brief respites, as islands of pleasure in the otherwise inexorable confrontations the soap opera format demands that they have with one another. They have to forget the inevitable consequences since sex is their only relief. Also, they must be constantly tempted so as to contribute to the soap's ongoing creation of suspense, as Ruth Rosen (1986) has noted. This temptation is especially evident in the costumes. Soap characters, women in particular, are always dressed to elicit sexual responses. Yet while these clothes are attractive and glamorous, they are so heavily constructed through artifice as to seem a sort of armor. Shoulder pads are nowhere so required as on soaps. This clothing is inviting yet protective, ironically signalling the double nature of sexuality in nighttime soaps.

Portrayals of intimacy also have a place on soaps, though the intimacy has a desperate quality to it. In this problematic world, everything in relationships is volcanic; everything is changing and unstable. On "Dynasty" Blake and Krystle are a solid couple, untiringly affectionate, but Krystle can be kidnapped and replaced by a look-alike and Blake doesn't notice. Val and Ben on "Knots Landing" are very close, but Ben's former ties to the CIA can destroy their honest communication. Miss Ellie and Clayton Farlow on "Dallas" are usually sweetly affectionate, but one plot has Miss Ellie's former husband returning from the grave to reassert his claims on her. In the world of the nighttime soap opera intimacy is even more fragile than it is in real life. A fling is easier and more exciting. Because intimate relations happen within the context of

ongoing stories whose continuous nature requires change and suspense, they must change rapidly, thereby exaggerating the sense of
anxiety that accompanies them.

DETECTIVE AND ACTION-ADVENTURE SHOWS

Detective and action-adventure shows are yet another pole apart
from the nighttime soaps. While the consequences of sex on the
latter are inexorable and inescapable, on detective shows and
action-adventures, sexual attraction and sexual relations are fleeting
and ephemeral, primarily because in these programs the plots are
related to crime. Thus, we are often dealing with the shady side of
sex—prostitution, blackmail through sexual photos, seduction for
criminal purposes. We are in a world where things are most often
not as they first appear.

The basic plot of the detective show, as Newcomb (1974) described it, is the occurrence of disorder, that is, the crime, which
must be solved or cleaned up so that order is reinstated. Frequently,
in this plot sexuality is the source of disorder. One episode of
"Mike Hammer" concerned the title character's efforts to get the
D.A. off the hook after he has committed a drunken indiscretion
that has been photographed by a blackmailer. In another episode of
"Hammer," called "Deirdre," the title character has been killed.
It turns out that her look-alike has actually been killed as a result of
having taken compromising videotapes of an evangelical preacher.
In this episode Mike himself is somewhat smitten with the heroine,
whom we do not see in person until the end of the program. Mike
has been intrigued by her photographs alone.

This remote quality to Mike's attraction is representative of the
most frequent way in which the detective heroes seem to conduct
their emotional-sexual lives. There is a good deal of sexual display
on crime shows, what with arresting prostitutes and going to discos
to look for suspects and informers, as well as the display provided
by women undercover cops who dress as prostitutes, like Gina and
Molly on "Miami Vice." Yet this downside of sexuality is also
reflected in the detectives' own sexual relationships, which are
most often fleeting and all too ephemeral. Typical plots feature the
detective attracted to someone who turns out to be a criminal, who

betrays him and whom he has to do in somehow, or *she* has to do in as Gina does her Irish lover on one episode of "Miami Vice." Often the beloved is killed in a skirmish and then mourned by the detective. A number of "Miami Vice" episodes end with Crockett staring melancholically across Miami Bay from the deck of his boat. The detective is a loner in the tradition of Joe Friday; the fight against crime is a lonely one in which a sexual partner, an intimate one, is too much baggage. Even Kennedy on the short-lived "Heart of the City," who was shown as a tender, intimate father, was not allowed a mate; his wife had been killed and her absence was one of the foundation premises of the show.

Crime fighters and adventurers are not without intimacy altogether, however. Their police-detective partners or their secretaries are their intimates. Mike Hammer has his Girl Friday; Crockett and Tubbs have each other as well as Gina and Molly. "Spenser for Hire"'s title character actually has a girlfriend, and this moves "Spenser" into a more global form of representation, integrating an intimate dimension of personal life into the program. "Spenser," "L.A. Law," "Cagney and Lacey," and "Hill Street Blues" all participate more fully in the constellation of sexual relations and display than do their counterpart crime programs, and may certainly be called intertextual, combining as they do aspects of various genres. On "Hill Street," as in most crime shows, sex is most often of the marginal, deviant sort. We often see prostitutes brought into the precinct; LaRue helps film a porno movie, and Howard, the right-winger, is seduced by a transsexual. Yet against these episodes of the shady side of sex and its commodification stands the relationship between Furillo and Joyce Davenport, in whose bed the show often concludes as they comfort and enliven each other. After a hard day of fighting on the front lines of crime and justice, they come home to the refuge of their intimacy and the light goes out at the end.

NEWS SHOWS

News-oriented programs like "20-20" or "60 Minutes" participate in the sexual universe in a fashion most like that of crime shows. To be newsworthy, sexuality must be in some way extraordinary, often deviant. Pornography is an object of the news gaze; lurid shots of red-light districts, porn film houses and blacked-out photos allow the viewer into these venues under the guise of dispassionate investigation. Soft-core porn can come through news programs in this way as well. Stories about beauty pageants, for example, allow the viewer to regard the overt sexuality of the contestants as they parade in bathing suits, while inquiring with the reporter about matters such as whether or not the pageants are rigged. The psychological aspects of sex also undergo the scrutiny of the news format—various sex therapies may be investigated, for example. The news eye portrays its gaze as a dispassionate one which, because of its objectivity, may delve prurience and bring it into the living room. We are invited to descend with the newscast as "tabloid TV" presents ever-new nadirs to this journey.

TV MOVIES

TV movies, which constitute a good chunk of prime time hours, cannot be categorized easily because they can take the form of any of the extant genres and, thereby, participate in the sexual universe in the same way as do regular series of those genres. However, it remains true, as is often pointed out, that TV takes its greatest chances in the movie format. Social issues or personal conditions thought too risky to include in continuing programs are aired through the vehicle of the TV movie. AIDS, homosexuality, incest, rape, inter-racial relationships, and wife-beating have all been subjects of made-for-TV movies, so that we can say that sex as a social issue is their field. On the other hand, the mini-series, a combination of nighttime soap operas and the made-for-TV movie, generally gives us lots of skin and is a veritable festival of blouse unbuttonings and fallings backwards onto bed, hay, or ground. The length of the mini-series offers the opportunity to plumb the relationship between sex and intimacy, but it rarely does so, instead treating its characters' relationships as grand or blighted romances, fields of passion and power.

THE SUPERNATURAL

Several TV programs use the supernatural as the basis of their plots, as in "Amazing Stories," "Wizard," "Starman," and "Alf." The latter program is a sitcom, and so it shares with most sitcoms a sexual orientation toward the taboo and the accompanying innuendos and sniggering attitude towards sex. Alf likes to cozy up to bosomy women, for example. The wizard is himself completely outside television's definition of sexy, though his supernatural powers are attractive to some women. For the most part, however, he is rather like Howard the Duck, a novelty item not to be taken seriously in the sexual world. He can have intimacy, but no sex. "Amazing Stories" sometimes have sexual dimensions, but these generally play a part in the programs' greater urge towards ironic surprise and are not constituent elements. It can be said that in these programs sex is treated in a juvenile fashion. This quality also informs "Starman," who is portrayed as a naif, though one of the continuing motivations of the program is the hero and his son's search for the mother, the earthling with whom the being from outer space mated to produce the son. Starman is "true" to her, which gives him an asexual character despite his good looks and virility.

ROMANTIC COMEDY ADVENTURES

An active genre of contemporary television consists of programs we can call romantic comedy adventures, programs such as "Remington Steele," "The Scarecrow and Mrs. King," "Jack and Mike," "Moonlighting," and the recent "Snoops." While the characters of these programs are ostensibly private detectives, their cases and, in fact, the plots that structure the programs are often less important that the focus on the relationship between the main characters. It is the tension between them, sexual and intellectual, which motivates the programs. On "Moonlighting" Maddie and David's quick, witty repartee reminds us of Nick and Nora Charles (without their urbanity), but the conventions of this sort of "battle of the sexes" and the verbal one-upmanship descend at least from the time of Shakespeare whose Rosalind and Orlando in "As You Like It" and Beatrice and Benedick in "Much Ado about Nothing" participate in the same sort of badinage that makes "Moonlighting" interesting to many people. The creators of this program are quite consciously aware of this link, having presented a television *tour de force* when they created an episode based on "The Taming of the Shrew" complete with Renaissance costuming.

On contemporary TV's romantic comedies, chase and pursuit most often structure plots as well as structuring the main characters' relationships to each other. For example, David pursues Maddie relentlessly, teasing and taunting her, in one instance accusing both Maddie and their secretary Agnes Dipesto of having "UMS" — urgently missing sex. David lauds sex; Maddie accuses him of thinking of nothing else. Meanwhile, the audience has been kept on the hook wondering when they will "do it." There have been tantalizing kisses every once in a while, but "Moonlighting" remained a lengthy exercise in televisual foreplay until the 1987 season.

In this way these programs become more about what is sexy than about sex. The main characters have become archetypes of what is sexy. Cybil Shepherd, who plays Maddie, was a famous fashion model before her acting career, and her co-star Bruce Willis now regularly appears on lists of "most sexy men" along with "Remington Steele"'s Pierce Brosnan. In "Moonlighting," "Remington Steele," or "The Scarecrow and Mrs. King," we become attuned to the modes of modern American sexuality. Cybil Shepherd invariable appears in pastel silk dresses, blouses, jackets, and skirts liberally split up the side, her blond hair swooped over one eye. She is often photographed as if through a mist, a sort of angelic vision. The male's sexiness is less in his clothes, though these are "hip," than in his mannerisms, his knowing looks and husky voice.

Because TV's romantic comedies are about what is sexy, by implication they are also about what is not sexy, as one episode of "Moonlighting" amply demonstrated, an episode focused on the secretary Agnes Dipesto. Agnes's appearance directly contrasts with the definition of sexiness constantly elaborated through Maddie. Agnes is short. She has wide-open brown eyes, and she dresses in loose, layered clothing that reveals nothing of what her body is actually like. She is occasionally the naif, occasionally the idiot-savant, a lovable dimwit who also, occasionally, shows backbone.

She is lovable, but certainly not sexy according to the standards the program constructs through its hero and heroine.

Agnes yearns at the outset of one episode for love, sex and excitement. Maddie and David are sympathetic to her needs and send her to the Detectives' Ball hoping she will meet a man there. In preparation for the ball, Maddie takes Agnes home to "make her over." The ugly duckling is turned into as much of a swan as she can be under the hands of the experienced Maddie, who chooses a dress from her own closet and does Agnes's hair and makeup. When Agnes appears on the stairs at the ball, she is as sexy as she can be, that is, she as closely resembles Maddie as she can, yet there is still the urgent vulnerability and naivete that distinguishes her from the show's heroine. Agnes does, indeed, meet a man at the ball, but it turns out she is being used by him to escape his pursuers. Later he tells her she is "nice" right before he is killed.

Later this man's colleague takes Agnes to his apartment in order to drug her to find out what she knows about the whole situation. Again she is cast as a likable fool. However, this man, Doug, really does like her, and they exchange a passionate kiss, initiated by Agnes. Importantly, Doug matches Agnes; he is not sexy according to TV's definition either. He is nothing like "Moonlighting"'s hero David; instead, he is short and slight, his features undistinguished. This is someone the audience can believe would be interested in unsexy Agnes, given the show's definition of sexy.

In the end Doug turns out to be a secret agent who has to leave town, so there is no continuing sexual relationship possible for Agnes, an echo and reinforcement of the usually unspoken ideology that unsexy people do not deserve sex and cannot have it. As "Moonlighting" has developed, however, Agnes Dipesto has indeed been provided with a boyfriend, though he is another "unsexy" type named Herbert Viola.

SEX AND INTIMACY ON PRIME TIME

The popularity of romantic comedy adventures like "Moonlighting" points not only to the continuing fascination of the battle of the sexes, a battle at once exciting and frustrating, but also to the renewed importance of that theme in contemporary culture. Sex roles have been under scrutiny and this social phenomenon finds expression on television. One major theme whose enunciation has received emphasis from the sexual revolution (though, of course, present before it) is the identification or the antithesis of sex and intimacy. Romantic comedies are able to represent the push and pull, the attractions of each of these poles, and this closeness to the pulse of modern sensibility in part accounts for their popularity.

Dramatic tension, that energy which maintains our attention to fictions, is commonly described as deriving from conflict, conflict which is identified within stories as series of paired opposites. These oppositions are said to structure the fiction. When this form of fictional integrity intersects with a charged cultural theme such as the shifting and confusing relationship between sex and emotional closeness, itself a paired opposition, there exists the possibility for the creation of programs more powerful as fictions and more culturally relevant than TV programs usually are.

Such is the case with "Cagney and Lacey," one of the few programs brought back from cancellation because of viewer demand. Chris Cagney and Mary Beth Lacey are partners on the New York City police force, and while each episode focuses on some sort of crime, thereby provoking action and suspense, the ongoing action is filtered through and often comments on the relationship between the two women police officers, each of whom lives a quite opposite sort of lifestyle — Chris is a single woman who enjoys sex but doesn't want too much emotional involvement; whereas, Mary Beth has been happily married for seventeen years, has three children and lives a domestic lifestyle.

One episode of "Cagney and Lacey" specifically focused on the relationship between sex and intimacy. The story begins with Chris' reluctance to go on a four-day weekend with her boyfriend David. Her reluctance stems from her confusion and apprehension about what such a trip would mean. Chris says she fears it will "change their relationship somehow," but the real fear is of intimacy. The show makes it clear that Chris and David are involved in a sexual relationship already, but as the show makes equally clear, for Chris this is not "going all the way." Mary Beth, who is profoundly wedded, encourages Chris to go on the trip with David. "It could be a lot of fun," she says innocuously, promoting the trip as an opportunity to deepen the intimacy between two people. When Chris tells Mary Beth that David has suggested the Poconos as the site of the trip, Mary Beth reminisces that she and her husband Harvey went there for their honeymoon, where they had a "heart-shaped bed and pink sheets." Mary Beth equates marriage, sex and intimacy.

The plot of this particular episode fits neatly into the continuing tension between the two characters about lifestyle, an aspect of the show which accounts for some of its popularity; it is socially relevant because it explores the poles of choices recently available to women. Similarly, the contrast between sex and intimacy reflects the social world wherein people are lonely, and sex is easier to come by than emotional intimacy and commitment and often acts as a substitute for them.

The range of modern attitudes towards sex is further exposed in this episode as Cagney and Lacey investigate several robberies of doctors. The first doctor they interview is a marriage counselor who tells them he has never been married, that he and his companion of many years do not require the "benefit of paper" to sanctify their commitment. Mary Beth is skeptical and sightly contemptuous of this fellow; he is a nut. The other robbed doctor is a sex therapist presented as a quack who complains that "his fertility gods are gone" and pronounces that sex is mostly in the mind, and that it is possible to enjoy sex with anyone. Mary Beth later tells Chris, "That man's not a doctor. He's a licensed Peeping Tom." To her sex and intimacy are one and she is offended by their split.

In this episode of "Cagney and Lacey," as in sitcoms, sex sometimes assumes a theatrical aspect based upon the taboos surrounding it. Lots of jokes and innuendos fill the plot. Chris and David are sitting in a restaurant arguing about whether or not to go away on the trip when an electrical blackout occurs, presented to the viewer as a black screen. After a brief pause in the darkness, David exclaims, "That's not fair!" and Chris giggles. The audience is to understand that Chris has done something sexual to David to seduce him to her point of view, something she could not have done with the lights on. In fact, she has already offered to hole up in her apartment for the weekend with champagne and sex.

The sex therapist figures in a number of broader jokes as does the suspect who was visiting the sex therapist. Asked why he was going to both a marriage counselor and a sex therapist, he says, "When a relationship goes bad, it goes bad all over." More jokes and *double entendres* involve Detective Izbecki, who has previously been established as sexually interested in Chris, but getting nowhere with her. Izbecki dwells on the visual aspects of sex, dates "bimbos," and is immature in his orientation to sexuality-intimacy. When the widow of the homicide victim, on whose case Izbecki and his partner Petrie are working, telephones, it is implied that she is making a sexual advance to Izbecki, as later she will to Petrie in her apartment. Petrie asks Izbecki if she is interested in his "upper body work." Later the widow confesses that she and her husband were on separate vacations, and her husband was suspicious. "Walter always thought I was cheating on him." "Were you?" Petrie asks. "Not always," she replies. Here is a widow with a husband barely in the grave showing sexual interest in other men. She is firmly planted on the sexual side of the sex-intimacy continuum elaborated throughout the program to comment on Chris's conflict about whether or not to go on the trip with David.

Victor Izbecki is very interested in Chris' sex life. He has come on to her himself a number of times in the past, but she always puts him down, as she does in this episode. Izbecki tries to find out what is in the suitcase Chris has packed for her trip with David. He also wants to see David; he "wants to see what it takes to get her motor running." She says, "Trust me, you don't have the tools."

Everyone understands that "tools" refer to Izbecki's sexual skills or even his parts, and this kind of verbal symbolism is vastly amplified on the physical level in this episode. In fact, the program is an interpretive paradise for psychological analysis. First, it takes place during a heatwave. Everyone is sweating, and the city is described as "steaming" during a voice-over introduction which features a shot of a beach with a woman's bare leg projecting into the foreground.

Some aspect of Mary Beth's home life comes forward in each episode; in this one it furthers the "hot" theme. Harvey bought a microwave oven which Mary Beth is struggling to use but with little success. Here the popular saying of a pregnant woman that "she's got one in the oven" is relevant, for while Mary Beth is certainly successful reproductively — she has three children — she worries that her job deprives her family of care. She anxiously hopes that the microwave oven will "make their lives better." After a failed egg dish and a turkey her sons refuse to eat, Mary Beth tells Harvey they can use the microwave to make cocoa. Harvey says. "What will we do with the extra time?" Mary Beth replies, "We'll think of something," the implication being that they will do something sexual in that saved time.

In a striking parallel to Mary Beth's situation with the microwave oven in her home, the criminal investigations of the robberies and the homicide come together as Mary Beth and Izbecki are trapped between floors in an elevator. Izbecki is claustrophobic; the small enclosed space crazes him. He becomes violent and babbles while Mary Beth tries to calm him down. Victor takes off his shirt to reveal his hairy, muscular chest, another visual representation of stimulation. When he finally hears Petrie's voice, Victor clasps Mary Beth tightly and kisses her, which she reacts strongly against. Later, while they are still waiting to be freed, Mary Beth assumes the mother role in the womb-like space of the elevator, holding Victor's head in her lap and rocking him, again showing his immaturity, in fact, his fear of the developed female.

Besides the oven and elevator, which we can note as a classic symbol of sexuality as identified by Freud, another significant box appears in this episode — Chris' suitcase, which Izbecki tries so hard to see into. Speculating about its contents he says, "I figure you for black lace." Chris allows Victor no glimpse into the intimacy of her suitcase, but she confronts her own impenetrable "box" as she voices her confusion and ambivalence over the trip with David. She stares directly into her locker for some length of time as she says, "We're not getting married. We're just going away for four days."

At no time are we humans in a more intimate situation than we are as inhabitants of our mothers' bodies, so the repeated appearance of box-like structures within the steamy atmosphere of this episode helps to create and reinforce the major theme of the program — the often confusing contrast between sex and intimacy, a theme that is even echoed in the criminal cases under consideration: The crimes turn out to have been committed with the connivance of an answering service, an unseen intimate about whose operator Izbecki has said, "I dig a chick with an English accent." When he finally sees her, he finds she is vastly fat and ugly, again showing Izbecki's distorted judgement.

"Cagney and Lacey " foregrounds sexuality as a personal and social issue, using it both for titillation and as a device whereby to assess character. Through both visuals and the jokes that play upon sex's taboo aspects, as in sitcoms, the program displays a pervasive concern with sexuality on the overt and symbolic levels while never even coming close to displaying the act itself. Certainly, the fact that it has adopted a vitally relevant social issue as one of its thematic centers is responsible for part of its popularity, but that it does so through a fictional structure that reproduces the structure of the social conflict accounts for its power as drama.

CONCLUSION

Mark Crispin Miller (1986) has argued convincingly that genres are disappearing on television, that all of television is increasingly homogeneous. However, if one inspects treatments of sexuality on recent television, differences in these treatments according to program type remain quite evident, and so the ways in which sexuality comes through TV programs remain an indicator of their genres, and genre survives through these treatments. Finally, though it is true that each genre tends to elaborate repetitively its own orientation towards sexuality — sitcoms toward the taboo, detective shows towards the ephemerality of sex and intimacy, there remains the possibility for television programs to function not only as vital social commentary, but also as art when the antitheses of a contemporary polarity such as sex vs. intimacy are reproduced in a matching fictional structure such as that of "Cagney and Lacey."

REFERENCES

Marc, D. (1984). *Demographic Vistas*. Philadelphia: University of Pennsylvania.
Miller, M.C. (1986). Deride and conquer. In T. Gitlin (Ed.), *Watching television* (pp.183-228). New York: Pantheon.
Newcomb, H. (1974). *TV: The liveliest art*. New York: Garden City.
Rosen, R. (1986). Search for yesterday. In T. Gitlin (Ed.), *Watching television* (pp. 42-67). New York: Pantheon.
White, M. (1985). Television genres: Intertextuality. *Journal of Film and Video*, 38, 41-47.

Dr. Ruth Westheimer:
Upsetting the Normalcy
of the Late-Night Talk Show

Rodney A. Buxton, MA

The University of Denver

SUMMARY. For the most part, the late-night talk/variety television genre has been analyzed as little more than a promotional device for producers of popular culture products. Using concepts of dialogic discourse borrowed from M.M. Bakhtin and of star discourse theorized by Jimmie Reeves, this paper explores the ideological complexity available in the content of late-night programming. The various inflections of Dr. Ruth Westheimer within the broadcast context of the late-night talk/variety genre provide the focus of this analysis.

Hal Himmelstein (1984) describes the interview portions of the television talk show as a barter system providing producers of consumable cultural goods an opportunity to pitch their wares before the viewing public. These cultural goods include movies, other television programs, records, concerts and nightclub appearances as well as the cultural validation of each guest in terms of popularity. From this perspective, this programming format offers little in-depth discussion of these products. Dominant trends and celebrities are swept along by currents of popular fashion and passed off onto the viewing public through the framing device of television programming. When focusing upon economic elements, this analysis

Rodney A. Buxton is a visiting instructor in the Department of Mass Communications at the University of Denver. He is presently working on his dissertation research which deals with the representation of AIDS in fictional broadcast television narratives.

139

fails to examine the ways in which particular personalities and trends contribute to ideological struggle and transformation. For instance, Himmelstein relates his experience in visiting a taping of the "Late Night with David Letterman" show. Guests for the evening were Robin Williams and Peter Tosh. Himmelstein (1984) describes the situation thus:

> It feels like a large late-night business, which it is. The guests are there to plug their latest releases: Williams, his new film with Walter Matthau, *The Survivors*, and Tosh, his latest record album . . . .
>
> Williams, like most celebrity talk show guests, is there to merely display himself for twenty minutes, plug his latest commodity, which is himself, pick up his paltry $431 — the appearance fee is certainly not the inducement for appearance — and exit, stage left. (p. 286)

Such an analytical approach reduces the talk show format to little more than an economic system. While this argument may account for the appearance of a celebrity on a talk show, it does not explain why a particular celebrity is popular. Himmelstein does not analyze the relationship of particular trends and personalities or how these reflect and participate in ideological struggles and transformations. The format and the celebrities who appear in it are more ideologically complex than their economic function. Although the economic constraints of the American broadcast system partially define the late-night talk show genre, the programming's mode of production is dissimilar enough from that of prime-time programming to dislodge the parameters of appropriate cultural content. Lowered production costs provide an arena where ideological normalcy can be challenged. With lowered production costs and the same day live-on-tape broadcasts, this format depends a great deal upon the celebrity interview to fill up its programming content.

Because of the very nature of the dialogue found in these interviews, at least two perspectives are presented to the at-home viewer. While this does not insure conflicting ideological points of view, it does provide an arena for such confrontations. In addition, the individual ideological makeup of both the host/interviewer and the guest cannot be considered as non-contradictory. Individuals are not just the product of their economic class, but are constituted by a range of ideological positions which can be both complementary and contradictory (Morely, 1981). As a result, the talk show host and guest, who are essentially playing themselves rather than fictional characters, enact both the complementary and contradictory ideological positions which constitute their dispositions within the American ideological landscape. This increases the ideological complexity of the late-night talk show interview.

Although host and guest confront each other in "real" studio space and during live-on-tape "real" time, these personalities are not unlike characters within the format of a novel. Bakhtin (1981) argues that the representation of a character in a novel resonates with the cultural and social elements that comprise his or her personality. Reeves (1984) extends Bakhtin's argument to explore the popularity of celebrities. He suggests that cultural stars found within television programs are:

> *representations of socially typifying language* operating within a conflicted national language . . . Rather than treating the star as a sign, the star can be treated as *discourse* within *discourse* — meta-discourse, even. For as discourse, the star breaks traditional critical boundaries — narrative boundaries, generic boundaries, media boundaries — and weaves through diverse media texts, linking them, inflecting them, and reflecting their meaning. (p. 58)

From this perspective, celebrities are popular because they form a complex 'star discourse system' that taps into complementary and contradictory ideological positions. For Reeves, "star presenters" moderate between the common sense world of the layman — those who have relatively low knowledge of scientific, educational or cultural topics — and the specialized knowledge of those who have acquired varying degrees of professional expertise. Those "who, by virtue of the relevance of their social existence outside television discourse" (Reeves, 1984, p. 79), gain cultural significance within television discourse are defined as "star personalities." This includes individuals with legitimated scientific and educational expertise. As a professional sex therapist, Dr. Ruth Westheimer, a star personality/presenter traversing the late-night talk/variety show circuit, provides a useful example to illustrate Reeves' approach to celebrity.

Dr. Ruth Westheimer is a fairly recent addition to the cosmos of star discourse. As a radio and television sex therapist, she has tapped into the American ideological conflict centering upon sexual attitudes and behaviors. Consequently, her cultural visibility has grown with her success through the electronic media. Expanding beyond the framework of her own cablecast talk show, she has entered into the realm of broadcast television as a guest on both "The Tonight Show" and "Late Night with David Letterman." The interaction of Westheimer's persona with those of Johnny Carson, David Letterman, and Joan Rivers refracts differently depending upon which ideological points of references they chose to engage with her. At times, topics are discussed on a professional level: for instance, when a particular sexual problem such as birth control is framed in clinical terms. Sometimes topics—for instance, sex education—are discussed in a personal manner relating to a particular host's experience. Furthermore, some dialogues may deal more directly with differences between male and female points of view or differences towards sexuality associated with age.

While Dr. Ruth, as a cultural icon, has found her way into the various incarnations of the late-night talk show format, it has not always been within the guest interview context. According to Peter Sheen (personal communication, April, 1985), director of "The Tonight Show" videotape archives, Johnny Carson has never had Dr. Westheimer on as a guest. However, he has done several parodies with her as the subject of sketches. Even though Carson has not interviewed Dr. Westheimer, his ironic acknowledgment of her as a cultural icon provides an important index of Westheimer's incorporation into popular culture. In order to better understand how Dr. Ruth functions as a star discourse in popular culture, a deconstruction of one of Carson's parodies will illustrate some of the elements of her persona which are culturally significant.

Dressed in Dr. Ruth drag with accentuated broad shoulders, extremely short legs, and a sandy blonde coiffure, Carson mimics her German-Jewish accent as he dishes out absurd advice to staff-written questions about sexual problems. The discrepancies between idealized feminine sexuality and Dr. Ruth's sexual persona is intensified when a male caller tells the parodic therapist, "Dr. Ruth, once I have sex, I can't get enough. Ten, twenty times—I just can't stop!" In response, the parodic Dr. Ruth gives the man her phone number. Ironically, Carson plays the conventionality of Dr. Westheimer's physical appearance against an unconventional response. The unconventional strangeness of an older female assertively seeking sexual activity exposes the conditions attached by dominant ideology to proper sexual behavior concerning gender and age. From a dominant American ideological perspective, elderly persons, and especially elderly women, are assumed not to be sexually active. Dr. Ruth, as a sex therapist and a self-proclaimed sexually active older woman, undermines this assumption. The sketch also undermines the controlled conditions of professionalism (in this case, related to sex therapy) by undercutting the aura of professional distance with a humorous acknowledgment of personal lust.

Using Reeves' star discourse system to analyze Carson's parody, the most obvious characteristic the sketch foregrounds is Dr. Westheimer's position as a professional. In a fairly straightforward manner, the sketch positions Dr. Ruth as "America's foremost authority on sex." The second important characteristic of Carson's parody is sex, the subject of Dr. Ruth's expertise. Within the parody, Carson touches upon topics of sex clinics, menopause, frigidity, infidelity, sexual ignorance, pregnancy, and divorce. All of these are topics that Dr. Westheimer deals with in a serious manner. In part, Dr. Ruth's ascension as star discourse is implicitly tied with the appropriateness of these topics of American culture outside the realm of broadcast television. Following the upheavals in sexual liberation of the late sixties and early seventies, consumer markets have opened up for cultural materials which deal frankly with sexual pleasure and dysfunction. Within the past decade and a half, such topics have become the focus of books, magazines, therapy groups, and even radio broadcasts.

By overemphasizing the physical and verbal stylistics of Dr. Westheimer's personality, Carson underlines the paradox between having a grandmotherly-type act as an expert on sexual matters and the dominant ideological values placed upon appropriate sexuality. Within American culture, sexuality, as it has been presented in visual and verbal images, is portrayed as a domain of youth rather than senior citizens. Dr. Ruth, as well as Carson's parody of her, undermines the limitations of those portrayals. Carson's parody not only pokes fun at Dr. Westheimer's cultural incongruency against physical type, but also exposes cultural myths concerning the sexuality of older adults.

Carson's parody illustrates the conventional characteristics that have become closely associated with the star personality of Dr. Westheimer: professional expertise, sexual subject material, age, gender, and physical appearance. In addition, Carson hints at the possible contradiction between Dr. Ruth's professionalism and her private life when he portrays her as being sexually active. These six characteristics are presented as the most visible, but not necessarily inclusive, cultural values linked with the star personality discourse of Dr. Westheimer. While Carson's parody provides a humorous index of Dr. Ruth's characteristics, a comparative analysis of her interviews with Joan Rivers and David Letterman should demonstrate how Westheimer's ideological dispositions produce complementary and contradictory discourse in the context of the late-night talk show.

As one example of the interaction between Dr. Ruth and Joan Rivers, the April 12, 1985, installment of "The Tonight Show" provides a particularly rich text for analysis. At this time, Joan Rivers was the permanent substitute host for "The Tonight Show." Rivers' introduction begins in much the same manner as did Carson's parody. She ironically cites Westheimer's professional expertise and accomplishments concerning cable television and radio programs. As Rivers compliments Dr. Westheimer's appearance ("You look very pretty" and "You look so glamorous — you're all in sequins") she implies that professional success has enhanced Dr. Westheimer's personal appearance. Age is emphasized when Dr. Westheimer states that she is the oldest woman to have appeared on the cover of *People Magazine*. At this point, Rivers alludes to a previous interview in which Victoria Principal had lied about her correct age. Thus, in the process of this short discussion, the topic shifts from the effect of success upon personal appearance to the particular feminine cultural dilemma concerning beauty and aging.

Continuing the line of discussion relating professional success and female physical beauty, Dr. Westheimer talks about a new French movie in which she appears. The film's premise is based on the discovery of the skeleton of the first French woman — "She is short and well proportioned . . . they're like you and me." Taking her cue from Westheimer's comments on physical type, Rivers questions her about early anxieties of being single and small. The tone of the interview shifts here from a professional dialogue between star presenter and an expert to that of star presenter and a layman. As a result, the interview moves into a more personal, rather than professional, mode.

In response to Rivers' questions, Westheimer concedes her past anxieties concerning her physical appearance — "I'm so short" — and the problems it has created in her personal relationships. The following discussion of Westheimer's three marriages and two divorces implies a partial gap between Westheimer's successful professional image and her more troubled personal sphere. While she is considered an expert in sex therapy and interpersonal relationships, Dr. Ruth has not been completely successful at these endeavors in her own personal life. This then leads into questioning about the effect of being a sex therapist and the effect it has had upon Dr. Westheimer's relationship with her children. Contradictions between the frankness of her professional image and the restrictions of her private self appear as Dr. Westheimer explains her behavior in the domestic arena. She quickly reasserts her professional persona by stating that she does not interfere with her children's private lives, that they realize she works within the framework of professional expertise and that they are proud of her because of her work.

From this point on in the interview, Westheimer locks into her professional persona. In fact, it is Rivers who switches from her role as a star presenter to the layman. A therapist/patient relationship develops between the two women as Rivers asks for advice on how to inform her own daughter about sexual maturation and sexual practice. This relationship begins ironically because of Rivers' approach, but the underlying tone of her discussion seems to be sincere in her desire to approach the topic. She jokingly acknowledges her own sexual ignorance as a teenager: "My mother told me nothing, Dr. Ruth. You know, I thought the menstrual cycle was something sold by Schwinn." Rivers asks Westheimer if parents should enlighten their children about sexual matters and question them about intimate sexual behavior. Dr. Westheimer advises her to be frank but to forego interrogation: "Not for you to say, 'Where did he touch you last night?' Don't do that."

Reasserting her role as a presenter, Rivers abruptly changes the topic of discussion, possibly because it became too personal and didn't move in the direction she desired: that parents should know what their children are experiencing sexually. Consequently, an ideological contradiction develops between parental control and the value of informing adolescents about sexual behavior. As a result, different aspects of "the right to know" create conflict within the same discourse. The interview ends with both women in their professional social positions: Joan Rivers, star presenter, coaxing stories from Dr. Westheimer about her professional media experiences.

During a magazine interview in the fall of 1984, Rivers complained that she was not allowed to do her jokes about the Cathy Rigby Maxi-Pad commercial or address the issue of women's menstrual periods within the production constraints of "The Tonight Show" (Israel, 1984). In doing so, she pointed out the hypocrisy of airing the commercials without being able to discuss the material in a non-commercial context. This changed during this particular Rivers/Westheimer interview. At this broadcast moment, the gender positioning of the two women combined with Dr. Ruth's legitimized expertise in sexual therapy to break through the stated parameters of the late-night talk show. Because the two women could discuss a female bodily function if framed by Westheimer's professional credibility, Rivers' jokes finally found their way into the program and were broadcast on the live videotape uncensored. As a result, menstruation, outside the context of a commercial advertisement, became an appropriate topic for discussion.

While the Rivers/Westheimer interview shuffled from the professional to the personal back to the professional, David Letterman's approach to Dr. Ruth seldom swayed from the professional path. On November 7, 1984, Letterman started his interview with Dr. Westheimer by acknowledging her expertise and success in radio and television. Just as Joan Rivers had commented upon Westheimer's personal look of success, Letterman states, "The TV show must be doing very well. You have a very successful look about you tonight." Implying that success and physical appearance are important cultural aspects for getting guests to come on a television program, Dr. Westheimer uses this opportunity to ask Letterman to come on her cable program. Letterman hesitates, noting the subject material of "Good Sex": wrenching sexual and emotional problems. In American society, the ability to disclose emotional problems is a devalued asset for the male. Indeed, it is considered a liability by dominant ideological standards. While a few images of the sensitive male who is in touch with his inner feelings filter into mainstream popular culture content, they are more than overwhelmed by images of males who maintain a tight restraint on their emotions and feelings. Because he is to a great degree a typical American male, Letterman's hesitation may be viewed as a function of his own positioning within the socio-cultural milieu and part of his ideological disposition.

In response to Letterman's uneasiness in discussing personal sexual problems, Westheimer states that they will talk about something different, for instance, professional success. Inverting the interview and upsetting the show's controlling hierarchy, she asks him what it is like for him to be successful. In this moment, the professional and the personal are juxtaposed. Even so, Letterman is visibly uncomfortable discussing his private reactions to his public success. Letterman attempts to regain control of the interview by stating that he is flattered by the attention. He then moves the dialogue back into the realm of non-personal professionalism. This short introductory rapport is the only point at which non-professional characteristics of either Dr. Westheimer or David Letterman are approached: her physical appearance or his submerged private personality. The rest of the interview centers around two topics of sexual interest.

As the first topic to be explored, sensuality, as opposed to sexuality, creates a mild confrontation which stems from gender positioning within the dominant social structure. Dr. Westheimer, who as a discourse system partially positioned by her gender, argues with what might be construed in dominant ideology as a feminine attitude:

> . . . have sometimes this kind of just hugging and touching and caressing and good feeling and don't let it end in sex . . . Because what will happen is that they will discover some sensuous feelings of well-being—some feelings of real warmness. Of this cuddliness.

Letterman humorously questions the practice from two distinct social positions: gender and geo-cultural. When he asks Dr. Westheimer where this particular trend in sexual behavior germinated, she responds with "Denmark." Exhibiting distorted facial features and an ironic tone, he undercuts this sexual practice by drawing upon the mythical aura surrounding relatively extreme (by American standards) Danish sexual behavior. Letterman undermines the impact of Dr. Westheimer's statement concerning sensuality by poking fun at the foreignness of the cultural values.

Letterman also questions the practice from a ideological position of gender. He responds with what might be considered a culturally dominant male response. "Now explain to me why this is in lieu of sexual activity . . . Why shouldn't it just end up in sexual activity?" This creates a conflicted dialogue between sensuality without sexual release — the more feminine value in dominant male ideology — and the physical climax which has been, until feminists re-appropriated it, a particular element of male discourse.

Through her culturally legitimated position as an academic expert, Westheimer ideologically counteracts Letterman's response concerning hugging and orgasm. She points out that the continued pressure to perform sexually causes physical dysfunctions in both men and women. Unable to provide a counterstatement, Letterman uses his ultimate control as program host to change the subject. This may end the debate as a stop-gap measure, but it does not resolve the gender-based conflict.

In addition, the second topic of sexual interest in their interview focuses on male physical dysfunction occurring from prostate problems. This topic enters into the conversation via Letterman's interest in television viewing. After watching a "Donahue" segment on this particular problem, Letterman expresses his amazement at what subject matter can get through programming practices in particular broadcasting contexts. Paradoxically, he cannot discuss the topic in the context on his own program. But in the context of her legitimated expertise, Dr. Westheimer is able to reveal explicitly the subject by quoting Phil Donahue, "And he says, 'This morning we are going to look up a penis.'" She continues the interview with a discussion of penile implants and a desire for a sexually literate society in which problems such as this can be discussed without embarrassment.

In the broadcast context of this particular interview, Letterman's dominant control of "Late Night" becomes devalued. It is Dr. Westheimer who carries the greater ideological clout in this broadcast situation. Voicing his consternation over this particular irony, Letterman acknowledges the conflict between the authority of programming practices and the authority of Dr. Westheimer's professionalism. At the same time, he humorously undercuts Phil Donahue's cultural value as a social mediator by stating:

> Well, it will be interesting to see if this stays in. Now that you said it — a professional in the field — she said it — now will it stay in or not? . . . If Phil can say it, can't Dr. Westheimer say it?

After all, if an expert in sexual therapy can't discuss the subject of impotency, why should some individual without professional qualifications be allowed to approach the topic? By pointing out the inconsistencies of broadcast censoring practices, Letterman broke through the topical constraints of commercial television production.

In this particular Letterman/Westheimer interview, Dr. Westheimer's cultural value won out over that of programming practices because this installment of "Late Night" was broadcast without being censored. However, this was not entirely dependent upon her cultural value as an expert. Other extraneous elements beside her star personality factors did enter into the situation. In part, the discussion aired uncensored because the program was broadcast in a non-prime-time period. If the program had been broadcast during prime-time, especially the 7-9 P.M. period, it is highly unlikely that such a candid discussion would have gone unedited. Also, "Late Night" is a program targeted towards Baby Boomers (Merrill, 1984). If the program had a larger constituency espousing traditional religious values rather than the relatively more explicit sexual attitudes of the Baby Boomers, frank dialogue concerning sexual activities and problems would most likely not have been permitted.

Using Dr. Ruth's professional expertise as a catalyst, Letterman was able to subvert the constraints of television production by acknowledging the discrepancies between the ideological positions of the studio audience and the production people in the control booth. In addressing Dr. Ruth's explanations of penile implants, he focused on the gap between the studio audience's willingness to discuss impotency and the unwillingness of the broadcast standards representative to offend any potential viewers. By pointing out this discrepancy, Letterman disrupted the ideological constraints of television production.

Within the broadcast context of the late-night talk show format, Dr. Ruth Westheimer emerges as a complex ideological system whose greatest power stems from her legitimated expertise in sexual therapy. However, this asset does not go unchallenged in the course of the talk show interview. Indeed, they do not always go uncontested within the cultural text of "Dr. Ruth Westheimer." Differences appear between the professional and the personal Dr. Ruth — how explicit she is when she talks to or about social actors from the public arena and how she restricts the discussion of her own or her family's sexual behavior. As a result, she cannot be understood as an unproblematic discourse system but one crossed by conflict and producing contestation.

As Morely (1981) argues, discourse is constituted not only by the contradictions that traverse each individual, but in the institutional sites where individuals articulate their positions to each other as well. Within the context of the late-night talk show format, both Rivers and Letterman acknowledge Dr. Ruth's expertise in the field of sexual behavior. Beyond this cultural characteristic, the two diverge in their reactions and interactions with Westheimer. The institutional site of "The Tonight Show" with Joan Rivers as host or "Late Night with David Letterman" each has its own set of ideological positions. This is due in part to the ideological dispositions of the hosts, as well as the production format. Just as Westheimer is a product of many ideological positions, differences in the ideological dispositions of the two hosts account for alternative refractions of her star personality in their respective interviews with her. This helps to explain the more personal approach taken by Joan Rivers in interviewing Dr. Ruth in contrast to the more professional approach used by David Letterman. Consequently, their specific conjunctures with Westheimer produce different fields of cultural dialogue.

In the production of cultural dialogue, Rivers is able to connect with more elements of Dr. Westheimer's discourse system than Letterman. Beyond expertise in sexual therapy, Rivers intersects with Westheimer in the fields of gender and physical type. This leads to questions dealing with ideological struggles concerning the dominant image of the female objectification and to issues focused upon the domestic realm—marriage, divorce, parent/child relationships. Contrary to Himmelstein's implications concerning economic agendas, these issues are discussed as an emotional, rather than economic, agenda.

On the other hand, Letterman maintains a distance of professionalism which focuses on abstract discussions concerning sexual behavior or television censorship. As stated before, this is due, in part, to the ideological differences in gender positioning. This influences the direction his interview takes where even the credibility of Dr. Ruth's professionalism is called into question. For example, visual juxtapositions of Letterman exhibiting raised eyebrows and rolling eyes play against the audio track where Westheimer is explaining her theory of orgasmic abstinence. This juxtaposition creates an audio-visual dialogue which, within the late-night talk show format, can be as important as the verbal interview alone.

While such ironic exhibitions can work against Dr. Ruth's ideological position, some juxtapositions work to her advantage. Within the Letterman/Westheimer interview, competing discourses do offer each other invaluable aid in getting through institutional broadcast boundaries. Dr. Westheimer's explanation of prostate problems and their correction occurs in conjunction with Letterman's discourse on television censorship. Even though they are different topics, their presentation in the institutional site are interdependent upon each other. Letterman's interest in censorship is prompted by Phil Donahue's graphic depiction of prostate surgery on broadcast network television, and Westheimer's discussion is initiated by the very censorship that restricts Letterman's detailed description of that process. Without the interaction of these two individuals' ideological dispositions and the intertwining of their respective interests, it is doubtful that either topic of its own accord would have found its way into the programming content. Through the juxtaposition of these two dissimilar topics, the normalcy of television broadcast content is transcended. What was formerly inappropriate material has found legitimacy.

Within the context of broadcast television, the program discourse and the star discourse of the late-night talk show genre are more complex than Himmelstein's analyses of this format acknowledge. By using Reeves' approach, the complexity of the format is more fully uncovered when celebrities are analyzed for their cultural value rather than their economic value. Within this context, restrictions are recognized, but are not viewed as static. In the example of Dr. Ruth Westheimer, her expertise in sexual therapy defines her strongest ideological position and provides her initial entry into the realm of broadcast television. However, other factors from her ideological disposition influence the tenor and direction of her appearances within the late-night talk show format as well. It is the complexity of Dr. Westheimer's ideological makeup, not the economic impetus for her appearances, which accounts for the various inflections of her cultural persona within the different incarnations of this broadcast genre.

In spite of the constraints and modes of production of this particular programming format (the low-budget production costs, the late-night broadcasts, a relatively narrow definition of the target audience), this genre's content reflects more than the huckstering of new movies, records and concerts. The late-night talk show provides a programming arena in which ideological broadcast constraints may be tested and broken. Contrary to a basic economic critique of this commercial programming, the late-night talk show and the celebrities presented within it may be viewed as a complex enactment of ideological contradictions and confrontations present within American society itself. Instead of an unproblematic reinforcement of conventional ideology, Dr. Ruth provides an example of how the normalcy of the late-night talk show can be upset.

REFERENCES

Bakhtin, M.M. (1981). *The dialogic imagination* (C. Emerson and M. Holquist, Trans.) (Michael Holquist, Ed.). Austin: University of Texas Press.
Himmelstein, H. (1984). *Television myth and the American mind*. New York: Praeger Special Studies.

Israel, L. (1984, October). Joan Rivers and how she got that way. *Ms.*, pp. 108-114.

Merrill, S. (1984). David Letterman: Candid conversation. *Playboy*, pp. 65-80.

Morely, D. (1981). Texts, readers, subjects. In S. Hall, D. Hobson, A. Lowe and P. Willis (Eds.), *Culture, media and language* (pp. 163-173). London: Hutchinson University Library.

Reeves, J. (1984). *Star discourse and television: A critical approach.* Unpublished doctoral dissertation, University of Texas at Austin.

Of Mice and Men:
An Introduction to Mouseology
Or, Anal Eroticism and Disney

Arthur Asa Berger, PhD

San Francisco State University

SUMMARY. This essay deals with two important comics, Walt Disney's *Mickey Mouse* and George Herriman's *Krazy Kat*, and considers the social, cultural, psychological and symbolic significance of the main characters and their creators. In the discussion of Disney and his work (based, in part on writings about him) it is suggested that he exhibited traits associated with anal eroticism, which raises an interesting question about the popularity of his work with the American public. The two dominant themes found in *Krazy Kat* are described as "the triumph of illusion over reality" and "anti-authoritarianism." In a comparison of the two characters, it is shown they are polar opposites: Mickey Mouse is sadistic, asexual, and anal while Ignatz Mouse, the hero of *Krazy Kat*, is playful, sexual, and phallic.

A MOUSE TO MEET TECHNOLOGY'S NEEDS

Mickey Mouse is one of the most popular comic-strip characters in the history of American popular culture and one of the most significant creations in animated films. What significance does this squeaky-voiced rodent have? What does he tell us about ourselves, our culture, our society, our ethos and mythos, our pathos and ba-

Arthur Asa Berger is Professor of Broadcast Communication Arts at San Francisco State University.

Correspondence may be sent to the author at the Broadcast Communication Arts Department, CA34, San Francisco State University, 1600 Holloway Avenue, San Francisco, CA 94132.

thos . . . you name it. Why is this mouse such a monumental figure for pop culturists, mythologists, culture critics and Disneyologists?

This report should be looked upon as a contribution to the study of pop culture mice, a field to which I will give the neologism "mouse-ology." It also deals with Disney and, by implication, the American psyche. Let's allow Walt Disney himself to describe his origin tale:

> His head was a circle with an oblong circle for a snout. The ears were also circles so they could be drawn the same no matter how he turned his head. His body was like a pear and he had a long tail. His legs were pipestems and we stuck them in big shoes [also circular in appearance] to give him the look of a kid wearing his father's shoes. We didn't want him to have mouse hands, because he was supposed to be more human. So we gave him gloves. Five fingers looked like too much on such a little figure, so we took one away. That was just one less finger to animate. To provide a little detail, we gave him the two-button pants. There was no mouse hair or any other frills that would slow down animation. (Schickel, 1968, p. 95)

All of this was necessary because Disney, so Richard Schickel reports in *The Disney Version*, had to produce some 700 feet of film every two weeks; thus he needed a character who was easy to draw.

We already see here the germ of Disney's passion — his fascination with technology and his willingness to let the requirements of machines dictate what he would do with his creations. Technology's inner necessities shaped Mickey Mouse, Disney's first significant creation, just as they were to shape his other efforts, including Disneyland. Mechanization had already taken command, decades before the idea of audio-animatronics had entered his head.

Were I a doctrinaire Freudian (as I have been accused of being) I'd feel compelled to speculate, at the very least, about the significance of Mickey Mouse trying to wear his "father's shoes." Is there some kind of a hidden Oedipal aspect to this? And what about the symbolic castration — lopping off one of Mickey's fingers (on each hand) because five fingers looked like "too much" on a small character? Could these "birth traumas" be, in some way, connected to the sadism and cruelty one often finds in Mickey's actions (masked, of course, by a veneer of genial humor and nonsense)? And that squeaky voice of his? Is he one of the castrati?

The mouse is a familiar character in folklore and popular culture. A mouse gnawed through the ropes holding a lion, who had saved the mouse at an earlier time, and three blind mice, obviously not then castrated (even symbolically) ran after a farmer's wife—with disastrous results. (I will not go into the messy details about this matter.) We've also had a Mighty Mouse figure, and, of course, that remarkable and magnificent mouse, Ignatz (hero of the brilliant comic strip *Krazy Kat*) about whom I'll have more to say later.

Mice are small, timid, dirty rodents with a passion, so we are told, for peanut butter and cheese. They have been anthropomorphized for centuries, but they have not always ended up like Mickey Mouse, though to be fair, I would imagine that media mice (as well as other creatures) have mirrored many of their cultures' dominant values and preoccupations obediently and unobtrusively, like him.

It is hard to think that Mickey Mouse's great triumph in *Steamboat Willie* was in 1928, some sixty years ago. Since that time he has been a character of some consequence and he, as well as his celebrated creator, "Uncle" Walt Disney, are worthy of considerable attention.

THE ALL-AMERICAN RODENT: LIKE FATHER, LIKE MOUSE

The myth of America is that we can all be successful if we are willing to work hard enough. We can all emerge from the poverty and obscurity in which we are born and with a bit of luck, pluck, and virtue, reach a stage in which we can, like Benjamin Franklin (who is an important role model for us, here), dine with kings. Or at least with movie stars and other showbiz celebrities. This is the American dream, which argues that social class is irrelevant and that individual willpower is the crucial factor in determining success.

There is, in the American psyche, a voracity, a hunger for experience, a lust (and I use the word with its sexual connotations in mind) for success, and for the symbols of success so that others will know that one is successful, which generates tremendous energy and dynamism. But also some other, less wholesome, consequences.

Disney was a small-town boy from the Midwest with All-American values, whose life is a testimonial to the fact that some people, who are born in ordinary circumstances, can "make it." There seems little doubt, when you examine Disney's life and his work, that he was afflicted with a great and overwhelming desire to be a success, which might account for his well-documented compulsiveness. Much the same applies to Mickey Mouse, whose quest for experience seems Promethean or, at least, Kerouakian. Mickey's biography reads like something you might find on the dust jacket of a beat poet's book, describing his life and numerous occupations, travels, and adventures, before he became a member of the literary bourgeoisie.

Here is Schickel's (1968) description of Mickey Mouse's career:

> The temporary solution to the problem of keeping Mickey fresh and amusing was to move him out of the sticks and into cosmopolitan environments and roles. The locales of his adventures throughout the 1930's ranged from the South Seas to the Alps to the deserts of Africa. He was, at various times, a gaucho, teamster, explorer, swimmer, cowboy, fireman, convict, pioneer, taxi driver, castaway, fisherman, cyclist, Arab, football player, inventor, jockey, storekeeper, camper, sailor, Gulliver, boxer, exterminator, skater, polo player, circus performer, plumber, chemist, magician, hunter, detective, clock cleaner, Hawaiian, carpenter, driver, trapper, whaler, tailor and Sorcerer's Apprentice. In short he was Everyman and the Renaissance Man combined, a mouse who not only behaved like a man but dreamed dreams of mastery like all men. (p. 117)

In short, he was a kind of home-made Leonardo da Vinci — and like Leonardo, Mickey's sexual proclivities, and those of his creator as well, are of some interest.

It is pretty obvious that Disney can be described as having many personality traits of the anal erotic. In his famous essay of 1908 entitled "Character and Anal Eroticism," Sigmund Freud described anal erotics as follows:

> The persons whom I am about to describe are remarkable for a regular combination of the three following peculiarities: they are exceptionally *orderly, parsimonious,* and *obstinate.* Each of these words really covers a small group of series and traits which are related to one another. "Orderly" comprises both bodily cleanliness and reliability and conscientiousness in the performance of petty duties . . . "Parsimony" may be exaggerated to the point of avarice; and "obstinacy" may amount to defiance, with which irascibility and vindictiveness may easily be associated. (pp. 27-28)

These three characteristics are often connected with an eroticization of (and intense interest in) the anal zone.

In his essay "The Wonderful World of Disney — Its Psychological Appeal," psychiatrist Michael Brody (1975) discusses anality in Disney's work. (Ironically, this paper was delivered to a convention of psychiatrists at a meeting held at Disneyland.) Brody writes:

> The story of the two frivolous brother pigs and the contrasting hard-working pig [in "The Three Little Pigs"] chased by the hungry, big bad wolf, provides not only possibly a parable of the hard times of the early 1930's, but the virtues of obsessiveness. Plan, prepare, isolate and be orderly. Only the pig who builds a traditional house of brick saves the other two "silly pigs" from being eaten by the Big Bad Wolf. Anal themes are used defensively to lessen the anxiety of oral aggression, represented by the wolf's desire to eat the succulent pigs. . . . There is also the compulsive repetition in the story, going from house to house with the wolf and pigs saying the same phrase. This anality reaches its zenith when the wolf is punished by the huge mechanical spanking-machine. (pp. 2-3)

Brody points out that we find anal themes and messages in many other places in Disney . . . with the "often-kicked-in-the-butt Jiminey Cricket and the exaggeratedly buttocked Tinker Bell" (p. 3), to cite a couple of other cases. Schickel (1968) says much the same thing. He writes, "Disney's interest in the posterior was a constant. Rarely were we spared views of sweet little animal backsides twitching provocatively as their owners bent to some task" (p. 146).

Disney's anality really manifested itself in his great creations, Disneyland and Disneyworld. There, as Schickel puts it, Disney's "lifelong rage to order, control and keep clean any environment he inhabited" (p. 15) could really take hold. He had "sanitized" the classics in his films — sometimes injecting anal resolutions to stories (as in the case of "The Three Little Pigs" cited above). This was one of the ways he "cleaned up" various stories (and "cleaned up" at the box-office as well, of course).

Beneath that folksy "Uncle" Walt exterior, beneath his pseudo-geniality and amiability, dark forces were at work. Disney's need to control and manipulate would eventuate in Disneyland and Disney-world (the latter the same size as San Francisco). In these parks, the ultimate in "clean" family entertainment, people could be (generally, without being aware of it) controlled, directed, regulated . . . whatever you will. As Brody (1975) put it, "Disney strove for control over his work and destiny. What could be more natural than a huge, controlled playground where all could be Disney-regulated" (p. 6). Employees in these parks attend training school for "smile and behavior regulation," and it is "control, not amusement, [that] seems the central theme in both the California and Florida parks" (p. 6).

This marked a new development in Disney's desire for mastery and control. The very art form he chose to work in, animation, is one in which the creator has great control. You can make animated figures do whatever you want them to do. As Schickel (1968) writes:

Of course, for a man as intense as Disney in his desire to control his environment, animation was the perfect medium, psychologically. You can redraw a character, or even a line in his face, until it is perfect; you need never settle as the director of the ordinary film must, for the best an actor — imperfect human that he is — can give you. . . . animation, to borrow from the unfortunate jargon of psychology, is a compulsive's delight. (p. 161)

Thus Disney progressed from animation to amusement parks, in his attempt to gain control over himself and others.

The ultimate move, for him, was the creation of those grotesque audio-animatronic figures. With them he does away with the vagaries of human personality and pushes the logic of control to its final and perhaps most absurd realization.

Disney also prided himself on the fact that Disneyland and Disneyworld were so clean. He is reputed to have come to Disneyland evenings to pick up litter that his sanitation workers had missed. What he created, "his" antiseptic wonderlands, were gum free, dirt free, and only slightly totalitarian. It may be, of course, that without recognizing it, Disney tuned into something buried in the psyches of his patrons — a desire to be controlled as a means, unconscious of course, of dealing with their conflicts — pre-genital and otherwise. We must ask ourselves whether the various aspects of anal eroticism found in Disney struck some kind of chord buried deep in the American psyche . . . or, at least, in the psyches of a large number of Americans?

Children might find anal themes pleasant and take delight in barnyard humor. But what about adults who "love" Disneyland, the "happiest place on earth," and go there often? How do you explain the fact that many high schools celebrate proms at Disneyland? Does it provide a momentary regression, in the service of our egos, or is there something other than regression involved (namely recognition)?

THE MOUSE I LOVE

The mouse I love is Ignatz Mouse, Herriman's malevolent, antiauthoritarian, incorrigible hero who heaved a brick at a lovesick Krazy Kat for thirty years. The situation in *Krazy Kat* is complicated in the extreme. Ignatz loves throwing bricks at Krazy, who takes the bricks as signs of love. This is because thousands of years ago Cleopatra's cat was creased by a brick thrown by her lover and the memory has lingered on. There is a third major character, Offisa Pupp, who loves Krazy and hates Ignatz. Pupp spends his life trying to protect Krazy from Ignatz, and arresting him and throwing him in jail when he does "crease" Krazy with a brick.

We have, then, a mad and wonderful triangle of protagonists and antagonists and bricks. Ignatz is a brick-throwing menace who refuses to acknowledge the validity of authority and pays for his anarchistic, anti-social acts by spending a great deal of time in jail (separated from his wife and children, I might add).

There are, I would argue, two important themes in this strip: the triumph of illusion over reality (as shown by Krazy's belief that the bricks are signifiers of love) and anti-authoritarianism (as shown by Ignatz's brick throwing). Ignatz is, in many respects, the opposite of Mickey Mouse and has infinitely more personality and spirit . . . and good humor. Mickey (like his creator) is so enterprising and so conventional, despite his frenetic behavior, that he becomes rather boring. That is why Disney felt trapped by Mickey and had to push him into a voracious quest for experience . . . and to find other characters, such as Donald Duck.

Ignatz, on the other hand, is an autonomouse character, who seldom fails to interest us and has cosmic as well as comic significance. I think Ignatz is an infinitely greater mouse, a more interesting mouse, and despite his anarchism, a much less threatening and destructive mouse. Mickey represents pseudo-individualism and the illusion of freedom. Created to accommodate the necessities of mass production, designed to titillate the lowest-common denominator, he now rules a "magic kingdom" in which human beings are manipulated and controlled, without their being aware of it.

That Mickey Mouse is one of the most widely known "heroes" in the world of pop culture and entertainment is something I find troubling. For the Disneyean world-view, as reflected by Mickey Mouse and Disney's other creations, including his amusement parks — compulsive, conservative (if not reactionary), entrepreneurial, mechanistic and perhaps even sadistic (at times, at least) — is not the only way of showing what this country stands for. Ignatz Mouse would be, to my mind, a much more representative and appealing "hero." There is, of course, an element of compulsiveness in his behavior. He did, let us remember, spend thirty years throwing bricks at a poor, lovesick Kat and doing whatever he could to evade the rules and regulations of his society.

He was not a "Disneyfied" or even "dignified" character. But that, precisely, is his strength. And there was an element of playfulness and humor about his behavior that showed he was not a victim of compulsions. If Mickey was the instrument of what Schickel describes (1968) as a "rage to order" (p. 15), then Ignatz was the instrument of what we might describe as a "love of disorder and chaos . . . of a messy world of wonderful, mixed-up characters." In the chart that follows I show the differences between these two mice:

MICKEY MOUSE	IGNATZ MOUSE
sadistic	playful
obedient	anarchistic
constrained	free
pseudo-individualistic	autonomouse (*sic*)
asexual	sexual
anal (reflects)	phallic

This chart suggests the differences between the two characters. I may have exaggerated things a bit, but I think it does a pretty good job of showing the dominant personality traits of each mouse — and what each mouse reflects about his creator and his psychological makeup.

If Ignatz Mouse had a themepark, it would be considerably different — and, I would imagine, a lot more fun. There certainly would be more of an opportunity to DO things (as opposed to spectate, go on rides, etc.) and test one's skills — at brick throwing, at the very least.

CONCLUSION

We are left with a problem. Does Disney's widespread popularity (in America and in many other lands, where Disney's characters are extremely well known) reflect some kind of a camouflaged and dif-

fused anality buried deep in our psyches? It has been argued by
certain Marxist media critics that Disney's work champions bourgeois capitalist values and is, ultimately, an instrument of cultural
imperialism. Is it possible that there is some kind of a connection
between bourgeois values, capitalism and anality? Is the anal personality type, then, one of the (if not the) basic personality types in
modern capitalist societies, which would suggest, in turn, that
Mickey Mouse is a symbolic figure who is truly representative?

   Let me conclude by pointing out a second consideration that
Freud discusses, relative to anal personality types. This has to do
with the fact that, as Freud (1908) puts it:

> The connections which exist between the two complexes of
> interest in money and of defecation, which seem so dissimilar,
> appear to be the most far-reaching. . . . In reality, wherever
> archaic modes of thought predominate or have persisted — in
> ancient civilizations, in myth, fairy-tale and superstition,
> in unconscious thoughts and dreams, and in the neuro-
> ses — money comes into the closest relation with excrement.
> (pp. 30-31)

There is, then, reason to believe that the character traits connected
to anality by Freud — orderliness, parsimoniousness, and obsti-
nacy — have a certain functionality in the modern world as far as
making money is concerned. The cost, in terms of other aspects of
life, is another matter.

   Freud concludes his essay by suggesting how people cope with
anality in their lives . . . either by "unchanged perpetuations of the
original impulses, sublimations of them, or reaction-formations
against them" (p. 33). That is, some people (such as Disney) never
abandon their anal personalities; some redirect the energy from their
anality into other areas; and some turn against anality, and like a
drunk on horseback, swerve over to opposite extremes.

   I would like to think that most of us outgrow our anality, though
residues of it linger in our psyches and are sometimes activated.
Disney, his creations like Mickey Mouse and Disneyland, do not
help us deal with anal eroticism but, instead, reinforce this element
in our psyches. Mickey Mouse is not like that mouse that gnawed

the ropes that constrained the lion in the famous folktale. Instead, Mickey Mouse helps forge the chains that we use to bind ourselves.

REFERENCES

Brody, M. (1975). The wonderful world of Disney—Its psychological appeal. (Unpublished Manuscript),

Freud, S. (1903). Character and anal eroticism. In Philip Rieff (Ed.), *Sigmund Freud: Character and culture*. New York: Collier Books.

Schickel, R. (1968). *The Disney version*. New York: Avon Books.

The Magazine of a Sadomasochism Club: The Tie That Binds

Rick Houlberg, PhD

San Francisco State University

SUMMARY. The monthly magazine of a sadomasochism club was investigated as a means of describing important issues for club members. The magazine was selected for this exploratory study because it is: (a) The club's only recorded history; (b) the only repository of club members' writings and photographs; and (c) the only link to the club for about 15% of the membership who do not attend meetings or other club activities because they reside some distance from the club's two West Coast chapters. A descriptive content analysis was performed on 47 issues of the club's magazine, published between October 1983 and January 1988, and the results were combined with the findings of a December 1987 magazine readership survey completed by 44% of the 812 dues-paying club members. The author's nonparticipant observations of club programs are also reported. The results indicate the magazine's space is filled by seven subject categories: S/M media reviews (2% of space), S/M poetry (5%), S/M issues (10%), S/M "how-to" (12%), S/M photography (14%), fantasy and real S/M stories (17%), and organizational reports (40%).

The study of sadomasochism has only recently emerged as a legitimate endeavor for social researchers. Weinberg (1987) stated: "It was not until the late 1970s that a body of sociological research

Rick Houlberg is Associate Professor of Broadcast Communication Arts at San Francisco State University.

Correspondence may be sent to the author at: BCA Department, San Francisco State University, 1600 Holloway Avenue, San Francisco, CA 94132. The author wishes to thank Dr. Michelle Wolf for her help with earlier drafts of this manuscript.

on S&M began to appear" (p. 51). Weinberg goes on to note that earlier published research focused on sadism and masochism as individual pathologies and not as interactions between people. Recent publications Weinberg argues, differ in issues addressed and in methods used but have as a unifying theme that S/M is "dependent upon meanings, which are culturally produced, learned, and reinforced by participation in the S&M subculture" (pp. 51-52). It is the social subcultures of S/M that are now receiving some study (Breslow, Evans & Langley, 1985, 1986; and Naerseen, Hoogveen & Zessen, 1987).

The S/M social subculture of this study is a West Coast sadomasochism club. The Club has over 700 members in two West Coast chapters, and almost 100 other members scattered across the United States, Europe and Australia. The Club produces a monthly magazine, and in each issue the Club's manifest is detailed. In addition to educating the public in the "understanding, interpretation, and appreciation of erotic art by providing commentary and literary review of eroticism in the arts," the Club will conduct lectures and group discussions in order to foster "the development of understanding and appreciation of erotic art" and the improvement of communication between erotic artists and the public. Finally, the Club provides instruction in the use of interpersonal erotic "psychodrama as a means to explore, share, and express erotic fantasy."

The Club's statement of purpose also indicates the organization is self-proclaimed as the "second-oldest group of its type in the United States." In discussions with the author, the Club's founders indicated they thought only one New York City organization had preceded the Club.

The only "cardinal" rules which the Club's membership insists each member must uphold are that all S/M activities must be consensual, non-exploitative, and safe. As children are not considered to be able to consent, all activities must be between adults. The consensual and safety rules of the Club are constantly being reinforced. Safety and etiquette issues, including restrictions on overt and heavy drug use, are strongly stressed at new-member orientations and in all written materials produced by the Club.

Perhaps the most concise and articulate expression of the Club's function was written by one of the Magazine's editors in 1986:

> Importantly, sexual and/or practice preference was not and is not a criterion for admission to [Club] membership. We have always had a gay, lesbian, hetero, bi, TS [transsexual], TV [transvestite], B&D [bondage and discipline], D&S [dominance and submission], infantilist, scatologist, etc., mix in [the Club]. One needed only a personal, non-judgmental, supportive interest in safe, consensual, non-exploitative S&M activities.

THE CLUB'S MAGAZINE

This study focuses on the Club's Magazine as a means of understanding the subculture represented within the Club. The Magazine is a periodic, primarily monthly, print publication which contains letters, stories, reports, poems, and photographs from Club members; financial, membership, and business meeting actions; reports from Club officers; and material from non-members such as reprints of newspaper articles and reports from other S/M organizations.

The publication was selected for study because: (a) The Magazine is the only recorded organizational history containing records such as membership reports and business meeting actions; (b) the publication provides a mediated forum for reflecting the S/M interests of Club members (stories, poems, photographs, interviews, etc.); (c) major conflicts within the Club, such as resource allocation and the dominance of one chapter over another, are played out in the Magazine; (d) approximately 15% of the Club's members reside more than one hour's drive from the two West Coast chapters and the publication is their *only* contact with the Club; and (e) the Magazine's editor is an important gatekeeper and an officer of the Club.

Two other types of print media are also created by the Club. Printed flyers for special events such as parades and parties are occasionally mailed to Club members. A calendar of upcoming events was contained in an approximately monthly publication which was separate from the Magazine. At the end of 1987, the calendar was incorporated into the Magazine. Neither of these publications contain any record of the Club's activities or any members' ideas or concerns.

CLUB MEMBERS' CONFIDENTIALITY

The organization in this study will be identified throughout this report as the "Club."[1] A proper name will not be used as the Club requires confidentiality with regard to reports of group activities or identification of any individual member. The publication under study will be referred to as the "Magazine." Both reporting devices are used to try and conform to the Club members' desires for some secrecy about their often described "socially unacceptable" sexual expressions.

All material published in the Magazine is copyrighted by either the individual author or the Club. When a letter was received complaining that the Magazine had a copyright policy which was meant to protect the possible economic interests of the authors, the Club's Communication Secretary wrote, "In fact, we have an entirely different reason for copyrighting [the Magazine], and that has to do with the right of privacy of all our members."

Another example of confidentiality is the approval process necessary for using an audio or video recording device at a Club function. Prior approval for an electronic recording must be sought and granted during a Club business meeting, and all individuals appearing or heard on tape must sign a release which is then held in the Club's files. In addition, only clearly defined and marked spaces may be included in the video recording. Finally, all video equipment must have a real-time monitor separated from the camera's viewfinder so the recording process may be regulated by a Club officer.

The need for privacy seems to be an essential and overriding concern of the Club's members starting with new-member orientations. During this introductory process, potential new members must sign a form which states the person may not reveal the names and other identification information about other people at the orientations. All potential members are told they may be known by an assumed name, an S/M name, or simply by a first name. During this study, very few Club members used a full and real name for identification purposes.

DEFINITIONS

~~Some definitions will be helpful in understanding this report.~~ A "scene" is an event in which two or more people engage in some type of "erotic power transference" for a predetermined period of time. The terms S/M (sadomasochism), B/D (bondage and discipline), and D/S (dominance and submission) will be used somewhat interchangeably. "Vanilla" is a term used to indicate heterosexual, middle-of-the-road, generally accepted sexual activity sanctioned by a majority of the general population and devoid of experimentation. The person engaged in a "scene" who is "in control" is called a "top," "master," or "mistress"; the person being controlled is termed a "bottom," "submissive," or "slave" (although, in fact, both actors are engaged in control, power transference, and the direction of the "scene").

METHOD

A descriptive content analysis by theme (Stempel and Westley, 1981; Wimmer and Dominick, 1986) was completed on 47 issues of the Magazine published by the Club between October 1983 and January 1988. The somewhat discontinuous nature of this monthly publication, which published 47 issues over a 52-month period, is due to its dependence totally on a volunteer production staff. Utilizing descriptive categories, a numeric analysis was completed on the contents of the 47 issues. The results contain both percentages of the space allocated to subject categories and examples of the contents of those categories.

The December 1987 issue of the Magazine contained a 26-question readership survey as a means of gathering information about the publication's future. The survey was initiated by the Club in response to internal organizational conflict between the two West Coast chapters. The January 1988 issue of the publication contained the survey results as 358 readers responded (representing 44% of the 812 dues-paying members). The survey results are used to support the content analysis.

As a supplement to the content analysis and the readership survey, this report includes information gathered by the author as a nonparticipant-observer of the Club's activities during the period covered by this study. The author attended a mandatory orientation session and approximately four program meetings each calendar year. The author discussed the Club and the Magazine with Club members during the orientation and programs.

MAGAZINE FORMAT

From October 1983 to January 1987, 35 issues of the Magazine were produced in a magazine format sized 7 inches by 8 1/2 inches. In this format, the issues averaged 27.5 pages per issue, with a range of 22 pages to 46 pages. In February 1987, the Magazine's editor adopted a new format to allow for the easy use of desk-top publication computer software. The editor claimed the new format would be cost effective and would allow for a "more glitzy" publication. From February 1987 through January 1988, the format size changed to 8 1/2 inches by 11 inches, the issues averaged 16 pages, and the range was from 8 to 20 pages. All issues were black ink on white paper stock.

READERSHIP SURVEY RESULTS

Almost the entire content of the January 1988 issue of the Magazine was dedicated to the results of the December 1987 readership survey. In addition to the survey question numeric results, ten of the publication's 16 pages were filled with members' letters concerning the publication's future. In the letters, two major reasons were indicated as to why the survey was necessary: (a) The founding chapter produced the Magazine, all the Magazine's editors were from the founding chapter, and the other West Coast chapter's members complained the publication served little purpose to their interests; and (b) the publishing and mailing costs of the Magazine increased over time and some members questioned the ever-increasing expenditures.

The first seven questions of the readership survey were concerned with the Magazine's continuation and format. When asked if the Magazine should be eliminated, 10 readers marked "yes" and 339 marked "no." Four format questions elicited similar response patterns as the elimination question, with the vast majority of responses supporting the magazine format adopted in February 1987. The responses to cost questions were also favorable but more mixed. The founding chapter members responded positively by a 6 to 1 ratio when asked if $18 of the yearly $25 Club membership fee should be used to support the Magazine. The other West Coast chapter members were almost evenly divided on the fees question. When asked if the format should be changed to allow the magazine to fit in a 25-cent envelope, the founding chapter members marked "no" by a 6 to 1 ratio, while the other West Coast chapter members marked "no" by a 3 to 1 ratio.

The ten pages of readers' letters included in the January 1988 issue indicated the writers were very strong in their support of the publication. The following statements came from several letters and reflected support sentiment:

> [The Magazine] should be recognized for what it is — the finest ongoing historical record of an S/M community ever compiled . . . . [The Club] will survive well without [the Magazine], but its history will be lost forever. . . . An incredible and refreshing diversity of material has been presented. . . . [The Magazine] is an important erotic event in my life. . . . [The Magazine] is an important part of my membership. . . . It is a publication far superior to any other in the field. . . . Let's use this publication as a voice and a focal point.

"At-large" members, those living some distance from the Club's two chapters, also wrote in strong support of the publication:

> I live in a foreign country [and] the whole [Club] to me is represented in the contents of [the Magazine]. . . . Thus [the Magazine] is my only tangible link to [the Club] and to the S/M community at large. . . . For individuals like me in extremely isolated areas, [the Magazine] is the only connection to the S/M

world. . . . [The Magazine] is my sole connection to [the Club].

CONTENT ANALYSIS RESULTS

The content analysis results of the 47 issues are reported under seven subject content areas: media reviews, poetry, S/M issues, how-to articles, photography, stories, and organizational reports. The seven areas are reported starting with the smallest amount of space utilized per category and continuing to the largest amount of space used.

Media Reviews

Reviews of books, films and videos with S/M themes appeared in about every second issue of the Magazine, averaged .5 items per issue, and accounted for about 2% of the space in the Magazine. Included in this category were reviews of S/M related story lines on "Hill Street Blues" (February 1986 - all reference dates for materials from the Magazine refer to the publication date of that issue) and the "Oprah Winfrey Show" (August 1987), and the best locations near the two Club chapters to purchase books, movies and other S/M media materials. The readership respondents overwhelmingly indicated the media reviews category should be retained by a vote of 304 to 13.

Poetry

Poems appeared an average of 1.2 times per issue, with a range of no poems in several issues to six poems in one issue, and accounted for about 5% of the Magazine's space. Poems tended to concentrate on the feelings (both physical and emotional) expressed by a "top" or "bottom" with regard to a "scene." Several poems were written by "slaves" to their "masters" or "mistresses." The readership respondents indicated poems were least favored content area with 139 votes for continuation, while 131 voted against continuation.

S/M Issues

Several types of S/M issue related articles appeared in the Magazine between 1983 and 1988. S/M issue articles and columns averaged 1.5 items per issue, ranged from a low of none in three issues to a high of six in two issues, and accounted for about 10% of the Magazine's space. Among the various discussions included in this category were long-term S/M relationships (June 1985), different levels of dominance (November 1985), masochistic "survival" (February 1985), a definition of torture (June 1985), and definitions of S/M terms (June 1985).

One recurring interest area was the concept that D/S was a more inclusive term than S/M. As noted in an October/November 1984 article:

> D/S is a broader term inclusive of S/M just as both are included in a still broader category of 'creative sexuality.' While inclusive of S/M, D/S is not higher or better than S/M. On the contrary, S/M is a special (some feel 'elite') subgroup within the broader context of D/S.

In July 1985 another writer agreed to the ideas expressed in the October/November 1984 article and added: "D/S doesn't have to be physically rough, nor does it require pain, fetishes — or even sex!"

Legal action against people engaged in S/M activities were reported. Information about a Sacramento, California, professional dominant who had been arrested for prostitution was included in issues starting with October 1983 and running until the middle of 1985. The cases of a Pennsylvania couple and a Michigan couple who ran into problems with the legal authorities were included in 1985 and 1986.

When asked about reporting legal actions, 289 respondents marked "yes," while 22 respondents marked "no." The readers also responded they wanted "reprints of S/M materials from non-members" by a 244 to 37 margin, and they responded with 280 "yes" and 18 "no" when asked about inclusion of "clippings of relevant S/M materials."

How-to Information

How-to information appeared in virtually every issue. This category averaged 2.4 items per issue, ranged from no items in one issue to seven items in six issues, and took up about 12% of the Magazine's space. How-to article titles indicated the subject matter, including: "Building Clothes Pins with a Screw Device" (October/November 1983) for attaching to a "bottom's" body, "Fur Braiding" (January 1985) for braiding rope in pubic hair, and "An Example of a Slavery Contract" (November 1986). In the how-to category, safety and health issues received a great deal of attention. The health problems related to AIDS received the most attention.

A readership survey question asking if how-to articles and "doing S/M" articles should be included received an overwhelmingly positive response with 320 readers marking "yes" and 15 respondents marking "no."

Photography

Over the 47 issues which were content analyzed, the average was 7.5 photographs per issue, the range was no photographs in nine issues to 39 photographs in the October/November 1984 issues, and these images accounted for 14% of the Magazine's space. The photographs were primarily of erotic images by members and of local and national S/M events.

Accounting for almost half of all photographs, erotic images included one or more individuals tied in tight bondage with various devices attached to their bodies. Other photographs included both the "top" and the "bottom" at play in either private or public settings. Facial expressions ranged from the exhibitionist who seemed pleased that his or her picture was being taken, to the grimaces of "bottoms" who were in some type of painful scene.

Results of the readership survey indicated members wanted "erotic photographs by members" by a rate of 283 "yes" to 23 "no," and "photos of local or national S/M events" by a margin of 229 "yes" to 52 "no."

Stories

Stories, both real and fantasy, averaged 1.5 per issue, ranged from no stories in five issues to three stories in three issues, and accounted for 17% of the Magazine's space.

Fantasy stories tended to fall into those with "vanilla" titles and those with very explicit titles. The first group included stories titled "Wednesday Afternoon" (May 1985) and "The Plan" (May 1987). More explicit titles included "Nocturnal Emissions from a Submissive" (August 1984) and "Scat 'n Shower Delights" (October 1987) focusing on scatological and "golden shower" interests.

Stories of real scenes tended to be forthright in their titles, subject matter, and accompanying photographs. One real column, titled "A Slave Girl Writes," was included in five 1985 issues and was written by female "slaves." "Viola's Slave Diary" was included in the October through December 1987 issues. As noted earlier, all the stories were copyrighted with 93% including an author's name and 7% indicating the Club held the copyright.

"Erotic fiction" should be included by a vote of the readers of 297 to 25, and "real-life S/M experiences" should be continued by a response of 297 "yes" to 25 "no."

Organization

The largest content category, both in terms of space and number of items, was devoted to Club organizational activities. Organizational items accounted for an average of 6.5 items per issue, ranged from 3 items in four issues to 12 items in 9 issues, and accounted for 40% of the Magazine's space.

Among the most common organization reports were: Complete monthly statements from the Club's treasurer, a column from the editor, reports from the Club's co-ordinator(s), membership reports, and extensive reports from the Communication Secretary (July 1984 to November 1987) or "Comm Sexy" as the column was signed.

A column titled the "Slave Trader's Marketplace" was included in each issue. Professional "play for pay" advertisements were not allowed because it was felt this type of advertising would bring the magazine and the organization to the attention of law enforcement agencies.

The Magazine reported on Club sponsored meetings. Approximately two theme programs were presented by the Club each month during the period of this study. The subjects of these programs, as presented in the Magazine's coverage, included: an ask-a-lawyer discussion (October/November 1984), a flagellation discussion/demonstration (December 1984), a founders' panel (February 1985), a body piercing demonstration (October/November 1984), a use of electricity demonstration (December 1985), an ask-a-chiropractor discussion (January 1987), a male genital torture discussion/demonstration (April 1987), and various panels by and about dominance and submission (March 1985, July 1985, and August/September 1985).

Several readership survey questions asked about organizational presentations in the Magazine. When asked if the readers wanted to read about "local club events and programs," 296 marked "yes" and 22 marked "no." When asked about the inclusion of the "Treasurer's reports and other club business reports," the respondents marked "yes" 171 times and "no" was checked by 86 readers. Even "classified or display advertising" should be kept in the Magazine according to 295 respondents who marked "yes" as opposed to the 12 readers who marked "no."

The seven subject categories outlined in these results include virtually all the material published in the Magazine from 1983 through early 1988 (which indicates that the content analysis categories were exhaustive). In the 47 issues which were investigated, the Club's activities and organizational information accounted for almost one-half of all publication space. Additionally, in descending order of the publication's space utilization, stories accounted for 17%, photography accounted for 14%, how-to information accounted for 12%, S/M issues accounted for about 2%.

The readership survey results published in the January 1988 issue indicate the respondents want to keep all the subject categories. While poetry received almost an even split vote, all the other subject areas received enthusiastic support from the survey respondents. The results indicate the Club members wish to continue the Magazine with 358 respondents (representing 44% of the total Club membership) responding positively by almost a 20 to 1 ratio.

EDITORS

All four of the Magazine's editors who worked during this study called for contributions to the Magazine by the Club's members, and they all stressed the participatory nature of the publication. One editor called in June 1985 for more members' input and then promised to "remain aware of the printed word's iconic powers and to remain sensitive to members' feelings." Another editor called in April 1987 for material which was not mediocre but was "brought to life by being handled with verve, originality and some skill." The problem, that editor continued, was trite storylines and "doggerl" poetry that tended to make the contributions less interesting.

One editor indicated in October 1986 his editorial stance by writing that the Magazine was a tool for communicating. In a particularly lucid moment, this editor wrote about the worth of the publication:

> [The Magazine] brings the membership an arena of common experience and concern. Each month of appearance is evidence of our energy and our pride — and our power. Because it is controlled by us, [the Magazine] can tell the evolving truth: no advertisers, governmental agencies, or professional practitioners! . . . We know the feelings of guilt, bewilderment, and isolation; we also know freedom and happiness when we can admit, discuss and demonstrate those feelings. [The Club] and [the Magazine], if you will, smooth a few steps on the road to happiness.

This editor went on to explain the publication operates as the only legacy and historical document of the organization, and about half of the yearly dues go into the support of the publication.

DISCUSSION

The results of this study indicate that the Magazine is a creation of the Club's membership and that membership is satisfied with the publication's format and contents. The January 1988 readership study and the content analysis results point toward strong support for the publication's place in the lives of the Club members.

In addition to being the only repository of the Club's history and the importance of the Magazine to individual members, the publication may serve to help create "shared meaning" for Club members. Researchers Berger and Luckman (1967) argue that a social institution "can only be understood in terms of the 'knowledge' that its members have of it, [and] it follows that the analysis of such 'knowledge' will be essential for an analysis of the institution in question" (p. 65). These writers further assert that once the body of social knowledge is given meaning by the collective understanding of the group, that meaning "has the capacity to act back upon the collectivity that produced it" (p. 85). As stated by one Magazine editor, "Through [the Magazine], we share experiences which few people in the world understand, and develop new vocabulary and concepts. Shared, our experiences become a legacy for every newcomer" (October 1986). The Magazine's editors and readers seem to agree that the publication is vital and provides opportunities to explain and explore their sadomasochistic experiences.

The "shared" experiences of Club members which is chronicled in the Magazine is a legacy to increasing numbers of Club members. During the period of this investigation, October 1983 to January 1988, the Club's membership increased by over 400%. The change in membership was of type as well as number. During the author's discussions with long-time members and through the author's nonparticipant observations of the audience composition for Club programs, the Club's membership was primarily male homosexuals at the end of 1983. Indeed, members' comments indicated male gays comprised virtually the entire membership between the Club's founding in 1974 and the early 1980's. From 1983 to 1988, a dramatic increase of both gay and heterosexual women was witnessed at program meetings. Male-female couples were at the end of this study about one-third of all participants at program meetings. By the start of 1988, a majority of the Club members were heterosexual men, women and couples; of course, many members were still homosexual men and women. The approach taken in this study is not appropriate to explicate the changes brought about by the changes in the makeup of the membership of the Club; however, the demographic changes are interesting and would provide the basis for a future study.

An issue highlighted through this research concerns the forces acting on an organization dedicated to alternative sexual practices. Contained in the Club's purpose statement is that the organization should attempt to help the public understand the S/M subcultures. Yet access to the Club and its Magazine is restricted. Only dues-paying Club members receive the publication, copyright and confidentiality statements are prominent in the Magazine, entrance into programs and meetings is granted to card-carrying members and their guests only, and most members use either an S/M "name" or are called by their first names. Personal questions about a member's employment and residence, even in the most general terms, are greeted with some suspicion. The call for public education is clearly restrained by the need for individual members to retain some measure of privacy as a means of escaping scorn.

The duality of public knowledge versus the private rights expressed in the Magazine reflects the conflicting forces of the larger society with respect to sexual expression. Respondents to a 1987 Associate Press poll thought pornography was not generally harmful to adults, 80% admitted to having looked at and enjoyed a magazine featuring nudity, and 60% had seen an X-rated movie on video cassette ("Poll says most Americans unoffended by pornography," 1987). The newspaper article which outlined the poll findings also pointed out the war on "smut" launched by U.S. Attorney General Edwin Meese and the increasing number of attempts to ban magazines such as *Playboy* from retail store shelves. What the people of the United States may like and practice in private does not seem to be acceptable when expressed or available in public.

The emergence of social science research on sadomasochistic activities which is just now appearing (Weinberg, 1987) may be due, in part, to the muting of emotions raised by the study of so-called "deviant" individuals that has plagued social science researchers in the past. Even now the way is not clear and unprejudiced. Many of the highly educated and sophisticated people the author encountered during this research were embarrassed or otherwise incapable of discussing the subject matter.

SUMMARY

The research reported here is broadly descriptive in nature. Focusing on the activities of a sadomasochism Club as detailed in the pages of the Club's magazine, this study combined a readership survey and a subject content analysis to reveal: (a) The Magazine is the Club's only record, (b) the publication is a legacy for new Club members and others interested in this S/M subculture, and (c) the Magazine is the codification of "shared" meanings created by Club members.

The major weakness of this investigation is the lack of actor viewpoint data. As noted by Berger and Luckman (1967), a group's participants create their shared realities. In addition, sadomasochism subcultures are, by necessity, somewhat secretive. For those reasons, the participants' viewpoint is necessary in understanding the subculture. Despite the inclusion of the author's nonparticipant observations, this study lacks understanding from the actor's point of view. Future research could concentrate on the members' communication strategies as a means of understanding the creation of group-shared meanings. The interpersonal power negotiations utilized by S/M interested people is also a fertile area of future study. Utilizing qualitative data gathering methods, the "secret" S/M groups could be better understood. Value-free approaches must be used or the researcher will fall victim to the negative opinions concerning "deviant" sexual expressions held by the society at large.

This study does suggest that this type of magazine and other "house organs" of S/M groups are sources for understanding the activities of group members. It would seem that this Magazine, for the members of this Club, is truly a "tie that binds."

NOTE

1. The term "Club" was selected to identify the organization as many club-like attributes have been adopted by the organization under investigation. A prospective member must be 18 years of age, must pay a fee to join and a fee to continue yearly membership. S/he must be issued and use a membership identification card to gain entry to Club activities. If the prospective member lives within

an hour's drive of either of the two West Coast chapters, s/he is required to attend a "mandatory" orientation.

REFERENCES

Berger, P.L., & Luckman, T. (1967). *The social construction of reality.* Garden City, NY: Doubleday.

Breslow, B., Evans, L., & Langley, J. (1985). On the prevalence and roles of females in the sadomasochistic subculture: Report of an empirical study. *Archives of Sexual Behavior, 14*(4), 303-317.

Breslow, B., Evans, L., & Langley, J. (1986). Comparisons among heterosexual, bisexual, and homosexual male sado-masochists. *Journal of Homosexuality, 13*(1), 83-107.

Naerseen, A.X. van, Dijk, M. van, Hoogveen, G., & Zessen, G. van. (1987). Gay SM in pornography and reality. *Journal of Homosexuality, 12*(2/3), 111-119.

Poll says most Americans unoffended by pornography. (1987, April 12). *The Stockton Record,* p. A-7.

Stempel, G.H., & Westley, B.H. (Eds.), (1981). *Research methods in mass communication.* Englewood Cliffs, NJ: Prentice-Hall.

Weinberg, T.S. (1987). Sadomasochism in the United States: A review of recent sociological literature. *The Journal of Sex Research, 23*(1), 50-69.

Wimmer, R.D., & Dominick, J.R. (1986). *Mass media research: An introduction.* Belmont, CA: Wadsworth.

It's gettin' hot in h

The Gay Voice in Popular Music: A Social Value Model Analysis of "Don't Leave Me This Way"

R. Brian Attig, MA

SUMMARY. The gay voice in popular music and its potential to create positive social change regarding societal values about homosexuality is the focus of the present study. The historical development of the gay voice in popular music is reviewed as an introduction to a critical analysis of the Communards' music video "Don't Leave Me This Way." Using a modified version of the Social Value Model proposed by Rushing and Frentz, the video is analyzed on three levels: (a) narrative content, (b) use of symbols in the narrative, and (c) lyrical content. It is suggested that this video effected a dialectical synthesis of mainstream and homosexual values because it achieved mainstream commercial success while realistically expressing a gay perspective.

Until very recently, gay people's contributions to society have not been given much formal recognition. With regard to the arts, Rudy Grillo (1982) wrote, "Since the Stonewall riots of 1969, gay writers, and some non-gay ones, have concerned themselves with reporting on the current and historic roles of gay men and lesbians in the fields of painting, literature, dance, photography, motion pictures, and so on. Yet relatively little attention has been directed to the field of music, particularly popular music and song, though that situation seems to be changing" (p. 23). Grillo traces the gay influence on popular music with an emphasis on the 1930s, '40s, and

---

R. Brian Attig is affiliated with Wake Forest University, Winston-Salem, NC 27109.

185

'50s, and concludes, "Gay echoes can be heard in cowboy songs, love songs, comedy songs, rock, folk, jazz, and opera too—in short, across the musical spectrum" (p. 26).

In popular music since the rock and roll era began in the early 1950s, however, the gay voice has been expressed to much more of a degree and with much more of an influence on mainstream culture than it ever has been before. This is not to say that popular music since the advent of rock and roll has always served as a forum for free gay expression. As recently as 1982 Adam Block wrote, "The fact is that to this day I can't think of one rock artist who has been gay and proud, erotic and liberating—seizing the airwaves and giving the boys boners" (1982a, p. 43). In fact, it wasn't until Bronski Beat in 1984 that the gay voice was openly and realistically expressed in popular music on a commercially successful level. This, of course, has much to do with the fact that homosexuality is still highly taboo in our society.

Before going any further, an issue which has to do with the focus of this study needs to be addressed. Although this paper is titled "The Gay Voice in Popular Music: A Social Value Model Analysis of 'Don't Leave Me This Way,'" a more accurate title would begin, "The Gay Male Voice in Popular Music." The reason for this is not to denigrate or dismiss the efforts of lesbian popular music artists, but is simply a necessary constraint imposed by the focus of this study. The intent of this study is to focus on the gay voice in popular music as it has come to be expressed in an open, realistic, and commercially successful manner. Unfortunately, for reasons ranging from underlying societal attitudes to the reality of popular music being a male-dominated industry (Gill, 1986), lesbian artists have had less of an opportunity to express themselves than have gay male artists. Recent lesbian popular music artists Phranc and Sweet Honey and Rock have enjoyed some success, though, at a level far below that of mainstream commercial appeal (e.g., Gill, 1986). Although the author in no way intends to equate commercial success with inherent social value, the potential for creating positive social change possessed by a commercially successful piece of popular music provides the basis for this study. As a result, the focus of this study will necessarily be limited to the male homosexual voice in popular music.

In order to place the gay voice in popular music in a historical perspective, this study will first trace its development from the beginning of the rock and roll era up to the present time. Following this review, the Communards' music video "Don't Leave Me This Way" will be critically analyzed using a modified version of the Social Value Model methodology proposed by Rushing and Frentz (1980).

HISTORICAL DEVELOPMENT
OF THE GAY VOICE IN POPULAR MUSIC

The beginning of the rock and roll era marked a significant emergence of the gay voice in popular music. Little Richard was "the self-proclaimed Georgia Peach . . . an apparition in a zoot suit" (Block, 1982a, p. 44), and led the way in assaulting traditional ideas about sexuality. Even Elvis Presley's classic "Jailhouse Rock" includes a fairly straightforward reference to the homosexual behavior prevalent in prisons: "Number 47 said to Number 31/ You're the cutest jailbird I ever did see/I sure would be delighted with you pumpin' me/Come on and do the Jailhouse Rock with me" (Grillo, 1982, p. 25). That this reference to homosexual behavior would be expressed in such an anti-social context (i.e., "jailbirds," soliciting homosexuals) is a telling reflection of the social attitudes of the time. From a purely historical perspective, however, that there was a gay influence on rock and roll from the beginning is not surprising—the artistic community in general has always included a greater proportion of homosexuals than has mainstream society. This is particularly true as regards men, as an important component of art is the expression of emotion—a trait not characteristic of the "traditional" male personality. As Howard Klein put it, "The world of rock'n'roll—a world of glamor and relaxed moral attitudes—is as gay as the world of the hair salon" (1978, p. 25).

As rock and roll grew in popularity and influence during the 1960s and '70s, some of its performers flaunted the boundaries of traditional sexuality to an even greater extent. The Rolling Stones, one of the most popular rock and roll bands of all time, gained notoriety for their "swaggering, debauched albums" (Klein, 1978, p. 25). One controversial song, "Cocksucker Blues," was "a completely unambiguous rock'n'roll paean to a facet of the homosexual lifestyle'' (Klein, 1978, p. 25). Other performers began to address sexuality in explicitly non-traditional ways: Groups like AC/DC, Queen, The New York Dolls; David Bowie and Elton John publicly declared their bisexuality; The Velvet Underground sang "Sister Ray" and "Walk on the Wild Side"; the Kinks sang "Lola," a song about a famous drag-queen; and Alice Cooper actually performed as a drag-queen. However, even though popular performers were now flaunting images of ambiguous sexuality, the flaunting remained at the level of a commercial pose. This period of rock and roll has been disparagingly dubbed by some critics as the "bisexual chic" phase (Avicolli, 1979, p. 184). Although artists now appropriated "bisexual chic" for sensational effect in their persona and their songs, the images they created were overwhelmingly negative. An article written by Tommi Avicolli titled "Images of Gays in Rock Music" made this point: "Though there have been both positive and negative treatments of homosexuals in rock, the overall picture is still not very pleasant. There is surely a lot of consciousness-raising to be done" (p. 193).

During the late 1970s, disco music became a significant force in the popular music industry. Here there was not only a gay influence, but the gay community was the driving force behind this music. "The crucial role gays played in launching disco music was an open secret in the music industry," wrote Adam Block in 1982 (1982b, p. 44). It was through disco music that the gay voice was not only expressed openly, but was also expressed in a positive way. In 1978, "I Was Born This Way" by Carl Bean was released on the Motown label and was the first time a major record label had released a disco song with a specifically gay theme (Conlon, 1978). Also in 1978, although not a disco song, Tom Robinson's embittered anthem "Sing If You're Glad to Be Gay" became a minor hit in Britain (Block, 1982a). As open and positive expressions of the gay voice in popular music, these two songs represented major breakthroughs. However, mainstream commercial success still eluded gay popular music artists.

It was Village People who made the greatest strides during the late 1970s toward putting the gay voice on the popular music charts. Their two albums, *Village People* and *Macho Man*, both contained songs that became #1 hits on disco charts in the United States and about a dozen other countries (Herschberg, 1978). Similar to the artists in the "bisexual chic" phase, though, the Village People only went as far as to create an image of homosexuality. Wrote Charles Herschberg, "Their sexual preferences were not and have not been labeled" (p. 31). John Schauer (1978) observed, "Without ever mentioning the word gay or singing same-sex love songs, they have managed to create albums as obviously gay as any I could imagine" (p. 32). Howard Klein summarized the general situation thusly, "Few mainstream rockers have been willing to express overtly autobiographical sentiments about their own homosexuality" (1978, p. 26). It remained for the gay voice in popular music to be expressed in an open, positive and commercially successful manner.

In 1984 and 1985 three English groups emerged which, to varying degrees, marked historic breakthroughs in the expression of the gay voice in popular music. Frankie Goes To Hollywood enjoyed major commercial success in Britain with their #1 single "Relax" (which was the fourth biggest-selling single in Britain ever) and their #1 album *Welcome to the Pleasure Dome* (Sullivan, 1985). Their popularity spread to the United States, with their album reaching #19 on the Top Fifty Album Chart (Wing, 1985a). Despite this major commercial success, Frankie Goes To Hollywood was a negative development in terms of the gay voice in popular music. In their music videos and onstage persona the group used negative stereotypes of gays—portraying promiscuous and leather-clad gays cruising bars in search of carefree sex (Frith, 1984). Music critics and fellow performers alike harshly criticized the group's posturings and even Boy George said about them, "If you're going to go out and say you're gay, why don't you present to people an intelligent side to homosexuality, instead of going out and saying, 'Look, I'm a seedy queer who screws in gay bars?'" (Sullivan, 1985).

More positive strides have been made by The Smiths, whose lead singer and song writer Stephen Morrissey is gay. They, too, enjoyed major commercial success in Britain, with their debut album *The Smiths* becoming a #2 British album and producing three successive hit singles for the group (Henke, 1984). Following the same pattern as Frankie Goes To Hollywood, their popularity spread to the United States as their second album *Meat is Murder* became a #1 College LP and produced a #1 Dance Tracks single (Wing,

1985c). Unlike Frankie Goes To Hollywood, however, The Smiths dealt with gay themes in a realistic and thought-provoking manner. A review in *Rolling Stone Yearbook 1984* described their first album as follows: "Lead singer Morrissey's memories of heterosexual rejection and subsequent homosexual isolation were bracing in their candor, and Johnny Marr's delicately chiming guitar provided a surprisingly warm and sympathetic setting" (p. 56). Their #1 Dance Tracks single, "How Soon Is Now?", provides a good example of Morrissey's thoughtful lyrics: "You shut your mouth/ How can you say?/I go about things the wrong way/I am human and I need to be loved/Just like everybody else does" (The Smiths, 1984). The Smiths have enjoyed continued commercial success; their latest album, *The Queen Is Dead* reached #25 in the United States Top Fifty Albums (Hamilton, 1986), but to the chagrin of some Morrissey has stopped short of addressing gay themes in a completely open and autobiographical way (Gill, 1986).

The third group to emerge was Bronski Beat, led by lead singer and song writer Jimmy Somerville. Their album *Age of Consent* was released in late 1984 and reached #5 on the British Albums chart (Wing, 1985b), generating four hit singles ("Bronski," 1985). Its popularity spread to the United States and by early 1985 had become a #1 College LP (Wing, 1985b), had produced a #1 Dance Tracks single (Wing, 1985b), and had reached #41 in the Top Fifty Albums chart (Wing, 1985c). This was a historic breakthrough because, as John Gill wrote, "Bronski Beat was the group that could, and perhaps did, prove that musicians could be matter of fact about their gayness" (1986). Bronski Beat expressed the gay voice in a positive and openly autobiographical way and, as Simon Frith of the *Village Voice* wrote, "Their real ambition is to make the realities of gay sex (hostility, anxiety, love) as normal a concern of chart pop as disco/leather fantasies" (1985, p. 78). Jimmy Somerville himself expressed the concern behind Bronski Beat's music when he said, "Gayness has not so much become a non-issue in pop. It's been dismissed rather than accepted" (Gill, 1986, p. 49). In April of 1985 Jimmy Somerville left Bronski Beat for reasons described as his inability "to resolve the conflicts between his devout socialism and the wealth that came with the group's success" ("Bronski," 1985, p. 39).

Bronski Beat has continued to make hit records (Israel, 1986;

"MTV," 1986a), but it has been Somerville's progress that has been followed by the gay and musical communities with the greatest interest. It was Somerville's "piercing, idiosyncratic voice . . . achingly intense vocals" (Aletti, 1986, p. 63) and his musical conviction to "forcefully . . . carry on the gay pride banners" (Aletti, 1986, p. 63) that gave Bronski Beat its emotional impact. Soon after leaving the group, Somerville teamed up with friend and classically trained musician Richard Coles to work on a new album (J.D., 1986). They called themselves and the album *The Communards*, in a tribute to the 19th-century French political dissidents (J.D., 1986). *The Communards* was released in the fall of 1986 and has met with significant commercial success. The album reached #7 on the British charts ("Hits of," 1986b, p. 77) and was in the Top 20 on half a dozen European charts ("Hits of," 1986c; "Hits of," 1986d; "Hits of," 1986e). There were several singles that were released from the album, but one in particular became a major hit. This single was "Don't Leave Me This Way," and it became a #1 song in Britain ("Hits of," 1986a), #1 in the Netherlands ("Hits of," 1986e), #2 in Australia ("Hits of," 1986e), #5 in West Germany ("Hits of," 1986c), and a top ten hit in several other countries ("Hits of," 1986f; "Hits of," 1986g). Its popularity spread to the United States becoming a #1 Club Play ("Hot Dance," 1986a) and a #3 12-Inch Singles Sales record ("Hot Dance," 1986b). Following what is now established convention in popular music, the Communards made a music video of their hit single "Don't Leave Me This Way." The video received airplay on the MTV (Music Television) cable network from October 15 to November 26, 1986, and its highest position was in MTV's "medium rotation" ("MTV," 1986b). It is this music video which serves as the critical object for this study.

THE SOCIAL VALUE MODEL

In a two-part essay titled "The Rhetoric of 'Rocky': A Social Value Model of Criticism," Janice Hocker Rushing and Thomas S. Frentz (1980) set forth a critical methodology called the Social Value Model. As an introduction to this methodology by way of summary, Rushing and Frentz's aim in positing this model is to "gain insight into the overall process of social change" (1980,

p. 262). They work from the assumption that film and societal values influence each other in a reciprocal way. On this basis they advance a five-part model of value change which describes this interactive process and also serves as a framework through which to explicate the "rhetorical force underlying both film and more general social processes" (Rushing & Frentz, 1980, p. 254).

The Social Value Model is an ideal critical methodology for analyzing the gay voice in popular music for two reasons. The first is that the gay voice in popular music (or, for that matter, in anything) exists in opposition to the prevailing social values of our society, which is exactly the situation Rushing and Frentz address with their five-part model. Secondly, an important consideration of the gay voice in popular music is its potential to positively influence societal values regarding homosexuality. It is this type of reciprocal relationship between rhetorical messages and societal values that the Social Value Model attempts to illuminate.

Rushing and Frentz (1980) explicate five elements of the Social Value Model as follows: Value Opposition, Symbolic Conflict, Dialectical Resolution, Psychological Prerequisites, and Audience Role. The value opposition element is rooted in the assumption that "the values basic to a culture's thought and rituals exist frequently in . . . a state of tension, real or potential conflict or change" (p. 248). As a result, "symbolic conflict is the necessary condition for value re-orientation" (p. 253). This symbolic conflict can result in two different patterns of resolution—dialectical transformation or dialectical synthesis. Dialectical transformation "entails an inversion from one prevailing set of values to the other" (p. 251). In dialectical synthesis "there are no 'losers' . . . but rather an integration of the old with the new is formed" (p. 252). The Psychological Prerequisites for dialectical transformation only require that the change agent have knowledge of one of the two competing sets of values; dialectical synthesis requires that the change agent have knowledge of both sets of values. The audience is most actively involved in the process of dialectical synthesis: "Ideally, they are contributors to the generative process; they both learn and vicariously help create that which did not exist before the pattern was enacted" (p. 253).

With regard to Rushing and Frentz's comment in the conclusion of their article that "the model needs to be conceptually and methodologically refined" (1980, p. 262), the present study will make three methodological refinements in the Social Value Model: (a) collapse the Value Opposition and Symbolic Conflict elements into one co-existing pair, (b) collapse the Psychological Prerequisites and Dialectical Resolution elements into one co-existing pair, and (c) exclude Audience Role as a formally stated element in the model.

As regards Value Opposition and Symbolic Conflict, the relationship between these elements is one of concept and symbol. Given that there are values in opposition, symbolic conflict will be the expression of these opposing values. The Psychological Prerequisites and Dialectical Resolution elements demonstrate this same relationship. The Psychological Prerequisites to any situation will be manifested in the resolution of that situation. Because Value Opposition and Psychological Prerequisites are purely conceptual in nature, they do not exist as rhetorical expressions. Symbolic Conflict and Dialectical Resolution, respectively, are their rhetorical expressions. It is suggested that the concept-symbol relationship between the elements of these two pairs makes their application in a rhetorical analysis more effective as two pairs than as four separately considered elements.

The third refinement made here is to exclude Audience Role as a formally stated part of the model. Although the role of the audience certainly plays an important part in determining the extent to which any form of mass communication affects value change, its rhetorical expression in that process is implicitly addressed in the Symbolic Conflict and Dialectical Resolution elements of the model. Thus, the role of the audience in the present analysis will be considered as it manifests itself in the Value Change/Symbolic Conflict and Psychological Prerequisites/Dialectical Resolution elements.

"DON'T LEAVE ME THIS WAY": *VALUE OPPOSITION/SYMBOLIC CONFLICT*

The Communards' video "Don't Leave Me This Way" is a musical statement about a gay experience from a gay perspective. Since this kind of musical expression is potentially controversial, it

had to be made in a subtle way or else the video would not have
received airplay. The opposing values that the video addresses are
society's repression of gay people versus gay people's struggle for
acceptance from society and with themselves. The video's symbolic
conflict between these opposing value systems is manifested on
three levels: (a) narrative content, (b) use of symbols in the narrative, and (c) lyrical content.

Narrative Content

   In the narrative, the Communards perform as themselves (accompanied by some supporting musicians) in a warehouse which has
been converted into a music hall. The video begins with a shot of an
unidentified hand opening a book labeled "Ministry of Culture."
The hand turns to a page marked "music banning order" in regard
to the Communards and rubber-stamps the order "approved." In
the next scene, a small group of young people are making their way
to the warehouse and filing into this crowded makeshift club. One
young man in particular is singled out in a close-up shot and he is
shown making his way through the crowd to get a good view of the
Communards, who are already performing. He finally finds a place
in the crowd and fixes his gaze intently upon the stage, showing no
expression in his face and standing motionless. Everyone else
around him is jumping and dancing to the music and their attention
is not focused in any directed way; they are caught up in the music.
Next, it is established that this young man has a specific interest in
the lead singer. This is accomplished by cutting the scene three
times directly back and forth from this young man to the lead
singer. The shots of the young man are close-ups of his face, which
has remained expressionless. His gaze has remained intent on the
lead singer and his eyes have become glassy and project a sense of
longing. The shots of the lead singer accentuate the reciprocity of
this connection as he is shown singing, "My heart is full of love
and desire for you," and "You started this fire down in my soul."
After the third close-up of the young man, the scene immediately
cuts to the young man being chased down a hallway by two men.
Both men look rather ominous, each having slicked-back black hair
which matches their black leather jackets, black shirts and pants,
and black army boots. One is carrying a black nightstick. These two

men finally catch the young man and escort him to another ominous-looking man sitting behind a desk at the end of a hallway. This man is also dressed all in black, is bald-headed, has a Fu Manchu mustache, and is wearing small round black spectacles. Apparently, he represents the Ministry of Culture as a book that matches the one in the opening shot in the video is sitting on his desk. Also sitting on his desk is a walkie-talkie which these men want the young man to take back into the crowd with him and use to help them carry out their "music banning order." The young man appears reluctant to do so, looking down and not moving toward the desk, but the man with the nightstick pushes him toward the desk. Both men then stand behind him as the leader slides the walkie-talkie across his desk toward the young man. Finally, the young man picks it up, conceals it in his overcoat and walks slowly back down the hallway. During this segment, the scenes cut several times between this encounter and close-ups of the lead singer. In these close-ups the lead singer looks directly into the camera and sings, "Don't leave me this way." When juxtaposed with the action involving the young man and the three men, this creates an association between these scenes in which the lead singer seems to be exhorting the young man not to acquiesce to the pressure that is being put on him. The next scene shows the young man back in the crowd, still gazing at the lead-singer, but now also pulling out the walkie-talkie. He talks into it, puts it back into his overcoat and turns away from the stage. Another cut is made to a close-up of the lead singer looking directly into the camera, this time singing, "Set me free." That line foreshadows the following action, which is a spotlight being flashed on the crowd in the club and everyone clearing out in a panic. The video ends with close-ups in quick succession of the two men, the young man looking despondent with his eyes downcast, and finally the leader. This final close-up of the leader zooms in on his face and finally the shot fades to black.

Use of Symbols in the Narrative

Throughout "Don't Leave Me This Way" use is made of symbols and symbolic action which tie in with the narrative to accentuate the video's message. There is an interesting contrast of contexts in which the Communards' emblem appears. This emblem is a five-point red and black star, with silhouette profiles of a red and a black man in the star's center. The Communards actually used this emblem as the cover art for their album and in the video this version of the emblem appears on the cover of the "Ministry of Culture" book, being distributed at the door of the club as the crowd files in, and on the front of the drummer's bass drum. However, in the other two instances where this emblem appears in the video it is black and white in color. The first instance is in the opening scene with the "Ministry of Culture" book. When the book is opened to the page marked "music banning order," the Communards' emblem is reproduced on that page in black and white. The second instance is in the segment where the two men from the Ministry of Culture are escorting the young man to their leader. Painted on the wall behind the leader is a large black and white Communards' emblem. This association of the black and white emblem with the Ministry of Culture (a general title for several branches of the British government) appears to symbolize a limited mentality demonstrated and fostered by the government in their dealings with homosexuals. This point is reinforced by depicting the Communards' red and black version of the emblem on the cover of the "Ministry of Culture" book, while on the "music banning order" inside the book the emblem is black and white. This "can't tell a book by its cover" metaphor infers a mentality that is hypocritical, as well as limited.

Another interesting use of symbols is the setting for this video — a deserted warehouse converted into a makeshift club. This setting echoes the repressed nature of the gay community. The ending of "Don't Leave Me This Way," when the three men from the Ministry of Culture turn the spotlight on everyone in the club and clear them out in a panic, suggests that this was also a surreptitious performance, further reinforcing the video's message that the gay community is repressed by mainstream society.

Some interesting symbolic action takes place in the scene where the crowd is filing into the club. As each person files into the club the Communards' red and black emblem is affixed to their shoulder. The first two people to file in get the emblem on the front of their shoulder. When the young man files in, however, he gets the emblem on the side of his shoulder. Since it is later established that the young man is a homosexual, one possible interpretation of this scene is that homosexuals are being differentiated from heterosexuals. The context of this differentiation, however, is not one of segregation and persecution. Even though the emblems are being affixed differently, everyone is still getting the same emblem. Also, this entire proceeding is carried out in a completely unaffected manner by everyone involved. The point seems to be that everyone who comes to the club is free to enjoy the tolerance at the root of this video.

Lyrical Content

The Communards were not the first to record "Don't Leave Me This Way"; the song was originally recorded by Thelma Houston in 1976 and was also a hit for her. The Communards' cover version, however, brings new meaning to the song's lyrics. Now the line which is the namesake of the song, "Don't leave me this way," takes on meaning beyond that of a plea for romantic reconciliation. As mentioned earlier, the line "Don't leave me this way," is sung by the lead singer directly into the camera during the segment when the three men from the Ministry of Culture are pressuring the young man to take the walkie-talkie. As a part of the narrative, the line functions as a prosopopoeiac exhortation from the lead singer to the young man. Interpreted in terms of the larger context of the Communards' musical concerns, though, the line takes on meaning as broad exhortation for gay people not to allow society to pressure them to change or to feel that they should change.

The lyrics "So come on down and do what you've got to do," and "I don't understand how I'm at your command," also take on broader meaning when interpreted in the larger context of the Communards' musical concerns. In this context, the lines become an expression of the gay voice in an issue which is central to the gay rights controversy: Homosexuality as a conscious choice or a naturally occurring sexual orientation. From this perspective, both of these lines express the gay position that their sexuality is a naturally occurring orientation and not a consciously made choice.

Finally, the line "Set me free," also takes on additional meaning in the Communards' cover version. The lead singer sings it repeatedly at the end of the song, again while looking directly into the camera. Juxtaposed with the narrative action of the crowd being dispersed by the three men from the Ministry of Culture, this line becomes a broad verbal plea for society to treat homosexuals with more tolerance.

"DON'T LEAVE ME THIS WAY"
PSYCHOLOGICAL PREREQUISITES
DIALECTICAL RESOLUTION

The symbolic conflict depicted in "Don't Leave Me This Way" indicates that the Communards have assimilated the value structures of both gay and mainstream society; in the words of Rushing and Frentz (1980), they "have 'psychologically previewed' the synthesis process to be enacted in the socio-political arena" (p. 252). In addition to the previously cited evidence from the video's narrative, use of symbols in the narrative and lyrical content, the Communards' choice to do a cover version of "Don't Leave Me This Way" indicates a keen ability on their part to strike a balance between the expression of gay concerns and commercial marketability. It is actually a common practice for gay groups to do cover versions of originally heterosexual songs. Barry Walters writes, "Let's consider what makes a record speak the queen's vernacular . . . a cover version can radically alter an interpretation" (1986, p. 61). "Don't Leave Me This Way" was an especially effective choice for a cover version for two reasons. First, the song had already been a hit for Thelma Houston in 1976 and so its potential marketability had been established. Secondly, even though the song can be understood from a homosexual perspective, its lyrics are gender-neutral and, thus, there are no explicit homosexual overtones which could have limited (or destroyed) the potential audience. As a result of their ability to produce a commercially successful musical expression of gay people's struggle for acceptance from mainstream society and with themselves, the Communards were able to achieve a dialectical synthesis of mainstream and homosexual values with "Don't Leave Me This Way."

In terms of the video's narrative, a dialectical transformation is depicted—the Communards surreptitiously perform in a converted warehouse; one of their gay fans comes to see them and is pressured into helping the Ministry of Culture break the performance up; and finally the performance is broken up. Mainstream society represses the homosexual community. Thus, the narrative is a realistic portrayal of the existing conflict between mainstream and gay society. However, given that "Don't Leave Me This Way" realistically portrayed this conflict and also became commercially successful, the video itself functioned as a dialectical synthesis of mainstream and homosexual values. "Don't Leave Me This Way" is a rare example of an instance where the expression of a gay perspective (or any minority perspective) found a large mainstream audience. Of course, it is only possible to speculate in this analysis upon the extent and long-term influence of the dialectical synthesis of values effected by this music video. Assuming, however, that mass media can affect the attitudes of those who consume it, it appears that this type of musical expression could be a positive influence toward a dialectical synthesis of mainstream and homosexual values. Perhaps the success of "Don't Leave Me This Way" is a sign that progress is being made toward this end.

FUTURE RESEARCH

One potentially interesting avenue of future research in this area might be the empirical examination of music video's impact on attitudes about sexuality in general and/or homosexuality in particular. In "Music Videos: The Look of Sound," Aufderheide (1986) observes:

> Music videos are powerful, if playful, postmodern art. Their raw materials are aspects of popular culture; their structure those of dreams; their premise the constant permutation of identity in a world without social relationships. Androgyny may be the most daring statement that an entire range of sex roles is fair game for projecting one's own statement of the moment. Gender is no longer fixed; male and female are fractured into a kaleidoscope of images. (pp. 111-135)

Although Aufderheide expresses concern over music videos' potential negative impact on viewers' sex role identities, it is also conceivable that exposure to the "androgyny" portrayed in music videos could nurture acceptance in viewers for a wider range of self-expression in the male and female personality. As a result, the viewers of music videos might develop sexual identities that are more balanced and stable than those fostered by "traditional" ideas about the male and female personality. To the best of the present author's knowledge, empirical research in this area has yet to be undertaken.

REFERENCES

Aletti, V. (1986, June 24). The single life: Voices Parry. *The Village Voice*, p. 63.
Aufderheide, P. (1986). Music videos: The look of sound. In Todd Gitlin (Ed.), *Watching Television* (pp. 11-135). New York: Pantheon Books.
Avicolli, T. (1979). Images of gays in rock music. In K. Jay & A. Young, (Eds.), *Lavender Culture* (pp. 182-194). New York: Jove.
Block, A. (1982a, April 15). Rebel, rebel: The confessions of a gay rocker. *The Advocate*, pp. 43-47.
Block, A. (1982b, December 23). Cracks in the rock closet. *The Advocate*, pp. 43-47,61.
Bronski Boys Minus One. (1985, July). *Record*, p. 39.
Conlon, D. (1978, April 19). Carl Bean was 'born this way.' *The Advocate*, p. 30.
Frith, S. (1984, October 16). Britbeat. *The Village Voice*, p. 102.
Frith, S. (1985, February 12). Britbeat. *The Village Voice*, p. 78.
Gill, J. (1986, July 22). British Beat: Bronskis, Communards confront prejudices at home. *The Advocate*, pp. 47-49.
Grillo, R. (1982). Gay moments in straight music. *Gay Books Bulletin* 8, 22-26.
Hamilton, T. (1986, October 23). Charts. *Rolling Stone*, p. 120.
Henke, J. (1984, June 7). Oscar! Oscar! Great Britain goes Wilde for the 'fourth gender' Smiths. *Rolling Stone*, p. 45.
Herschberg, C. (1978, April 19). Prophets or profits? The Village People. *The Advocate*, p. 31.
Hits of the World. (1986a, September 20). *Billboard*, p. 68.
Hits of the World. (1986b, October 11). *Billboard*, p. 77.
Hits of the World. (1986c, November 8). *Billboard*, p. 65.
Hits of the World. (1986d, November 15). *Billboard*, p. 77.
Hits of the World. (1986e, November 29). *Billboard*, p. 57.
Hits of the World. (1986f, December 6). *Billboard*, p. 30.
Hits of the World. (1986g, December 13). *Billboard*, p. 56
Hot Dance/Disco. (1986a, November 22). *Billboard*, p. 30.
Hot Dance/Disco. (1986b, December 6). *Billboard*, p. 30.
Israel, D. (1986, May 8). Charts. *Rolling Stone*, p. 100.

J.D. (1986, October). New in London. *Interview*, p. 21.

Klein, H. (1978, April 19). They're playing our song: Rock grooves on gay. *The Advocate*, pp. 25-26.

MTV Programming. (1986a, September 3 to October 8). *Billboard*.

MTV Programming. (1986b, October 15 to November 26). *Billboard*.

Rolling Stone Yearbook 1984, p. 56.

Rushing, J. and Frentz, T. (1980). The rhetoric of "Rocky": A Social Value Model of Criticism. In B.L. Brock & R.L. Scott (Eds.), *Methods of rhetorical criticism: A twentieth century perspective* (pp. 244-263). Detroit: Wayne State University Press.

Schauer, J. (1978, April 19). Waxing gay at the Waxworks. *The Advocate*, pp. 32-33.

The Smiths (1984). "How Soon Is Now?," Hatful of Hollow, Rough Trade Records, Rough 76.

Sullivan, J. (1985, February). Frankie says Buzz Off. *Record*, pp. 17-19.

Walters, B. (1986, June 3). Playing it both ways. *The Village Voice*, pp. 61-62.

Wing, E. (1985a, January 31). Charts. *Rolling Stone*, p. 56.

Wing, E. (1985b, March 14). Charts. *Rolling Stone*, p. 64.

Wing, E. (1985c, April 25). Charts. *Rolling Stone*, p. 64.

APPENDIX

"Don't Leave Me This Way"

(Gamble, Huff, Gilbert)

Don't leave me this way
I can't survive, I can't stay alive
Without your love, oh baby
Don't leave me this way
I can't exist, I will surely miss
Your tender kiss
So don't leave me this way.

Oh baby, my heart is full of love and desire for you
So come on down and do what you've got to do
You started this fire down in my soul
Now can't you see it's burning out of control
So come on down and satisfy the need in me
Cos only your good loving can set me free

Don't leave me this way
I don't understand how I'm at your command
So baby please don't leave me this way

Don't leave me this way
I don't understand how I'm at your command
So baby please don't leave me this way

Oh baby, my heart is full of love and desire for you . . .

Don't leave me this way
Cos I can't survive, I can't stay alive
Without your love, oh baby
Don't leave me this way
I can't exist, I will surely miss
Your tender kiss
So don't leave me this way

Oh baby, my heart is full of love and desire for you . . .

SEXUAL MINORITIES AND COMMUNICATION LAW

Lesbian and Gay Rights as a Free Speech Issue: A Review of Relevant Caselaw

Paul Siegel, PhD

Gallaudet University

SUMMARY. The legal struggles waged by lesbian and gay male litigants almost invariably involve issues of freedom of expression, broadly construed. To illustrate this point, a wide array of caselaw is examined—ranging from classic "access to a forum" controversies to those concerning symbolic conduct and freedom of association (including marriage and child custody law), employment discrimi-

Paul Siegel is Associate Professor and Chairperson of Communication Arts at Gallaudet University, and an Associate Editor of the *Free Speech Yearbook*.

The author gratefully acknowledges the assistance of Professor Richard Mohr of the University of Illinois, Leonard Graff, the staff of Lambda Legal Defense and Education Fund, Mary C. Dunlap (who argued the "Gay Olympics" case before the Supreme Court), as well as the staffs of numerous affiliate offices of the American Civil Liberties Union, with special thanks to Claire Ebel, Martha Kegel, and Matthew Stark. The author dedicates this article to the loving memory of Peter Michael Siegel (1959-1987).

Requests for reprints should be sent to the author at the Department of Communication Arts, Gallaudet University, Washington, DC 20002.

nation, and proscriptions against deviant sexual conduct. In each category, claims to a right of freedom of expression are manifested.

Cautionary notes are offered concerning those cases in which gay litigants try to protect their rights by inhibiting the speech of others. A brief concluding section assesses the long-term and short-term efficacy of raising First Amendment arguments (as opposed to privacy or equal protection arguments) in lesbian/gay male litigation.

A state employee whose gay activism attracts a modicum of media coverage that comes to the attention of his employer is told to seek psychiatric examination or be terminated (*Gish v. Board of Education*, 1976). A lesbian couple is told that they may retain custody of one of the women's children, but is warned that if they spend "too much time" in lesbian rights advocacy, that "would jeopardize future custody" (*Schuster v. Schuster*, 1974, p. 2004). A gay-oriented social service organization seeking tax exempt status is successful, but only on the condition "that none of the educational programs includes any substantial advocacy of the position that homosexuality is a mere preference, orientation, or propensity which is on par with heterosexuality or should otherwise be regarded as normal" (Coleman, 1978).

In each of these instances and in many others to be recounted here, lesbian and gay male individuals or organizations encounter "judicial homophobia" (Dressler, 1979) as a direct result of their affirmation and expression of their identity or "personhood" (Gomez, 1983) as a member of a sexual minority.

This Article assumes that the legal struggles faced by lesbian and gay litigants almost invariably involve issues of freedom of expression. In one sense, this is a trivial and obvious truth. Gays are, after all, often described as an "invisible minority"; implicit in this characterization is the unlikelihood of suffering anti-gay discrimination in the absence of some kind of communicative action that ends the invisibility. Whether such an act takes the form of directly "coming out" to a potential employer (or landlord, etc.) or living an "openly gay lifestyle" that might by itself or through media coverage come to the attention of such an employer, issues of free speech and freedom of association are clearly implicated.

Perhaps a more substantive argument in support of the thesis that gay rights are, first and foremost, a First Amendment issue, would center not on the mechanism by which gays are "found out" but instead on the nature of the official reaction to such discovery. As Richards (1986) cogently points out, anti-gay prejudice cannot any longer be justified in an intellectually honest way on the basis of the traditionally asserted "harms" (homosexuality as unnatural, or as mental illness, or equated with pederasty, etc.). When such prejudice manifests itself in official sanctions, Richards argues, gays confront "the functional equivalent of a heresy prosecution" (p. 905).

Support for this view can be gleaned from social science findings in the area of anti-gay prejudice, which clearly indicate that one of the best predictors of such prejudice is an attitudinal rigidity concerning the family and gender roles. Lesbians and gays, according to this view, are devalued because they are perceived as agitators, questioning traditional roles (Lieblich & Friedman, 1985; MacDonald, 1976; MacDonald & Games, 1974; Siegel, 1981; Weinberger & Millham, 1979). As Richards (1986) puts it:

Homosexuality is today essentially a form of political, social, and moral dissent on a par with the best American traditions of dissent and even subversive advocacy . . . Those that support criminalization find today in homosexuality what they found before in the family planning of Sanger, the atheism of Darwin, the socialism of Debs, or the Marxist advocacy of the American Communist Party. (p. 905)

It is no surprise, then, that on the few occasions when the United States Supreme Court has reviewed a controversy involving gay rights, the First Amendment was implicated in almost every instance (*Board of Education v. NGTF*, 1985; *Manual Enterprises v. Day*, 1962; *Mishkin v. New York*, 1966; *New York v. Uplinger*, 1984; *Pope v. Illinois*, 1987; *San Francisco Arts and Athletics v. United States Olympic Committee*, 1987).

What follows, then, does not constitute an argument for the proposition that lesbian and gay male liberation necessarily *should* be seen as a First Amendment struggle; rather, the review of caselaw provided herein is offered as just that—a descriptive review of relevant litigation. It is hoped that a taxonomy of sorts will emerge from that review that may help us to sort out the communication-relevant facets of what one commentator refers to as "queer law" (Rivera, 1985, 1986).

Two points concerning the scope of this taxonomy should be made at the outset. First, the reader should be alerted that discussions of lesbian and gay speech as it applies to immigration and naturalization, the prisons, and the military will be eschewed here, although all certainly raise important and relevant issues for gay litigants (Fowler & Graff, 1985; *Inosencio v. Johnson*, 1982, aff'd sub. nom., *Brown v. Johnson*, 1984; "Miscellaneous News Notes," 1986, p. 59; *Matthews v. Marsh*, 1985; "Newsbriefs," 1987; Reynolds, 1980; Rivera, 1986). This exclusion is based upon the reality that the First Amendment, to the extent it has any impact at all upon those areas of law, surely applies with diminished force and would therefore require separate treatment.

Second, although this volume is devoted to sexuality and *mass* communication, the review of caselaw here will not be limited to legal controversies involving the mass media. Rather, we will try to examine all the caselaw from the gay rights movement that concerns the communication act, broadly construed. The decision to adopt this broader focus is based largely upon the fact that the most fundamental tenets of "media law" actually have their roots in landmark First Amendment cases from decades past that themselves did not involve media litigants. For example, while media lawyers often trace the "prior restraint" doctrine in First Amendment law (which claims that pre-publication censorship is even more odious than post-publication punishment) back to *Near v. Minnesota* (1931), a case that did involve the mass media, the philosophical basis for the doctrine can actually be found in Justice Brandeis' concurring opinion from the earlier *Whitney v. California* (1927) case, which did not deal with the mass media at all. Similarly, the notion that the broadcast media's obligation to provide for a "marketplace of ideas" would permit such special regulations as the Equal Time Rule and the Personal Attack Rule (*Red Lion Broadcasting v. FCC*, 1969), stems from an earlier invoking of the marketplace metaphor from Justice Brandeis's famous dissenting opinion in a World War I era Espionage Act case (*Abrams v. U.S.*, 1919).

Numerous other examples could be cited, but instead suffice it to say that although the Supreme Court has on occasion suggested that the First Amendment applies with different force to the mass media and to face-to-face communication (e.g., *Zauderer v. Office of Disciplinary Council*, 1985), such cases are unusual, and the Court often has stated that the First Amendment should apply equally to mass media representatives and to ordinary citizens (*Branzburg v. Hayes*, 1972; *Dun and Bradstreet v. Greenmoss Builders*, 1985; *Zurcher v. Stanford Daily*, 1987). Thus it is no surprise that most of the leading textbooks in mass media law (Francois, 1986; Middleton and Chamberlin, 1988; Pember, 1987) boast lengthy chapters on the history and philosophy of the First Amendment, examining more than cursorily the landmark cases that may themselves not have involved the mass media but whose outcomes are nonetheless of importance to today's media litigants.

Keeping the above issues in mind, we are now ready to present a typology of free speech caselaw emerging from the lesbian and gay rights movement. The typology will begin on solid ground with the *inarguable* "free speech" cases, those which request the judiciary to come to terms with the most basic First Amendment values in the most traditional settings, what I refer to as the "access to a forum" cases. Next we will review the caselaw on freedom of association and the right to engage in symbolic conduct. A separate section will assess the relevance of the communication act to the protection of the rights of employees. The next area of caselaw to be confronted—that dealing with the constitutionality of sodomy statutes themselves—is typically not argued on First Amendment grounds, but is, it will be asserted here, by no means irrelevant to the study of communication.

Next we will examine cases in which the gay litigants are involved in free speech cases, but are cast in the role of anti-speech advocates, espousing the view that their rights are being abridged by the speech of others. A concluding section will offer thoughts concerning the efficacy, short-term and long-term, of arguing for lesbian and gay male rights as communication issues.

THE "PURE" SPEECH CASES: ACCESS TO A FORUM

Toward a Gayer Bicentennial Committee v. Rhode Island Bicentennial Foundation (1976) is one of those few cases whose citation alone gives a clear indication of the legal controversy involved. The state of Rhode Island was gearing up to do its part in commemorating the 200th anniversary of the Declaration of Independence. The gay plaintiffs wanted to participate by, among other things, having a parade, a prayer vigil, a town meeting, and a listing in the Foundation's directory as a sponsoring organization. The Foundation refused, citing the state's sodomy statute, arguing they did not want to be put in the position of associating themselves with an organization that advocates illegality (a charge denied by the gay group). Judge Pettine, in ruling that the Foundation could not preclude the gay group's participation without running afoul of the First Amendment, had this to say about the irrelevance of Rhode Island's criminalization of sodomy:

> I cannot help but note the irony of the Bicentennial Commission expressing reluctance to provide a forum for the plaintiff's exercise of their First Amendment rights because they might advocate conduct which is illegal. Does the Bicentennial Commission need reminding that, from the perspective of British loyalists, the Bicentennial celebrates one of history's greatest illegal acts? (p. 642)

The forum sought by the gay litigants in *Alaska Gay Coalition v. Sullivan* (1978) was a listing in the "Anchorage Blue Book," a government publication described by the court as a paperback guide to services and organizations in the greater Anchorage area (p. 953). At trial, Mayor Sullivan had expressed a "personal aversion" to homosexuality and a concern that Alaska's sodomy statute made it "improper" for a government publication to include a listing for the Gay Coalition (p. 955). The Alaska Supreme Court ruled that the Blue Book was a public forum and that the city of Anchorage had violated the First Amendment rights of the Coalition.

At issue in *Gay Activists Alliance v. Washington Metro* (1979) was whether commuters on the District of Columbia's subway system would have to confront posters provided by GAA that pictured a wide array of Washingtonians of different races and ages with the one-sentence caption, "Someone in your life is gay." The Transit Company refused to display the posters, arguing that some commuters would be upset by the message. Judge Pratt did not find the argument convincing, and pointed out that commuters had already seen posters placed by the Unification Church, the Church of Scientology, and by both pro- and anti-abortion rights groups on the Metro system:

> Many riders will undoubtedly take umbrage at the message that "SOMEONE IN YOUR LIFE IS GAY . . . ." Although we are sympathetic to the [the transit company's] interests in raising advertising revenue and its natural desire to protect its riders from offensive messages, and to avoid controversy, we are nonetheless compelled to hold that it has run counter to the requirements of the First Amendment in its pursuits of these interests. (p. 11-12)

During the author's tenure as Executive Director of the American Civil Liberties Union's affiliate for Kansas and Western Missouri, the *Washington Metro* case proved an invaluable precedent for an ACLU case involving a local Kansas City gay group that wanted to advertise on that city's transit system. The proffered poster in the latter case—perhaps a reflection of Midwestern vs. Eastern sensibilities—more tentatively asserted that "SOMEONE IN YOUR LIFE *MAY BE* GAY" (H. Isaacs, personal communication, March, 1983).

The AIDS crisis has led to another round of confrontations between gay activists and the protectors of mass transit commuters' sensibilities, this time in the city of Chicago. Initially, the Chicago Transit Authority had refused to sell advertising space to the Kupona Network, a non-profit organization targeting the Black community with AIDS education messages. The specific ad depicted a couple holding a condom package, and a drug user with a "NO!" slash through the whole scene. The caption read in part, "Sex without Condoms and Drug Abuse = AIDS." The CTA backed down after the local ACLU affiliate filed suit (ACLU AIDS Project, 1990). As of this writing, at least one member of the Chicago City Council is scrambling to find a constitutional means to keep yet another AIDS related poster off CTA vehicles ("Content," 1990). This ad campaign, familiar to commuters in several other large American cities, depicts 3 couples (one Male/Male, one Male/Female, and one Female/Female) kissing, with a caption alerting readers that "Kissing does not cause AIDS — Greed and Indifference Do."

One of the forums often sought out by gay rights groups is the ubiquitous "Yellow Pages." Two early cases heard by California's Public Utilities Commission are noteworthy. In the first case — *Council on Religion and the Homosexual v. PT&T* (1969) — a gay group had already been advertising in the Yellow Pages under "Religious Organizations" but sought to be listed instead as a "Homophile Organization." The telephone company denied the request, claiming that the suggested heading was too narrow, too limited; moreover, the word "homophile" did not appear in most dictionaries. The PUC majority deferred to the telephone company's judgment, finding it was not arbitrary or discriminatory.

Commissioner J. P. Vukasin, Jr., wrote a stingingly anti-gay concurring opinion. After making reference to the "disorders of drug addiction, alcoholism *and homosexuality*," he admonished the plaintiff organization that their time and effort "would be far better spent in the dedication of time and financial resources to the restoration of their members as respected and dignified citizens of the community" (p. 476, emphasis added).

The dissenting opinions provided by Commissioners Gatov and Moran point out the inconsistencies in the telephone company's reasoning. As Gatov put it:

> PT&T has no objective criteria by which to determine whether or not a heading is too limited. Such decisions . . . are capricious and dictated by the whims, prejudices, or vagaries of an individual or individuals in PT&T's directory sales department. For example, the PT&T directory sales supervisor testified that he would not approve a separate classification heading for clarinets, as he felt such a listing really belonged under the heading of musical instruments. He was unable to adequately explain, however, why violins, accordions, and pianos were permitted separate classifications . . . . Furthermore, the majority's attempt to hide behind the fortress of Webster is futile. It is true, as they point out, that the word "homophile" does not appear in Webster's Third New International Dictionary. On the other hand, neither does "Scientology" or "Per-

sonology," both of which have headings in the current San Francisco yellow-page section. (p. 477-478)

The very next year, California's Public Utilities Commission was again confronted by a controversy in which a gay group wanted to advertise in the Yellow Pages (*Society for Individual Rights v. PUC*, 1970). The display ad S.I.R. sought to place was rejected by PT&T, which this time argued more forthrightly that the subject matter raised by the ad ("Homosexuals—know and protect your rights. If over twenty-one, write or visit . . .") was offensive. Again, the majority deferred to the judgment of the phone company, and again an eloquent dissenting opinion penned by Commissioner Gatov cut to the heart of the issue:

> My view that PT&T has no reasonable standards by which it measures good taste can perhaps be best illustrated by comparing the innocuous little proffered ad with those which PT&T has published and which presumably have met its lofty standards. One advertisement in the San Francisco telephone book, issued September, 1970, is for a night club which features topless and sometimes bottomless nude girls in the bedroom, and another tastefully advertises that it features topless-bottomless gun molls and has nightly raids. For music lovers, another club advertises, with illustration, that it has a nude girl on the piano. Out of deference to the wives of America, I have avoided outlining the details of six pages of massage parlor advertisements. (p. 627)

More recent legal conflicts surrounding access to the Yellow Pages have produced less discriminatory results than did the early California cases ("Newsfront," 1988). In *Ashley v. Ameritech Publishing* (1984), the owner of a Detroit bookstore called "Chosen Books" won the right to make mention in his Yellow Pages ad of the fact that the store carries "Gay-Lesbian Literary Books." The next year, a state appellate court in Georgia refused to find any constitutional infirmity in the refusal on the part of the publisher of a local Yellow Pages to carry an ad for a similar bookstore, "Christopher's Kind" (*Loring v. Bellsouth Advertising and Publications Co.*, 1968). Despite this ruling, based largely upon the court's conclusion that the publishing company was too indirectly related to the regulated phone company to provide the requisite "state's action," Bellsouth eventually changed its policy in response to political pressure from the gay community (Fauntleroy, 1986; Westheimer, 1985). Even more recently, the Gay and Lesbian Alliance Against Defamation, without having to resort to litigation, obtained from the Nynex corporation the right to be listed under a new heading in regional phone books, "Gay and Lesbian Services" (Hays, 1989).

Another public forum sought out by lesbian and gay litigants are newspapers. Defendants here tend to be state university newspapers, thus at least providing the opportunity to raise the argument that "state's action" is involved. That argument was unsuccessful in *Mississippi Gay Alliance v. Goudelock* (1976), wherein the gay group sought to place an ad in the Mississippi State University's *Reflector* to the effect that the group offered "counseling, legal aid, and a library of gay literature." The majority found that student-editor Goudelock functioned with sufficient autonomy to preclude a finding of state's action. Judge Coleman was not content to leave the issue there, however. In an almost comic exchange of dicta with dissenting Judge Goldberg, he expressed concern about the ad's offer of "legal aid": "Such an offer is open to various interpretations," he claimed, "one of which is that criminal activity is contemplated, necessitating the aid of counsel" (p. 1076, n. 4). Judge Goldberg's reply: "The suggestion . . . that the criminal taint in the ad is demonstrated by the offer of 'legal aid' implies a presumption of illegality whenever lawyers are involved — surely the level of respect for the profession has not reached this nadir" (p. 1078).

More recently, a federal district judge in Nebraska found no state's action in the refusal of *The Daily Nebraskan* (the student newspaper of the University of Nebraska at Lincoln) to publish "roommate wanted" ads from a gay male and a lesbian student (*Sinn v. Daily Nebraskan*, 1986). The student editors claimed further that permitting such ads to run would violate the paper's non-discrimination policy. (Different versions of plaintiffs' ads either identified the sexual orientation of the advertiser or specified the desired sexual orientation of any potential roommates.)

In at least one case (*Robertson v. Anderson*, 1985), editors of a public *high school* newspaper were more open to gay ads than most of their college counterparts. When the student editors were held accountable for having accepted for publication in *The Arrow* (the newspaper at Minneapolis' Southwest High School) a paid ad from a local gay rights group, the court prohibited the school administration from further enforcement of the regulations used to deny publication. More recently, a gay youth group in Washington, DC, sought, with mixed results, to place ads in dozens of area high school papers (Baker, 1990).

Perhaps the most interesting "access to the newspapers" cases will be those not involving state's action at all. These will be the cases in which a local anti-discrimination ordinance attempts to define the advertising pages of a newspaper as a "public accommodation" access to which cannot be denied on the basis of, among other traits, sexual orientation. The only court so far to rule on the issue has refused, not surprisingly, to negate the traditional First Amendment rights of the newspaper publishers (*Hatheway v. Gannett Satellite Information Network*, 1990; Kane, 1989) and this may not be a bad thing. After all, the same ruling that would allow a gay group to force a small town paper to accept an ad can be used to force a big city gay newspaper to accept an ad for a group of fundamentalist "ex-gays." Nonetheless, this is certainly an area of litigation to watch for future developments (Freiberg, 1987a).

The public school itself was the forum sought by litigants in *Solmitz v. Maine School Administrative District* (1985), a case with a tragic history and a depressing outcome from the perspective of the gay and pro-gay plaintiffs. Teacher Solmitz, deeply troubled by the killing of a young gay male by three Bangor high school students, decided to seek support for a "Symposium on Tolerance" to be held during the school day at Madison High School. Representatives of various minority groups—the aged, the disabled, etc., as well as a local lesbian activist—would all take part in the day long program. When word of Solmitz's invitation to lesbian Dale McCormick became public, the school received numerous threatening calls from parents and others. There would be a picket, children would be kept home from school, there would be bomb threats. As a result, the School Board cancelled "Tolerance Day" altogether. The trial judge, whose decision was upheld by the state Supreme Court, found it was the Board's genuine and understandable fear of violence, and not its own alleged anti-gay sentiment, that led to the cancellation.

A final genre of pure First Amendment case involves not so much access to a forum as freedom to utter a specific message. Frequently litigants with an explicitly gay message have run afoul of obscenity laws and have in so doing prompted the Court to fine tune accepted definitions of obscenity (*Mishkin v. New York*, 1966; *Pope v. Illinois*, 1987). Moreover, much concern has been expressed within the gay community surrounding recent actions by the Federal Communications Commission which may suggest that even non-obscene gay speech is less protected than heterosexually oriented speech ("Federal Censorship Commission," 1987; Vandervelden, 1987a). In one such action, the FCC moved against Pacifica station KPFK-FM of Los Angeles, finding that its broadcast of excerpts from the play "Jerker" was indecent, and possibly obscene (*in the matter of Pacifica Foundation*, 1987). Concerns about the FCC's new aggressiveness against such broadcasts are all the more warranted since January, 1989, when a Congressional action requiring the FCC to enforce its anti-indecency policies 24 hours a day went into effect (Enforcement of prohibitions against broadcast obscenity and indecency, 1988).

Arts patrons in New York, Washington, DC, and Cincinnati experienced censorship of gay messages recently. The Corcoran Gallery in the nation's capital cancelled a scheduled showing of photographs (some with homoerotic and sadomasochistic themes) by the late Robert Mapplethorpe, out of fear that the National Endowment for the Arts would cut its funding. Although the Gallery's actions were much criticized by gay activists and by the art community generally (Richard, 1989), the Corcoran's fears became reality when Congress passed a version of the "Helms Amendment" into law, which prohibits the NEA from giving monies to exhibits of homoerotic art lacking "serious" value. The new law, in turn, resulted in the Endowment's decision to withhold promised funding to an exhibit of AIDS-related art at the Artists' Space gallery in New York, an action which created controversies anew (Kastor, 1989). That decision was eventually rescinded and the funding restored after John Frohnmayer, NEA's chairman, viewed the exhibit. Even so, he insisted that NEA's monies not be used to fund the exhibit's catalog, which included pointed criticisms of, among others, Senator Jesse Helms (Botkin, 1989).

When the Mapplethorpe exhibit reached Cincinnati, local authorities decided to prosecute the offending gallery under the state's obscenity laws. Although the museum director was acquitted (Parachini, 1990), the bringing of the case itself added new fuel to the NEA controversy, leading many well-known artists and prestigious museums to refuse previously awarded grants (Masters, 1990a; Weintraub, 1990). The controversy gathered even further momentum when the NEA rejected four grant applications that had been approved by their respective review panels. That three of the four artists involved are openly lesbian or gay, and that their performance art deals explicitly with gay, lesbian, and feminist themes, has not escaped the notice of NEA critics (Masters, 1990b).

At issue in a recent U.S. Supreme Court "access to a message" case (*San Francisco Arts and Athletics, Inc. v. United States Olympic Committee*, 1987) were sections of a federal law giving the U.S. Olympic Committee exclusive rights to use the word "Olympics," which the Committee invoked in its suit against the sponsors of the "Gay Olympics."

The majority found no constitutional infirmity in the extraordinary powers granted the USOC by the statute. An inescapable irony of the case is that the most cogent argument raised by the gay litigants — that their choice of the label, "Gay Olympics," and their close modeling of their games after *"the"* Olympics was intended to make a political statement protected by the First Amendment — provided the basis for the majority's anti-gay ruling. The more closely your games are modeled after their games, the majority concluded, the more likely confusion as to sponsorship is to develop. Congress' wish to avoid any such potential for confusion, the Court ruled, was precisely the reason it gave the U.S. Olympics Committee such extraordinary powers over the word "Olympics," especially over those who would use the word to promote an "athletic performance or competition."

FREEDOM OF ASSOCIATION

Although the phrase "freedom of association" appears nowhere in the United States Constitution, it is incontrovertibly established by the caselaw that such a right does exist as a corollary First Amendment right (Emerson, 1970). In its earliest form, this freedom of association was seen as a means to an end only; our right to freedom of speech could most efficiently be exercised if we could freely form political associations. More recent decisions (e.g., *Griswold v. Connecticut*, 1965) and commentaries (Karst, 1980; Raggi, 1977) recognize a freedom of association that need not necessarily be linked to the exercise of freedom of political expression. Gay litigants have often had to go to court to seek both kinds of associational freedoms.

Political Associations

As we have already seen, the existence of a sodomy statute is often used by a state as an argument for the denial of other rights — including First Amendment rights — to gay litigants. Such an argument was raised by the state of New York in *Gay Activists Alliance v. Lomenzo* (1973), wherein the gay group sought state recognition as a non-profit corporation. The trial court, whose judgment was eventually reversed, found that

> by identifying themselves as a "homosexual civil rights organization," [plaintiffs] are professing a present or future intent to disobey a penal statute of the State of New York . . . It would seem that in order to be a homosexual, the prohibited conduct must have at some time been committed or at least presently contemplated. (pp. 996-997)

The trial judge in the *Lomenzo* case was referring to a sodomy statute then on the books, since found unconstitutional (*People v. Onofre*, 1980). Yet even the absence of such a statute did not stop the Ohio Supreme Court from refusing to accept the articles of incorporation proposed by the Greater Cincinnati Gay Society (*State, ex rel., v. Brown*, 1974). Without explanation, the per curiam opinion stated that "although homosexual acts between consenting adults are no longer statutory offenses . . . the promotion of homosexuality as a valid lifestyle is contrary to the public policy of the state" (pp. 113-114).

The plethora of non-profit gay-oriented organizations in existence today suggests that cases such as *Brown* are mostly of historical interest; indeed, even the Greater Cincinnati Gay Society was granted official status as a non-profit organization upon resubmitting its articles (Rivera, 1979, p. 911, n. 674).

Once granted non-profit status by the state, an organization's next logical step is often to seek the most favorable tax-exempt status provided by law. As numerous gay-oriented organizations discovered up until at least the late 1970s, the Internal Revenue Service was often a tremendous hindrance. A typical ruling concerned the Lambda Services Bureau of Colorado Springs. In a letter to the organization from the IRS District Director in Austin, Texas, dated March 25, 1976, Lambda was warned:

> The unqualified promotion of the tenet that homosexuality is not a sickness, disturbance or other pathology in any sense but is merely a preference, orientation or propensity on par with and not different from heterosexuality, carries a serious risk of encouraging or fostering homosexual attitudes and propensities . . . Therefore, the unqualified promotion of such a proposition would prevent an organization from qualifying for exemption. (District Director, 1976)

This state of affairs apparently came to a halt in 1978 as a result of Revenue Ruling 78-305, 1978-2 C.B. 172, which indicates that "a non-profit organization formed to educate the public about homosexuality in order to foster an understanding and tolerance of homosexuals and their problems qualifies for exemption." Even this ruling, however, continues to suggest that to achieve tax exempt status an organization's educational activities regarding homosexuality must "present a full and fair exposition of the facts"; thus the dramatic increase in the number of tax-exempt gay-oriented organizations since the late 1970s is best attributed to an informal decision on the part of the IRS to liberalize its interpretation and application of its prior rulings (Bros, 1981; Rivera, 1981, p. 342).

By far the most litigious situs for politically oriented gay groups seeking to preserve their freedom of association has been the college campus. Student groups at such schools as Virginia Commonwealth University (*Gay Alliance of Students v. Matthews*, 1976), the University of Georgia (*Wood v. Davidson*, 1972), Austin Peay State University in Tennessee (*Student Coalition for Gay Rights v.*

Austin Peay State University, 1979), Texas Tech University (*Student Services for Lesbians/Gays v. Texas Tech University*, 1986), the University of South Carolina (*Gay Students Association v. University of South Carolina*, 1983) and Texas A&M University (*Gay Student Services v. Texas A&M University*, 1984) have all been successful plaintiffs.

Representative of such cases is *Gay Lib v. University of Missouri* (1977), in which a federal appellate court overturned a trial court finding, based upon "expert" psychiatric testimony, that granting official recognition to the gay group would lead to an increase in sodomy violations. Justice Rehnquist, in his dissent from the Supreme Court's decision not to review the appellate decision, analogized the question posed by the case to one of

> whether those suffering from measles have a constitutional right, in violation of quarantine regulations, to associate together and with others who do not presently have measles, in order to urge repeal of a state law providing that measles sufferers be quarantined. (p. 1084)

Three additional cases dealing with recognition of gay student groups, but presenting unique legal postures, also bear mentioning. In *Department of Education v. Lewis* (1982), the Florida Supreme court struck down a law denying funding to any state university that permitted approval of sexual relations outside marriage. (The legislative sponsors admitted their aim was to persuade state universities to deny recognition to gay student groups.)

The second case found the Eighth Circuit Court of Appeals, reversing the trial court below, ruling that "content-motivated" reasons could not constitutionally be used by a student senate to deny funding to the gay student group at the University of Arkansas (*Gay and Lesbian Students Association v. Gohn*, 1988).

Concerning this latter case, it is probably worth noting that, as in the early *Gay Lib* case from Missouri, the University of Arkansas tried to justify the denial of funding at least in part by calling attention to the state's sodomy statute. The Circuit Court of Appeals had little difficulty in refuting the argument:

True, sodomy is illegal in Arkansas. However, GLSA does
not advocate sodomy, and, even if it did, its speech would still
be protected by the First Amendment. People may extol the
virtues of arson or even cannibalism. They simply may not
commit the acts . . . . Conduct may be prohibited or regulated,
within broad limits. But government may not discriminate
against people because it dislikes their ideas, not even when
the ideas include advocating that certain conduct now criminal
be legalized. (p. 368)

The University of Arkansas ruling should perhaps best be viewed
as a narrow one, restricted to situations wherein student senators
provide the reviewing court with a trial record "replete with evidence that the Senate's action was based on viewpoint discrimination" (p. 366). Had the senators withheld funding for more neutral
reasons, such as the gay group's inability to attract large numbers of
students to its meetings, the court's ruling may have been different
(cf. *Wallace v. Jaffree*, 1985). The Arkansas precedent nonetheless
proved helpful to ACLU attorneys in California, whose threat of
legal action against the State University's Fresno campus resulted in
restoration of funding to that campus' Gay and Lesbian Students
Alliance ("Out on campus," 1988b).

Completing the category of political association cases is a legal
controversy so complex that the ACLU engaged in an extended internal debate concerning whose side to support. The national ACLU
filed an amicus brief in support of the students in *Gay Rights Coalition of Georgetown University Law Center v. Georgetown University* (1987), while the legal director of the organization's local affiliate for the National Capitol Area filed an amicus brief on behalf of
the university. At issue was whether Washington's Human Rights
Act could be used by gay litigants to compel the university to grant
the group full "university recognition" status. Georgetown argued
that such an application of the law would violate the First Amendment in two ways. First, the Free Exercise Clause would be
abridged, the university alleged, in that it is a Catholic institution
that cannot on religious grounds embrace pro-homosexual advocacy. Second, forcing the university to recognize the group would

be tantamount to forcing it to publicly endorse the group, a violation of the institution's right "not to speak."

The 7-judge appellate court, in an en banc decision handed down more than 2 years from the date of oral argument, produced 7 separate opinions taking up 171 pages. A 5-2 majority held that the university may be compelled to provide the gay group with all the tangible benefits (including a campus mailbox, the use of a computer label service and of mailing services; and the right to apply for, but not necessarily receive, university funding) usually accruing only to groups that have been granted full "university recognition" within Georgetown's by-laws. A differently constituted 5-2 majority held, however, that the university would not be compelled to officially award the gay groups the status of "university recognition."

Of special relevance to our subject matter is a dialogue between Judges Belson and Ferren. Belson tried to draw a distinction between the possibility that Georgetown refused to grant the gay group full rights because of the sexual orientation of group members (which would be clearly forbidden by the DC Human Rights Act) and the alternative possibility that Georgetown instead meant to move against the pro-gay advocacy engaged in by the group. The latter motivation, Belson concluded, might be protected by the First Amendment, a view soundly rejected by Judge Ferren. "The distinction between discrimination based on advocacy and on status will not work," he argued, in that "part of who a person is, is what he or she says; to deny the right to speak is to deny an essential aspect of one's person" (p. 56).

Most gay activists reacted to the complex array of opinions produced by the appellate court with cautious optimism pending certain Supreme Court review. Indeed, Chief Justice Rehnquist granted the university an emergency stay on December 24, 1987, in effect temporarily nullifying the lower court decision. But the stay was rescinded in January of 1988, and two months later the university signed a consent decree which forfeited its right to appeal the decision further (Harding, 1988; Taylor, 1988).

A complex postscript to the Georgetown case must be added. The 100th Congress, in a heavily lopsided vote, responded to the court ruling by requiring the District of Columbia to rescind that portion of its Human Rights Ordinance that could apply to religiously-affiliated schools such as Georgetown (Ayres, 1988; "Congress mandates," 1988). This legislative action would not affect Georgetown itself, because of the signed consent decree alluded to above. Members of the DC City Council were nonetheless sufficiently angered by what they saw as this Congressional infringement upon their "home rule" that they challenged the "Nation's Capital Religious Liberty and Academic Freedom Act," as it was called (aka the Armstrong Amendment) in federal court. On December 13, 1988, Judge Royce Lamberth ruled that the Act was indeed unconstitutional. It might have been constitutional, Judge Lamberth reasoned, for Congress itself to rescind portions of the DC Human Rights Act, but to coerce the DC City Council into doing so, under threat of loss of funding to the District, violated each Council member's First Amendment right *not* to speak (*Clarke v. United States*, 1988). A unanimous decision from a 3-judge panel of the Court of Appeals for the D.C. Circuit affirmed Lamberth's ruling, suggesting again, however, that had Congress itself "done the dirty work" and rescinded the District's ordinance, there might not be a constitutional infirmity. As of this writing, Congress has done precisely that, and the full Court of Appeals, sitting *en banc*, has therefore vacated the previous rulings. It is not at all clear whether a plausible legal theory can be constructed to challenge Congress' action (Chibbaro, 1989a, 1989b).

Non-Political Associations

In "Pre-Stonewall" times, there were few overtly political associations of lesbians and gay males. As such, it is not surprising that the earliest gay rights cases raising freedom of association issues concerned the granting or revocation of liquor licenses to bars with gay clientele. Most of the early caselaw did not result in favorable outcomes for the tavern owners or their patrons (Rivera, 1979, pp. 913-924).

That the liquor licenses of taverns are not in jeopardy nowadays solely on the grounds that their customers are gay is in part a function of more pro-gay caselaw (*Stoumen v. Reilly*, 1951; *Vallerga v. Dept. of Alcoholic Beverage Control*, 1959), but also a function of a more tolerant attitude generally on the part of local officials (Rivera, 1979, p. 920). Even some of the more recent, pro-gay caselaw is of interest by dint of the kinds of homophobic and voy- euristic testimony entertained at trial. What follows is a description of a gay bar, as provided to one trial court (*111 Wines and Liquors v. Division of Alcoholic Beverage Control*, 1967) by undercover investigators:

> They were conversing and some of them in a lisping tone of voice, and during certain parts of their conversations they used limp-wrist movements to each other. One man would stick his tongue out at another and they would laugh and they would giggle. They were very, very chummy and close. When they drank their drinks, they extended their pinkies in a very dainty manner. They took short sips; [it] took them quite a long time to finish their drinks. (p. 15)

That unfavorable rulings against gay bars are almost unheard of today does not mean that gays' freedom of association is unlimited. Thus, when health authorities in New York City sought an injunc- tion to close the New St. Mark's Baths in an effort to slow the spread of AIDS, New York County's Supreme Court granted their request, notwithstanding the freedom of association claims raised by defendants (*New York v. St. Mark's Baths*, 1986). Perhaps more disturbing is a decision from the Ninth Circuit Court of Appeals upholding the Washington State License Board's requirement that the managers of "the Sanctuary" — a church-affiliated club with a gay clientele — provide its membership list to the Board. The court rejected the appellant's argument that such forced disclosure was violative of the constitutional right to free association, and "would subject the members to harassment" (*Freeman v. Hittle*, 1984, p. 1303).

An interesting twist on the issue of freedom of association in eating and drinking establishments is found in *Rolan v. Kulwitzky* (1984), which held that a Los Angeles anti-discrimination ordi- nance forbade a restaurant owner from limiting the use of a semi- private booth to *heterosexual* romantic couples. The case, which had been brought by a lesbian couple denied use of the facility, ended with the restaurant owner permanently closing the booth rather than liberalizing his seating policy (McDonald, 1984).

No discussion of litigation over non-political associations brought by lesbian or gay male plaintiffs would be complete without at least brief mention of the related issues of same-sex marriage and child custody. Concerning the former issue, suffice it to say that the two published cases in which gay (male) plaintiffs argued that their constitutional rights were abridged by the state's refusal to officially sanction their relationship (*Baker v. Nelson*, 1971; *Singer v. Hara*, 1974) were unsuccessful. The courts — and some commentators (see especially Buchanan, 1985) — feel comfortable with the notion that a society's right to define marriage as an exclusively heterosexual union does not infringe unnecessarily upon rights of privacy, equal protection, or freedom of association. Other commentators have argued that the tangible benefits of marriage should not be denied to gay couples, even if the state refuses to recognize and sanction gay or lesbian relationships as "marriages" ("Comment," 1979; Karst, 1980).

The issue of child custody is complicated by the truism that custody law is a separate animal entirely, that the "best interests of the child" standard can and often is used to ignore or selectively outweigh what would otherwise seem to be dispositive claims to equal protection or freedom of association. As Rivera (1981) points out, courts often pay lip service to the notion that one parent's lesbianism should not be treated as an overriding consideration, then in the next paragraph proceed to treat the issue as precisely that.

The custody cases that are most clearly relevant to the scope of this Article are those in which custody or visitation is contingent upon the absence of the same-sex lover, or upon the litigants' relative political *in*activism (Rivera, 1981, p. 329, 334; *L v. D.*, 1982; *Scarlett v. Scarlett*, 1978; *Woodruff v. Woodruff*, 1979). The court in *M.P. v. S.P.* (1979) permitted the lesbian mother to retain custody, giving this reasoning:

> The evidence is affirmatively to the effect that she never displayed any sexual behavior in the presence of her children and that she refrains from *any demonstration of affection* toward other women when the girls are present. Moreover, she is not

a member of any homosexual organization. (p. 259, emphasis added)

Such judicial rulings not only ignore the associational freedoms of the parents; they also work against the best interests of the children, in that clinicians and social scientists who study lesbian and gay communities have shown that the freedom to express affection and to become connected in some way to the larger world of gay politics are signs of positive adjustment (Berger, 1980; Jacobs & Tedford, 1980; McDonald, 1982; Rand, Graham, & Rawlings, 1982; Susoeff, 1985). Thus, a gay parent's likelihood to retain custody may be negatively correlated with her own psychological adjustment.

Before leaving this issue, it should be noted that some commentators and legal advocates believe that the plight of lesbian and gay male parents in the courts has measurably improved in the past few years. A recent *New York Times* article reports that trial courts in many states, as well as appellate courts in Alaska, California, Colorado, Massachusetts, New Jersey, New York, Oregon, Texas, Vermont and Washington have all concluded that a parent's sexual orientation should be treated as irrelevant in custody disputes "unless it can be *demonstrated* to be harmful to the child" (Gutis, 1987, emphasis added).

SYMBOLIC CONDUCT: ANOTHER COROLLARY FIRST AMENDMENT RIGHT

Although the first Amendment prohibits government from abridging freedom of "speech," it is now well established that nonverbal expression, or symbolic conduct, is also protected by that constitutional provision (*Cohen v. California*, 1971; *Tinker v. Community School District*, 1969). Lesbian and gay litigants have frequently had to go to court to win the right to engage in non-verbal expression.

In one such case (*Gay Student Association v. Bonner*, 1974) the University of New Hampshire agreed to officially recognize the student group, but restricted the group's activities to the sponsorship of

strictly educational events. Purely social events, especially gay
dances, were prohibited. The court admonished university officials:

> There is some support for the proposition that dancing, the
> activity which the [university is] most confident in asserting
> [its] right to regulate, is itself a form of expression protected
> by the first amendment . . . . By holding a gay dance, GSO
> seeks to convey that homosexuals exist, that they feel re-
> pressed by existing laws and attitudes, that they wish to
> emerge from their isolation, and that public understanding of
> their attitudes and problems is desirable for society. (pp. 660-
> 661)

The *Bonner* precedent proved a helpful one six years later to
Cumberland, Rhode Island, high school student Aaron Fricke
(*Fricke v. Lynch*, 1980). Judge Pettine (the same magistrate who
ruled so eloquently in the *Toward a Gayer Bicentennial* case discussed earlier) recounted the facts of the case:

> Most of the time, a young man's choice of a date for the senior
> prom is of no great interest to anyone other than the student,
> his companion, and, perhaps, a few of their classmates. But in
> Aaron Fricke's case, the school authorities actively disapprove
> of his choice, the other students are upset, the community is
> abuzz, and out-of-state newspapers consider the matter news-
> worthy. All this fuss arises because Aaron Fricke's intended
> escort is another young man. (p. 382)

Judge Pettine went on, making clear what he saw as the First
Amendment relevance of the case:

> The proposed activity has expressive content. Aaron testified
> that he wants to go to the prom because he feels he has a right
> to attend and participate just like all the other students and that
> it would be dishonest to his own sexual identity to take a girl to
> the dance . . . . [He] feels his attendance would have a certain
> political element and would be a statement for equal rights and
> human rights. (pp. 384-385)

The significance of Judge Pettine's ruling is especially evident when it is contrasted with the *Solmitz* "Tolerance Day" case discussed earlier. There, it will be recalled, the Maine Supreme Court concluded that the school board had acted properly in cancelling the special program, that just because the angry townspeople who made threatening phone calls may have been motivated by violently discriminatory emotions did not dirty the hands of the school board.

Judge Pettine also had to rule on this "fear of violence issue," all the more plausible because Fricke had been the victim of a violent assault and battery by one of his classmates, requiring several stitches, shortly after his prom plans became public. Principal Lynch, however, would not be permitted to preclude Aaron's prom attendance on the basis of a fear of violence. Pettine explains:

> To rule otherwise would completely subvert free speech in the school by granting other students a hecklers' veto, allowing them to decide — through prohibited and violent methods — what speech will be heard. The First Amendment does not tolerate mob rule by unruly school children . . . Aaron's conduct is quiet and peaceful; it demands no response from others and — in a crowd of some 500 people — it can be easily ignored. (pp. 387-388)

So it was that the principal and assistant principal of Cumberland High School personally escorted Aaron and Paul to the prom, which transpired without incident (Fricke, 1981).

A right to dance in same-sex couples was won recently by two other gay males, this time in the context of a private amusement park (*Exler v. Disneyland*, 1984; Granelli, 1984; Shade, 1984). The cause of action, given the private setting, was not the First Amendment, but rather California's Unruh Civil Rights Act.

The symbolic conduct at issue in *Kristie v. Oklahoma City* (1983) was the Miss Gay America Pageant. The event's promoters had contracted with the city for the use of a municipal auditorium; the suit came about when the city abruptly cancelled the contract upon learning the nature of the event, claiming that it would be an "open expression of homosexuality" in violation of prevailing community standards. The trial judge rejected the city's reasoning:

[The city] contends that the Miss Gay America Pageant is not accorded constitutional protection because it is a commercial enterprise and not a noteworthy artistic endeavor such as a play or musical. They contend that a blatant showing of men parading in women's apparel is not artistic.

Such a judgment is subjective. While this court may agree that such a pageant may not rise to the level of artistic endeavor that HAIR or LA CAGE AUX FOLLES represents, it is still expression.

The First Amendment is not an art critic. (p. 91)

The court could not resist adding this bit of dicta, in response to the city's fear of an "open display of homosexuality":

In view of the acclaimed performances by Dustin Hoffman, Julie Andrews, Flip Wilson, Harvey Korman, Tony Curtis and Milton Berle in the roles of female impersonators, such impersonations may not be necessarily equated with homosexuality. (p. 92)

Gay litigants in the 1980s seem to have been at least as interested in marching as they were in dancing. Thus, in *Olivieri v. Ward* (1986), representatives of the gay Catholic organization "Dignity" won the right to demonstrate peacefully in front of St. Patrick's Cathedral during New York City's Gay Pride Parade. Judge Motley, whose order was upheld in slightly modified form by the Circuit Court of Appeals, showed a sensitivity to the expressive elements of the "Dignity" action:

By demonstrating on the sidewalk fronting the Cathedral as the parade passed by, Dignity sought to convey symbolically its love for the Church and its members' sense of themselves as integral parts of the Church's spiritual body. Dignity sought to communicate its belief that, notwithstanding the opposition of the institutional Church and its officials, Catholic gays need not choose between their homosexuality and their religion. (p. 855)

Contrast again is made to the "Tolerance Day" case from Maine, in that Judge Motley was confronted in *Olivieri* with the Police Department's argument that the demonstration should be enjoined because of possible violence from counterdemonstrators who would see Dignity's conduct as sacrilegious. The court gently accused the police of being less than truthful about their real motives. "Police sensitivity to the discomfort of . . . the Catholic Church, as well perhaps as discomfort within the Police Department itself with Dignity's message, are more credible explanations," concluded Motley (p. 873).

A more complicated and troublesome recent case also concerned a regularly scheduled parade in New York City. The parade at issue this time (*Gay Veterans Association v. American Legion*, 1985), was not the June Gay Pride Parade but the November Veterans Day Parade, the permit for which had traditionally been granted by the city to the American Legion. When the Legion, in response to an inquiry from the gay group, denied the group's request to march in the parade under a "Gay Veterans" banner, the Gay Veterans asked the city to revoke the Legion's parade permit. This the city refused to do, although Mayor Koch did send a strongly worded letter to the Legion asking them to reconsider their discriminatory posture. When the Legion refused to answer the Mayor's request, the gay group brought suit in federal district court, asking for an injunction to permit it to march in the parade. The court found no merit to the Gay Veterans' claim that their First Amendment rights had been violated, concluding that the American Legion did not act "under color of law."

The trial judge then offered the following dicta, which suggests to this author that the gay group here may be better off in defeat than it would have been in victory:

> [The city] reserves certain routes, dates, times and places for what have become annual events. For instance, a parade permit is reserved for the New York County Board of the Ancient Order of Hiberians for the St. Patrick's Day Parade on March 17. *A permit will be issued for no parade on Fifth Avenue other than the Gay Pride Parade on the last day of June.* (p. 1516; emphasis added)

Presumably the judge's point is that had he ruled otherwise, had the Gay Veterans won the right to march on Veterans Day, what then would stop the Moral Majority from petitioning for the right to march under its own banner as part of the Gay Pride Parade?

EMPLOYMENT DISCRIMINATION AS A FREE SPEECH ISSUE

That employment discrimination against perceived or actual homosexuals often implicates rights to freedom of speech and association should be seen as a self-evident truth. Generally, employers discover that an employee is lesbian or gay as a result of the latter's "coming out" directly to them (*Childers v. Dallas Police Department*, 1982; *Dorr v. First Kentucky National Bank*, 1986), or to their coworkers (*Rowland v. Mad River School District*, 1984), or as a result of some media attention (*Acanfora v. Board of Education*, 1973; *Gish v. Board of Education*, 1976), or at least some modicum of political activity engaged in by the employee (*Gaylord v. Tacoma School District*, 1977).

Unfortunately, courts have not always been progressive enough to recognize the First Amendment dimensions of anti-gay employment discrimination cases. The small but representative sample of cases to be reviewed here — more thorough treatments of lesbian and gay employment caselaw can be found elsewhere (Friedman, 1979; Rivera, 1979, 1981, 1985) — paints a rather discouraging picture. One very notable exception, however, is the bold step taken by the California Supreme Court in 1979.

Gay Law Students Association v. PT&T (1979) was an ambitious class action suit brought by "past, present, [and] future applicants" for employment with the utility company, which chose not to contest the factual allegations of discriminatory practices but rather to argue that it could not be barred from arbitrary employment discrimination against homosexuals (p. 595). The court's holding was two-pronged. First the court addressed those constitutional and statutory provisions that might prevent PT&T as a heavily regulated and monopolistic utility from engaging in employment discrimination. Employment discrimination by such a utility should not only be reachable by law because it manifested the requisite "state's action," but for other reasons as well. In the truly private sector, the court asserted, there is a market incentive, at least in theory, *not* to engage in arbitrary employment discrimination, lest the best workers vote with their feet and take jobs with your competition. Such an incentive is lacking when the employer at issue effectively has no competition. Moreover, the loss to the aggrieved employee is all the more, since many of the skills needed to be performed by the phone company are needed *only* by the phone company, so the employee will have no other job option. Finally, from the point of view of the public at large, such discrimination is especially odious because the public is deprived of the right to take their business elsewhere in protest over discriminatory practices.

This reasoning led the California Supreme Court to conclude that for a state employer (or one heavily regulated by state) to discriminate against gays would be violative of the state constitution's "equal protection" clause, as well as relevant sections of the state Public Utility Code.

Gay Law Students goes far beyond this holding, however, in that the court also looked to portions of the state's Labor Code ratified by the legislature in the early 1900s, portions of which make it illegal for *any* employer to take punitive actions against employees on the basis of the latter's political activities or affiliations.

The progressiveness of the California court's ruling can be found in Justice Tobriner's ability to see the relevance of the Labor Code to the gay plaintiffs' plight:

> The struggle of the homosexual community for equal rights, particularly in the field of employment, must be recognized as a political activity. Indeed the subject of the rights of homosexuals incites heated political debate today, and the "gay liberation movement" encourages its homosexual members to attempt to convince other members of society that homosexuals should be accorded the same fundamental rights as heterosexuals. . . .
>
> A principal barrier to homosexual equality is the common feeling that homosexuality is an affliction which the homosexual worker must conceal from his employer and his fellow worker. Consequently one important aspect of the struggle for

equal rights is to induce homosexual individuals to "come out of the closet," acknowledge their sexual preferences, and to associate with others in working for equal rights . . .

PT&T has adopted a "policy tending to control or direct the political activities or affiliations of employees" and has attempted to coerce or influence employees to "refrain from adopting a particular course or line of political activity" in violation of [the Labor Code]. (p. 610-611)

Gay Law Students, then, tells us that, at least in California, two things are true: (a) government employers may not discriminate against gays; and (b) *no* employer may discriminate against "open" or "manifest" gays (the only ones presumably involved in the "gay liberation movement" and whose political activism is thus in danger of being stifled). Actually, whether the second prong of the court's holding really would be limited to "manifest" gays was an open question—a gay plaintiff in a later case might argue that she *would have* been more politically active were it not for her fear of retribution, that her speech was "chilled."

Whatever ambiguity remained has been removed by a recently promulgated opinion by John Van de Kamp, California's Attorney General, who ruled (Office of the Attorney General, 1986) that the *Gay Law Students* holding should not be applied only to "manifest" gays:

> Initially, we find it quite improbable that the legislature could have intended that it would be permissible for an employer to discriminate against an employee on the basis of undeclared political beliefs, while at the same time the employer was prohibited from discriminating against an employee on the basis of openly expressed views.
>
> We cannot imagine that the Legislature intended . . . to grant permission to an employer to have a policy permitting discharge of employees on the basis of the employer's belief that an employee is a covert Republican or a secret Democrat . . . If an employer had a policy of discharging employees believed to be secretly associated with the Democratic Party, employees who were actually oriented in that direction would

feel pressured to either declare themselves publicly as Democrats in order to secure the protection of [the] Labor Code
sections for their political affiliation, or to declare themselves
as Republicans in order to placate their employer . . .

We conclude that the legislature's protection for political
activity extends to those who have not made a public issue of
their [sexual] orientation as well as those whose stand is
openly proclaimed. (p. 82)

It is worth noting that the *Gay Law Students* precedent, even
prior to Van De Kamp's opinion, proved a valuable one to young
Tim Curran, who sought not employment but continued affiliation
with the Boy Scouts, which discharged him upon learning of his
sexual preference (*Curran v. Mt. Diablo Council of the Boy Scouts*,
1983). After citing the earlier case for the proposition that coming
out as openly gay is protected political activity, the court found that
the Boy Scout's action was "distinctly contrary to public policy"
and illegal.

Not nearly so fortunate as the plaintiffs in the cases just discussed
was junior high school science teacher Joseph Acanfora. Acanfora's homosexuality came to the attention of his employing Maryland school district when an official of the Pennsylvania Department of Education held a press conference to alert the world that the
Department had decided, after much consideration, to grant Acanfora a Pennsylvania teaching license. (Acanfora had studied at
Pennsylvania State University, where his activism in the gay student group made the state somewhat reluctant to grant him a license; he then moved to Maryland, and obtained a license and a
position there.)

Upon learning of Acanfora's sexual preference, his Maryland
school board promptly transferred him to non-teaching duties – he
was kept at full pay, but was simply given "make-work" to do out
of the company of students. It was at this point that Acanfora filed
suit (*Acanfora v. Board of Education*, 1973; Siegel, 1987). By the
time the case was decided at the trial level, Acanfora had been
discharged. In a complicated ruling, the court concluded that the
initial reaction by the board – the transfer to non-teaching duties –
was unjustifiably arbitrary, but that its later decision to dismiss

Acanfora altogether was justifiable. How could a court have reached such a conclusion?

It seems that, in the interim between the transfer and the dismissal, Acanfora had taken his case to the public. He granted numerous interviews that appeared in both local and national media, including CBS' "60 Minutes." The court expressed much disfavor with Acanfora's new notoriety;

> The instruction of children carries with it special responsibilities whether a teacher be heterosexual or homosexual. The conduct of private life necessarily reflects on the life in public. There exists not only a right of privacy, so strongly urged by the plaintiff, but also a duty of privacy. (p. 855)

Acanfora was able to persuade the appellate court that his media appearances were not valid grounds for dismissal:

> There is no evidence that the interviews disrupted the school, substantially impaired his capacity as a teacher, or gave the school officials reasonable grounds to forecast that those results would flow from what he said. We hold, therefore, that Acanfora's public statements were protected by the first amendment, and that they do not justify . . . the action taken by the school system. (p. 501)

Yet even the appellate court upheld the school board's dismissal of Acanfora. This holding was based upon the manner in which Acanfora had filled out his initial application for employment in Maryland. The form required applicants to furnish information about "professional, service and fraternal organization" memberships and about extracurricular activities engaged in as an undergraduate. Acanfora failed to disclose his affiliation with the gay student group at Penn State. Based upon this omission, the court concluded that he did not have standing to challenge the school board's employment practices:

Acanfora purposely misled the school officials so he could circumvent, not challenge, what he considers to be their unconstitutional employment practices. He cannot now invoke the process of court to obtain a ruling on an issue that he practiced deception to avoid. (p. 504)

The appellate court's ruling is a puzzling one, in that not even passing reference is made to a directly relevant United States Supreme court precedent (*Shelton v. Tucker*, 1960) which struck down as unconstitutional the Arkansas practice of requiring teaching assistants to disclose all of their recent group associations. That requirement, in the Court's words, would tend to "impair a teacher's right of free association, a right closely allied to freedom of speech" (pp. 485-486).

Another gay public school teacher whose sexual orientation became known as a result of his political affiliations was Jim Gaylord, who gave time to a Seattle-based social service organization known as the Dorian Group (*Gaylord v. Tacoma School District*, 1977). When a student at the school where Gaylord taught contacted the Dorian Group for help with his own "coming out," he was referred to Gaylord, who counseled briefly with the student. Unfortunately for Gaylord, discretion was not one of the student's better virtues, and rumors of Gaylord's sexual orientation came to the attention of the school administration. When confronted directly, Gaylord informed his superiors that he was gay, and he was promptly dismissed. In refuting Gaylord's argument that he never proselytized in the classroom, that it was his superiors, and not he, who made an issue of his sexual orientation, the Washington Supreme Court said that "by seeking out homosexual company, he took the risk his homosexuality would be discovered" (p. 855-856).

An intriguing contrast with the *Gaylord* and *Acanfora* cases is found in *Rowland v. Mad River School District* (1984). After nontenured high school guidance counselor Marjorie Rowland "came out" as bisexual to a small number of her coworkers, she was transferred to "non-contact" duties, then not rehired at the end of her contract. The trial court ruled that her freedom of speech had been abridged, but the Circuit Court of Appeals ruled that unlike Joe Acanfora, whose speech might have been protected were it not for his lack of candor in filling out his employment application, Rowland's speech was private and did not touch upon a matter of public concern. It was, therefore, not protected speech. A clear "Catch 22" emerges for the gay school teacher—if she comes out too publicly, she will be fired because of the danger the classroom will be disrupted, but if she comes out quietly and selectively she can be dismissed because her speech was not the kind of speech protected by the First Amendment.

Justice Brennan displayed an awareness of this problem in his opinion dissenting from the United States Supreme Court's decision not to hear the case. Clearly, Brennan thought, speech about sexual orientation *is* speech about a matter of public concern, *is* "core political speech," and *is* protected by the First Amendment. For the school board to argue that gay liberation was not a volatile political issue until Rowland's disclosure made it one strains our credulity, but even if this were so we cannot abide

> a strict rule that an employee's first statement related to a volatile issue of public concern must go unprotected, simply because it is the first statement in the public debate. Such a rule would reduce public employees to second-class speakers, for they would be prohibited from speaking out until and unless others first bring an issue to public attention . . . . It is the *topic* of the speech at issue, and not whether a debate on that topic is yet ongoing, that [should be dispositive]. (p. 1012-1013; emphasis in original)

At least one lesbian teacher has found the old adage that "even when you win, you lose" meaningful. When Peggy Burton acknowledged her lesbianism in response to her superiors' questioning, she was dismissed under a statute providing for exclusion of "immoral persons" from the ranks of public school teachers (*Burton v. Cascade School District*, 1975). The trial court found the statute under which she was disciplined unconstitutionally vague and awarded money damages, but refused to reinstate Ms. Burton to the classroom, fearing possible disruption. One of the judges at the appellate level filed an opinion dissenting from the decision not to reinstate. We are sending the wrong message to the school district, he felt. Instead of putting them on notice that we will not tolerate employment discrimination, we are telling them that they can purchase the right to discriminate for a paltry few thousand dollars (pp. 855-856).

Completing the group of cases here that deal with gay teachers is a controversy that started in the Oklahoma state legislature and ended anticlimactically in the U.S. Supreme Court with a 4-4 tie vote — thus upholding the decision of the court below as good law *in the Tenth Circuit states only (Board of Education v. NGTF, 1985).*

At issue was a state statute that provided for the firing of public school teachers who engage in either "homosexual activity" or "homosexual conduct." The former construct referred to indiscreet acts of sodomy, and would thus hardly be a novel proscription. The free speech relevance of the case becomes apparent when we learn that "homosexual *conduct*" was in turn defined as "advocating, soliciting, imposing, encouraging, or promoting public or private homosexual activity in a manner that creates a substantial risk that such conduct will come to the attention of school children or school employees" (p. 1271).

The trial court judge found no constitutional infirmity in the statute, but the appellate court, whose majority struck down that part of the law dealing with "homosexual conduct," disagreed:

> A teacher who went before the Oklahoma legislature or appeared on television to urge repeal of the Oklahoma anti-sodomy statute would be "advocating," "promoting," and "encouraging" homosexual sodomy . . . even if all he or she said is, "I think it is psychologically damaging for people with homosexual desires to suppress those desires. They should act on those desires and should be legally free to do so." Such statements, which are aimed at legal and social change, are at the core of First Amendment protections. (p. 1274)

Although lesbian and gay teachers seem to comprise a disproportionately high ratio of plaintiffs in employment discrimination cases, they are by no means the only litigants in this area of the law.

For example, both of the gay marriage cases discussed earlier prompted related employment discrimination cases. Thus, plaintiff in the marriage case from the state of Washington, who was dismissed from his job as a clerk-typist for the federal government as a direct result of his activism — including his prior litigation — became plaintiff in *Singer v. U.S. Civil Services Commission* (1977). The Circuit Court of Appeals upheld Singer's dismissal on the grounds that his case "involved the open and public flaunting . . . of homosexual conduct" (p. 256). His employing agency, it was revealed at trial, had written to Singer in his letter of discharge that his "activities in these matters are those of an advocate for a socially repugnant concept" (p. 250, n. 3). The Supreme Court, however, vacated this ruling, and Singer was eventually vindicated (Rivera, 1981, p. 317-319).

Minneapolis gay activist Jack Baker's lover from the *Baker v. Nelson* (1971) marriage case cited earlier was involved in his own employment discrimination suit, this one against the Board of Regents for the University of Minnesota where he was soon expecting appointment as a librarian (*McConnell v. Anderson*, 1971). Although successful at the trial level, James McConnell found a most unreceptive ear on appeal. His was not a claim to a right of freedom of speech, he was admonished; rather, what he sought was the "right to pursue an activist role in implementing his unconventional ideas concerning the societal status to be accorded to homosexuals and thereby to foist tacit approval of the socially repugnant concept upon his employer" (p. 196).

Far more successful was plaintiff in the more recent case of *Van Ooteghem v. Gray* (1982). Van Ooteghem was an assistant county treasurer in the state of Texas, a position that provided flexibility in making his own hours. One day he indicated to his superiors his wish to testify in front of a local county commissioners' meeting on a gay rights issue. The official response was a written memo to him restricting him to the office during regular business hours, the only hours county commission meetings were held. Upon refusing to sign the memo as received, he was dismissed from his job.

Van Ooteghem brought suit, alleging a violation of his First Amendment rights. The Fifth Circuit Court of Appeals granted him reinstatement, back pay, and attorneys' fees. The court offered its view of the dispute:

It may be true that some treasury workers . . . found the prospect of an employee addressing the Commissioners on homosexual rights to be distressing. However, the ability of a member of a disfavored class to express his views on civil rights publicly and without hesitation — no matter how personally offensive to his employer or majority of his coemployees — lies at the core of the Free Speech Clause of the First Amendment. (p. 492-493)

Somewhat less successful was another Texas appellant, in *Childers v. Dallas Police Department* (1982). Childers took a civil service exam to become "storekeeper" for a Dallas Police station. Although he received the highest exam score of all applicants, his personal interview was a disaster. In it, he alerted his prospective employers that he was gay and politically active, that he had a leadership role in the Metropolitan Community Church, and that his male "spouse" was waiting for him in the car. (There was some factual dispute at trial regarding whether these revelations "came out naturally" in the course of the conversation or were thrust upon the Police by Childers.)

Childers' application was not processed further, which prompted his suit. The court allowed that the First Amendment is clearly implicated, but determined that deference must be paid to the employer in this case:

It must be remembered that the governmental entity involved here is the police department of a major metropolitan area. No one can disagree that the character and activities of those to whom we entrust the enforcement of our laws must be beyond reproach . . . The issue of homosexuality is one charged with emotion and anxiety. When activity of the sort in which Childers was involved is undertaken publicly, it undermines the legitimate needs for obedience and discipline within the police department. Such activity will undoubtedly foment controversy and conflict within the department. These considerations, as well as the concern of the police department to protect its public image and to avoid ridicule and embarrassment, are more than sufficient justification for the refusal in this instance to hire an admitted homosexual who actively publicized his lifestyle. (pp. 140-142)

One of the most intriguing and still unsettled questions of law with respect to gay public employees is the amount of deference the courts must pay to the employment policies of federal agencies. Of special note is a 1988 United States Supreme Court case, *Webster v Doe*, wherein Chief Justice Rehnquist wrote for the Court that even the Director of the CIA was not immune from the judicial review of a fired employee's constitutional claims. The employee, whose supervisors consistently rated him "excellent" or "outstanding" in formal evaluations, had been promptly dismissed upon acknowledging his homosexuality to a CIA security officer (p. 2049).

All of the cases in this section reviewed thus far concern employment in the public sector. This should not be surprising, of course. The "American Rule" in employment law — that, in the absence of some statutory rule to the contrary, employers are permitted to hire and fire for any reason whatsoever or for no reason whatsoever — still remains a formidable obstacle to plaintiffs. This is true notwithstanding a slowly evolving tendency among courts to question whether a firing is "against the public interest," as in the dismissal of a "whistleblower" (Lopatka, 1984).

Nonetheless, the literature does reveal a fair number of gay-related employment discrimination cases in the private sector (see Rivera, 1985), and some of these raise intriguing First Amendment issues. In *Dorr v. First Kentucky National Bank* (1986), the relevant clause of the First Amendment dealt with Free Exercise of religion, rather than Free Speech. Sam Dorr was dismissed from his position as manager of the Bardstown Branch of the First National Bank of Louisville, upon his assuming the presidency of the local chapter of Integrity (a group of gay Episcopalians). The trial court dismissed his claim that his discharge was motivated by religious discrimination. The Sixth Circuit Court of Appeals reversed, finding that the proper inquiry should not have been whether Dorr's sincerely held religious beliefs "required" him to become an active member of Integrity (the trial court's approach), but rather only whether they "motivated" him in that direction. The decision of the appellate panel was vacated upon the full court's grant of review. There has been no decision from the full court, however, and apparently Dorr has settled out of court ("Other discrimination law notes," 1986).

In some ways an even more intriguing case is *Madsen v. Erwin* (1984), wherein plaintiff Christine Madsen unsuccessfully fought her firing by the Christian Science Monitor, for whom she had been a reporter for seven years. The Massachusetts Supreme Court dismissed her constitutional claims, largely on the basis that to do otherwise would violate the newspaper's constitutional rights to function as a religious organization. "If Madsen were allowed to collect damages from defendants because she was discharged for being gay," the court held, "defendants would be penalized for their religious belief that homosexuality is a sin for which one must repent." The court refused to dismiss the tortious elements of the case, and granted Madsen her right to a trial on the merits, opining that "a clergyman may not with impunity defame a person, intentionally inflict serious emotional harm on a parishioner, or commit other torts" (pp. 1166-1167).

ASKING FOR IT AND DOING IT: SOLICITATION AND SODOMY STATUTES

Few readers of this journal are unaware of the fact that the United States Supreme Court, in its 1985-86 term, voted 5-4 to uphold Georgia's sodomy statute (*Bowers v. Hardwick*, 1986). The Court's central holding was that the privacy right found implicit in the Constitution two decades previously (*Griswold v. Connecticut*, 1965) did not extend to homosexual relations.

The legal arguments that gay litigants have traditionally hurled against sodomy statutes are that they violate rights of privacy (after *Bowers*, such arguments must be based upon *state* constitution privacy provisions), equal protection, due process (usually because of allegedly vague wording of the statutory prohibition), and even the Eighth Amendment protections from cruel and unusual punishment (an argument Justice Powell indicated in *Bowers* that he might have entertained had it been argued). When the First Amendment is raised at all in such cases, the Establishment Clause, rather than the Free Speech Clause, tends to be the issue, the allegation being that the only plausible state's interest in criminalizing same-sex love-making is an interest in fostering a morality based upon a particular religious ethic, thus "establishing" a state religion (*Baker v. Wade,* 1985).

Still, issues of freedom of expression are plainly implicated by the existence of sodomy statutes. Consider first Justice Douglas' opinion for the Court in *Griswold* (1965), wherein the Supreme Court first recognized a constitutional right to privacy. In overturning a Connecticut statute prohibiting the use or counsel of the use of contraceptive devices, Justice Douglas articulated the view that the "right of privacy" was to be found not in any one specific constitutional provision, but in a combination of provisions. Among these was the First Amendment right to freedom of association (pp. 482-484).

Douglas' opinion describes marriage (Ms. Griswold was convicted of counseling a married couple in the use of contraceptives) as an "association that promotes a way of life, not causes; a harmony in living, not political faiths; a bilateral loyalty, and not commercial or social projects." Despite these distinctions between the institution of marriage and the plainly political associations that were the focus of the early Supreme Court caselaw, Douglas concludes that marriage "is an association for as noble a purpose as any involved in our prior decisions" (p. 486). As Richards (1977) argues, this same freedom of association should extend to "the depth of human significance derived by *lovers* from [their own] association" (p. 1318).

Moving for a moment from the realm of judicial discourse to that of common parlance, it is significant that we speak of "sexual *expression*," as if by the use of the phrase we show an awareness that the sexual act *is*, above all, an act of communication. The equating of sexual activity with communication is a two-fold equation. First, the act itself can reasonably be seen as the non-verbal equivalent of verbal endearments, and can thus plausibly be considered "symbolic" conduct. A touch, a caress, can say "I love you" as or more effectively than the words themselves. Moreover, sexual conduct can be seen as a form of "selective disclosure," an imparting of intimate information about the lover to the loved one. Lovers know much about each other simply because of their status as lovers.

Sexual expression may be seen as First Amendment-relevant for yet another reason. In one of the most often cited treatises on freedom of speech, Emerson (1970) enumerates the functions that this freedom serves, the reasons why it is special and deserving of special protection. One of these reasons offered by Emerson is that the freedom to express oneself is a chief means by which humans achieve self-fulfillment. As British philosopher and jurist H. L. A. Hart points out (1963), much the same argument can be made on behalf of sexual expression. Writing in defense of the Wolfenden Report's call for decriminalization of homosexual behavior, Hart argued that "sexual impulses" are "a recurrent and insistent part of daily life." Moreover, Hart continues, any statute calling upon persons to suppress such sexual impulses would damage "the development or balance of the individual's life, happiness, and personality" (p. 22).

Far less controversial than the notion of sex-as-speech is the proposition that statutes prohibiting the verbal solicitation of "deviant sex" infringe upon the First Amendment. Yet much caselaw defies this truism, finding that such solicitations either border on the obscene, thereby forfeiting First Amendment protection, or fall into the First Amendment exception referred to as "fighting words." Some courts have even made such findings when the sex acts being solicited were themselves quite legal (e.g., *State v. Phipps*, 1979).

The Supreme Court balked at the chance to offer a definitive ruling in this area of the law in 1984. Before it was an appeal it had earlier granted—and which had been briefed and argued—from a New York state decision overturning the solicitation conviction of Robert Uplinger (*New York v. Uplinger*, 1984). The lower court's reasoning, while not clearly articulated, seemed to hinge upon the commonsense proposition that since sodomy was no longer a crime in New York (*People v. Onofre*, 1980), asking another to engage in sodomy could not be criminalized either (Siegel, 1985).

THE ANTI-SPEECH CASES:
A DISTURBING DEVELOPMENT?

The caselaw discussed to this point involved both gay rights claims and free speech claims. Moreover, both claims were raised by the same litigants in virtually every case. (The case against Georgetown University is a possible exception; there, it will be recalled, the university unsuccessfully set forth a "right not to speak" argument.)

There is a body of caselaw, however, in which the gay litigants are on the side of inhibiting, rather than furthering, speech. Libel suits emerging from assertions concerning another's sexual orientation are not unheard of. In one case from New York (*Stein v. Trager*, 1962), a university professor accused one of his former graduate students of being "a homosexual" (as well as "intellectually incompetent," "immoral," "a liar," and a fraudulent researcher). In that the plaintiff was unable to prove tangible damages, the court could only find for him if one of the charges hurled at him by his professor was "libelous per se," in New York restricted to charges of criminal wrongdoing. The only utterance even arguably libelous per se was the imputing of homosexuality, but the court found for the defendant, articulating a distinction between the status of being homosexual (not prohibited by law) and the commission of specific homosexual acts (then a criminal offense in New York).

A more recent libel case from Illinois (*Morricoli v. Schwartz*, 1977), represented the beginning of the end of that state's "innocent construction" libel rule, which had required courts confronting ambiguously worded libelous remarks to interpret the words in their most innocent possible meaning, however strained. Here a nightclub owner who publicly called an aspiring entertainer a "fag" moved for dismissal on the grounds that "fag" has several meanings, most of which are not defamatory. The court denied the motion, refusing to entertain the possibility that defendant intended to call the plaintiff a cigarette, or a British schoolboy.

Oliver Sipple's unsuccessful invasion of privacy suits are noteworthy additional examples of anti-speech actions pursued by a gay litigant. Sipple—who achieved notoriety when he saved President Ford from an assassination attempt—was upset at the media's matter-of-fact reportage of Sipple's homosexuality (*Sipple v. Chronicle Publishing Company*, 1984; *Sipple v. Des Monies Register and Tribune Co.*, 1978). In the more recent case, the court reached the merits of Sipple's privacy arguments, but rejected them for two main reasons. First, Sipple was such an openly gay activist that the media revelation was not publication of "private" facts. Moreover, the story of Sipple's heroism and of President's Ford's failure to offer his thanks to Sipple was deemed highly newsworthy:

> The record shows that the publications were prompted by legitimate political considerations, i.e., to dispel the false public opinion that gays were timid, weak and unheroic figures and to raise the equally important political question whether the President of the United States entertained a discriminatory attitude or bias against a minority group such as homosexuals. (p. 670)

From a pro-speech, civil libertarian perspective, defamation and media invasion of privacy suits are inherently troubling, no more or less so because of the sexual orientation of the plaintiff. This generalization, of course, applies also to situations in which pro-gay speech is the object of a defamation suit, as when Baltimore AIDS activist Stuart Caplan was sued for criticizing a private blood-testing center that sells ID cards "certifying" that the holder is HIV-negative (Harding, 1989).

More troublesome in a sense are those cases in which a valid gay rights claim is articulated, but in a legal posture that necessarily inhibits another's expression. One example of such a case is *Big Brothers, Inc., v. Minneapolis Commission of Civil Rights* (1979). Gary Johnson's interview to become a Big Brother was terminated, and his application delayed, when he admitted his homosexuality. After some internal consultations, the Big Brothers organization decided it would be proper to process Johnson's application, but that whenever the organization sent Johnson's name out to a single mother, it would affirmatively alert her about Johnson's gayness. At trial, Big Brothers produced a multitude of affidavits from local clients who argued that (a) they would want to know the sexual orientation of a prospective Big Brother for their child; and (b) they would — rightly or wrongly — assume that any "big brother" sent to them by the organization is heterosexual, unless otherwise advised.

At issue in *Big Brothers* was whether the organization is more like a "public accommodation" and thus reachable by local anti-discrimination ordinances, or rather nothing more than a conduit between individual "big brothers" and the client/mothers. The Minnesota Supreme Court decided upon the latter model, and ruled against Johnson. The case is a troubling one, from the author's perspective. Clearly it would be unconstitutional to prohibit an un-enlightened parent from excluding gay males from contact with her son in her own home. If we accept the court's holding that Big Brothers served as little more than an extension of the client's private home, we are compelled to accept the legal outcome as correct.

Whereas the *Big Brothers* organization did not refuse to process Johnson's application, the military does, of course, refuse to know-ingly enlist homosexuals. This fact became the central issue in *U.S. v. City of Philadelphia* (1986). A local anti-discrimination ordi-nance was used by the city to attempt to have Temple University ban military recruiters from its campus. The Court of Appeals did not even reach the military's and the university's First Amendment claims, basing its pro-military ruling instead upon the U.S. Consti-tution's Supremacy Clause. (Federal laws and regulations govern-ing the military must supercede any conflicting state or local laws or policies.)

We have seen many cases in which lesbian or gay workers have been fired after coming out on the job, and have also discussed the Oklahoma statute that seemed to make uttering a pro-gay statement an offense calling for termination. At least one recent case has pro-vided what some would see as a modicum of poetic justice, when an appellate court in Wisconsin upheld the firing of a member of the county board of health who made a public anti-gay statement (*Pawlisch v. Barry*, 1985; cf. Freiberg, 1988). In another, more recent incident, the publisher of the Dayton, Ohio *Daily News* was fired by the President of the Cox Newspapers chain for refusing to publish a classified ad from the local Gay Center (Jones, 1988). Still more recently, Andy Rooney was suspended (then prematurely reinstated) from CBS' "60 MINUTES" program as a result of rac-ist and homophobic statements made by him (Hentoff, 1990b).

Anti-speech litigation undertaken by gay or pro-gay litigants has taken on varied shadings in recent years. Two gay graduates of University High School in Irvine, California, obtained a court order temporarily restraining publication of their school's reunion year-book because the publisher refused to include a photo of the gay male couple along with all the heterosexual couples to be pictured ("Newsfront," 1987).

The pro-gay but anti-speech pressure on another anti-gay speaker in California came not from private parties, but from the city council of West Hollywood. Irwin Held, owner of a local restaurant called Barney's Beanery, was persuaded to remove a sign reading "Faggots Stay Out" from the restaurant, under threat of prosecution for violating the city's anti-discrimination ordinance (Mohr, 1988). Although the city council's action here was likely on sound constitutional footing (in *Pittsburgh Press v. Pittsburgh Human Relations Commission*, 1973, the U.S. Supreme Court found that the separate listing of newspaper classified ads under "Help Wanted — Male Interest" and "Help Wanted — Female Interest" *was* itself an act of employment discrimination), one cannot help but wonder if another hypothetical restaurant owner will be forbidden to verbalize *any* anti-gay attitudes even while complying with all applicable anti-discrimination ordinances.

Moving from the situs of the local restaurant to the local radio or television station, we recognize that whether or not the attempt to obtain "equal time" on TV or radio is a pro-speech or an anti-speech act is itself a controversial question ("Fairness Doctrine," 1985; *Meredith Corp. v. FCC*, 1987; Rowan, 1984; *Syracuse Peace Council*, 1987; *Telecommunication Research Action Center and Media Access Project v. FCC*, 1986). This Article contends that such statutory provisions as the Fairness Doctrine, the Equal Time Rule, and the Personal Attack Rule do in fact inhibit free expression. Entreaties to the FCC by anti-gay litigants complaining about pro-gay programming (*in re Brent Buell*, 1985; *in re James Robison Evangelistic Association*, 1981; *People for Better Education v. Station KAKM*, 1976) and by pro-gay litigants complaining about anti-gay programming (Freiberg, 1989; Gross, 1985; *in re Jack Baker*, 1973; *in re Daniel H. Smith*, 1974; *Council on Religion and the Homosexual v. Station KVOF-TV*, 1978; *in re Georgetown University*, 1977; "Newsbriefs," 1986; Vandervelden, 1987b), as well as cases in which listeners invoke the Personal Attack Rule when they feel they or their organizations have been "attacked" by being labeled gay or pro-gay (*in re Mae A. Junod*, 1974) all should be of concern from this perspective, because they will tend to make the media disinclined to cover gay issues at all.

A handful of additional controversies in which the gay advocates' stance may reasonably be seen as anti-speech have played themselves out in recent years on the campuses of some of our most prestigious colleges and universities. The first concerned Teresa Polenz, a student-reporter for the Dartmouth Review, who was charged by the College's Committee on Standards of having violated the school's regulation mandating "lawful and orderly conduct." The Committee's action was prompted by an article Polenz wrote based upon a meeting she attended of the college's Gay Students Association. The GSA was upset because it felt the confidentiality of its meetings had been violated and because Polenz had secretly tape recorded the meeting she attended (a fact that led to an independent investigation by New Hampshire's Attorney General to determine whether the state's wiretap law had been violated).

In that the college made clear to Polenz that its own charges against her would have been brought on the confidentiality issue alone, apart from the charges of clandestine taping, the Dartmouth controversy has much in common with ordinary invasion of privacy suits (*Munson v. Gaylord Broadcasting Company*, 1986). As in Oliver Sipple's suits against various newspapers, the Dartmouth Review would have a strong "newsworthiness" defense, especially in that the newspaper was seeking information from GSA's officers regarding how the gay group was using student funds allotted to it (Freiberg, 1984).

Concerning the breach of confidentiality issue, it is worth noting that nowhere in the Polenz article (1984) does she reveal the names of any of those in attendance at the GSA meeting. Moreover, GSA regularly advertised its meetings in the campus daily paper. As the Dartmouth Review editors coldly but accurately admonished its readers in an insert to Polenz' article, "people wishing to keep private their sexual strife would do well not to attend and speak out at a meeting where the public is invited."

More recently, an official investigation of Michigan State University's College Republicans by that campus's Anti-Discriminatory Judicial Board was instituted at the request of the MSU Lesbian/Gay Council. Prompting the request for the investigation was the Republicans' use of a "Straight Shirt Day" campaign to counteract what they saw as the negative effects of the gay group's annual "Gay Blue Jeans Day" ("Out on campus," 1988a; "Out on campus," 1987b).

The fliers distributed by the Republican club, which charged that "Blue Jeans Day" was a "ridiculous farce" and encouraged its supporters to "fight back" by wearing white shirts, should clearly enjoy First Amendment protection. Perhaps the real irony of the incident is that the gay group did not know how to deal with its own success. After all, the whole purpose of these "Blue Jeans Days" is to force homophobic heterosexuals who might wear blue jeans in the normal course of the day to feel a bit uncomfortable with the sudden attention paid to them and the assumptions made about them. "Blue Jeans Day" exists to make "closet homophobes" register and react to their own prejudices. Perhaps the MSU Lesbian/ Gay Council would have done better to use the counterdemonstrators' actions as grist for their own public education campaign, instead of calling for an investigation of the opposing side.

In another related incident, Yale University sophomore Wayne Dick was placed on two years probation—a sanction that was withdrawn upon appeal—"for drawing and distributing a poster that satirized Yale's annual Gay and Lesbian Awareness Days" ("Yale professors," 1986). C. Vann. Woodward, Chairman of Yale's Committee on Free Expression, acted as Dick's faculty adviser during the appeal process. In a guest editorial for the *New York Times* (Woodward, 1986), he offered these sobering thoughts for anti-speech litigants:

> Free speech skeptics of the present day might . . . reflect that outside the university walls . . . it is not the conservatives but their opponents who most need protection for their right of free speech. It is a principle that has to be applied consistently if it is to be defended at all. And it can be subverted from the left as well as from the right. (p. 27)

Woodward's op-ed piece was cited with approval recently by a federal judge asked to rule on the First Amendment implications of a university anti-harassment policy (*Doe v. University of Michigan*, 1989). The policy was overbroad both as written and as applied, Judge Cohn found. His ruling was based in large part upon one instance reported at trial, in which a social work student had been subject to a formal hearing after he expressed his view in class that homosexuality was a disease.

One reason for concern about these incidents — and related ones at Stanford (Dembart, 1989; Hentoff, 1990a; Lachenauer, 1990) and Harvard (Gold, 1988) — involving anti-speech gay litigants, implicit in Woodward's admonition to the offended Yale students, is the truism that the courts are intended to be counter-majoritarian, that it is the powerless who are most in need of free speech. (I consider all these college incidents "litigation," in that the gay student groups sought the help of an official fact-finding body with the power to impose sanctions.) The same kind of regulation that can be used today against Yale's anti-Gay and Lesbian Awareness protestor can be used next year against lesbians and gays protesting a Supreme Court Justice, or the Pope. Or, in another context, the same well-intentioned statute attempting to provide penalties for "degrading" depictions of women in pornography (*Hudnut v. American Booksellers Association*, 1986), can be turned against feminist supporters; to some juries, *any* depictions of lesbian sexuality are inherently degrading to women.

A related concern is that many of the controversies that spark anti-speech gay litigation tend to be ones where extra-judicial solutions might be preferable. The Gay Veterans group in New York was unsuccessful in its litigation seeking inclusion as part of the American Legion's parade. As it turns out, the Legion chose to change its policy anyway, "which resulted in a group of wet but happy gay vets marching in the November 11 downpour" ("Other discrimination law notes," 1986, p. 73). Recall too that it was protracted political pressure, and not the unsuccessful litigation brought by the owners of a gay bookstore, that persuaded the Bellsouth Corporation to change its policies concerning gay ads in the Yellow Pages. Similarly, gay activists in Urbana/Champaign, Illinois, obtained concessions from the publisher of that community's local newspaper that will permit gay groups to advertise their services; they did this through in-person meetings and public demonstrations, not litigation ("Out on campus," 1987a). And no lawsuits were needed (nor could they have succeeded) to persuade the *New York Times* finally to instruct its reporters that "gay" is to be preferred to "homosexual" as an adjective describing gay men (Freiberg, 1987b).

Litigation is a powerful tool, but it is not the only one available to gay litigants. Moreover, even successful litigation results only in forced compliance, not the level of re-education necessary to produce genuine change in the way that lesbians and gay males are treated by the larger surrounding community (Kelman, 1958).

EFFICACY OF FREE SPEECH: A CONCLUDING NOTE

A white-collar employee who happens to be lesbian arrives at her office one Monday morning, and engages in small talk with her coworkers prior to beginning her workday. "What did you do this weekend?" she is asked. "Nothing too exciting," she replies. "My lover and I spent most of the weekend refinishing furniture."

Has this woman just "flaunted" her homosexuality? Many of her heterosexual coworkers might believe she did, despite the fact that the real subject matter of her reply—other than the use of the word "lover"—dealt with nothing more risque than varnish and sandpaper. Had the woman's sexual orientation been different, and "husband" been substituted for "lover," no one would accuse the woman of flaunting her heterosexuality. (Note too that if we only slightly alter the details of the hypothetical, restricting our focus to office situations in which everyone has known each other for a while, the lesbian worker might be accused of "flaunting" her sexuality simply by making repeated reference over the months or years to "Sally," who may or may not ever be explicitly identified as her "lover.")

This is precisely Gomez's (1983) point in his essay on lesbian and gay "personhood," the expression of which often results in anti-gay epithets and official sanctions. Expressions of heterosexual personhood, in contrast, are "favored socially and legally by tacitly being seen neither as sexual *nor as speech*" (p. 128; emphasis added).

If expressions of heterosexual personhood are not seen even as speech, as Gomez correctly concludes, this must be a function of heterosexuality's ubiquity, its acceptance, its unremarkableness. "When one looks at a cavalcade of engagement and wedding photos, it never even crosses one's mind to think 'gosh, what a slew of heterosexuals'" (Mohr, 1987, p. 97).

Expression of *gay* personhood, then, derives its Free Speech qualities precisely from the unacceptability of same-sex conduct. More simply put, it makes no sense to protest against acceptance. Were we living in a near utopia in which differences in sexual orientation were not only tolerated or accepted, but actually celebrated, it ~~would make no sense to argue for gay rights from a First Amend~~ment perspective.

Recall the landmark California employment case, *Gay Law Students v. PT&T* (1979), in which Justice Tobriner was able to use a free speech analysis precisely because homosexuality is a controversial issue, because "coming out" at work is a defiantly political act. The analysis would collapse if society generally were not homophobic, if PT&T's hiring policies were an aberration.

Recall too the plight of the plaintiff in the Rhode Island prom case (*Fricke v. Lynch*, 1980). Judge Pettine's ruling was based in large part upon Fricke's testimony to the effect that his choice of prom partner was a political statement, that he wanted to say something to his classmates. How strained such an analysis would seem if we were living in that near utopia, if Fricke had no reason in advance to presume that the identity of his escort would produce any repercussions.

None of this should be read so as to negate the assumptions undergirding this Article. Gay rights are, in contemporary American society, a First Amendment issue. But the moment that the gay liberation movement achieves liberation, the free speech claims will lose much of their force. Whatever vestigial and isolated pockets of homophobia and anti-gay discrimination that persist will then be combatted on more intellectually defensible grounds with privacy and equal protection arguments. Fricke should have a right to attend his prom because his choice of partner is no one else's business. Employers should not discriminate against gays because to do so would be fundamentally unfair.

Perhaps, then, the best way to visualize the role played by free speech arguments in gay and lesbian litigation is to analogize it to that played by the plethora of non-profit organizations seeking a cure for a debilitating disease. The rhetoric of such groups, from the

Heart or Lung Associations to the Diabetes Foundation, often suggests that they would like nothing more than to be put out of business, to work themselves out of a job by finding the elusive cure. Similarly, gay rights litigants who make First Amendment claims are also seeking to cure a disease, the one we know as "homophobia." The review of caselaw presented herein suggests that the eventual cure is not currently on the horizon, however, and we can thus expect to see the continued interplay between free speech and gay rights claims in the nation's courtrooms for many years to come.

REFERENCES

Abrams v. U.S., 250 U.S. 616 (1919).
ACLU AIDS Project (1990). AIDS and the Law: ACLU AIDS Docket.
Acanfora v. Board of Education, 359 F. Supp. 843 (1973); aff'd on other grounds, 491 F. 2d 498 (1974), cert. den., 419 U.S. 836 (1974).
Alaska Gay Coalition v. Sullivan, 578 P. 2d 951 (1978).
Ashley v. Ameritech Publishing, #84-420259 (Circ. Ct., Wayne County, MI, 1984).
Ayres, D. (1988, July 9). District of Columbia home rule: The tug of the leash from those on the Hill. New York Times, p. 7.
Baker, P. (1990, February 13). Gay group's ad provokes dissent among student editors. Washington Post, B1.
Baker v. Nelson, 191 N.W. 2d 185 (1971).
Baker v. Wade, 353 F. Supp. 1121 (1982), rev'd, 769 F. 2d 289 (1985).
Berger, R. (1980). Psychological adaptation of the older homosexual male. Journal of Homosexuality, 5, 161-175.
Big Brother, Inc., v. Minneapolis Commission on Civil Rights, 284 N.W. 2d 823 (1979).
Board of Education v. NGTF, #80-1174 (W.D., OK, 1982), aff'd, 729 F. 2d 1270 (1984), aff'd by 4-4 vote, 470 U.S. 903 (1985).
Botkin, M. (1989, November 23). NEA restores AIDS show grant. Bay Area Reporter, p. 26.
Bowers v. Hardwick, 478 U.S. 186 (1986).
Branzburg v. Hayes, 408 U.S. 665 (1972).
Bros, P. (1981, February 5). Letter from IRS manager to the author.
Brown v. Johnson, 743 F. 2d 408 (1984).
Buchanan, G.S. (1985). Same-sex marriage: The linchpin issue. University of Dayton Law Review, 10, 541-573.
Burton v. Cascade School District, 353 F. Supp. 254 (1973), aff'd, 512 F. 2d 850, cert. den. 423 U.S. 839 (1975).

Chibbaro, L. (1989a, October 20). Activists: Armstrong must be challenged in court. *Washington Blade*, p. 3.
Chibbaro, L. (1989b, October 29). Could anything have thwarted the Armstrong amendment? *Washington Blade*, p. 1, 14.
Childers v. Dallas Police Department, 513 F. Supp. 134 (1982), aff'd mem., 669 F. 2d 732 (1982).
Clarke v. United States, 705 F. Supp. 605 (1988), aff'd., 886 F. 2d 404 (1989); vacated, 915 F. 2d 699 (1990).
Cohen v. California, 403 U.S. 15 (1971).
Coleman, E. (1978, January 9). Letter to The Pride Foundation, San Francisco, from IRS official.
Comment: Homosexuals' right to marry: A constitutional test and a legislative solution (1979). *University of Pennsylvania Law Review*, *128*, 193-216.
Congress mandates "overruling" of Georgetown case and letting D.C. insurers test for HIV antibodies (1988). *Lesbian/Gay Law Notes*, p. 55.
Content of AIDS poster angers officials (1990, August 16). *Washington Post*, p. D13.
Council on Religion and the Homosexual v. Station KVOF-TV, 68 FCC 2d 1500 (1978).
Council on Religion and the Homosexual v. PT&T, 70 Cal. PUC 471 (1969).
Curran v. Mt. Diablo Council of the Boy Scouts, 195 Cal. Rptr. 325 (1983).
Dembart, L. (1989, May 5). At Stanford, leftists become censors. *New York Times*, p. 27.
Department of Education v. Lewis, 416 So. 2d 455 (1982).
District Director (1976, March 25). Letter from IRS to Lambda Service Bureau.
Doe v. University of Michigan, 721 F. Supp. 852 (1989).
Dorr v. First Kentucky National Bank, 41 FEP Cases 423 (1986), pet. for reh. granted, 796 F. 2d 179 (1986).
Dressler, J. (1979). Judicial homophobia: Gay rights' biggest roadblock. *Civil Liberties Review*, *1979*, 19-27.
Dun and Bradstreet v. Greenmoss Builders, 472 U.S. 749 (1985).
Emerson, T. (1970). *The system of freedom of expression*. New York: Random House.
Enforcement of prohibitions against broadcast obscenity and indecency. 47 CFR 52425 (1988).
Exler v. Disneyland, #342021 (Superior Ct., Orange County, CA., 1984).
Fairness Doctrine, 102 FCC 2d 145 (1985).
Fauntlcroy, J. (1986, September 7). Ma lets queer fingers walk, too. *Gay Community News*, p. 2.
Federal censorship commission (1987, May 12). *Advocate*, p. 19.
Fowler, P. & Graff, L. (1985). Gay aliens and immigration: Resolving the conflict between *Hill* and *Longstaff*. *University of Dayton Law Review*, *10*, 621-644.
Francois, W.E. (1986). *Mass media law and regulation*. New York: Macmillan.
Freeman v. Hittle, 747 F. 2d 1299 (1984).

Freiberg, P. (1984, September 18). Secret antigay taping at Dartmouth. *Advocate*, p. 57.

Freiberg, P. (1987a, March 3). Rural gay group sues Wisconsin newspaper. *Advocate*, p. 13.

Freiberg, P. (1987b, July 21). The New York Times finally okays use of "Gay." *Advocate*, p. 14-15.

Freiberg, P. (1988, July 19). Classified material: Publisher fired after rejecting Ohio AIDS group's safe-sex ad. *Advocate*, p. 12.

Freiberg, P. (1989, September). Philadelphia gays ask FCC to yank city's TV permits. *Advocate*, p. 10.

Fricke v. Lynch, 491 F. Supp. 381 (1980).

Fricke, A. (1981). *Reflections of a rock lobster*. Boston: Alyson Publications.

Friedman, J. (1979). Constitutional and statutory challenges to discrimination in employment based on sexual orientation. *Iowa Law Review, 64*, 527-572.

Gay Activists Alliance v. Lomenzo, 320 N.Y.S. 93 (1971), rev'd 329 N.Y.S. 181 (1972), aff'd, 341 N.Y.S 108 (1973).

Gay Activists Alliance v. Washington Metro., #78-2217 (U.S. Dist. Ct., DC, 1979).

Gay Alliance of Students Association v. Matthews, 544 F. 2d 162 (1976).

Gay and Lesbian Students Association v. Gohn, 656 F. Supp. 1045 (1987), rev'd, 850 F. 2d 361 (1988).

Gay Law Students Association v. PT&T, 595 P. 2d 592 (1979).

Gay Lib v. University of Missouri, 538 F. 2d 848 (1977), cert. den., 434 U.S. 1080 (1978).

Gay Rights Coalition of Georgetown University Law Center v. Georgetown University, 496 A. 2d 567 (1985), vacated, 496 F. 2d 587 (1985), aff'd in part, rev'd in part, 536 A. 2d 1 (1987).

Gay Student Services v. Texas A&M University, 737 F. 2d 1317 (1984), cert. den., 471 U.S. 1120 (1985).

Gay Students Association v. Bonner, 367 F. Supp. 1088 (1974), aff'd, 509 F. 2d 652 (1974).

Gay Students Association v. University of South Carolina, #82-3030-0 (U.S. Dist. Ct., SC, 1983).

Gay Veterans Association v. American Legion, 621 F. Supp. 1510 (1985).

Gaylord v. Tacoma School District, 559 P. 2d 1340 (1977).

Gish v. Board of Education, 366 A. 2d 1337 (1976), pet. for cert. den., 377 A. 2d 658 (1977), cert. den., 434 U.S. 899 (1977).

Gold, A. (1988, October 12). At Harvard, guidelines on speech and dissent. *New York Times*, p. 24.

Gomez, J. (1983). The public expression of lesbian/gay personhood as protected speech. *Law and Inequality, 1*, 121-153.

Granelli, J. (1984, May 19). Disneyland ban on same-sex dancing upset. *Los Angeles Times*, Sec II, pp. 1, 8.

Griswold v. Connecticut, 381 U.S. 479 (1965).

Gross, M. (1985, November 15). Letter to M. Inyang of Philadelphia Lesbian and Gay Task Force.

Gutis, P. (1987, January 21). Homosexuals winning some custody cases. *New York Times*, pp. 13, 15.

Harding, R. (1989, April 23). HIV test firm sues activist over interview. *Advocate*, p. 12.

Harding, R. (1988, May 10). Georgetown University won't fight pro-gay ruling. *The Advocate*, p. 20.

Hart, H.L.A. (1963). *Law, liberty and morality*. Stanford: Stanford University Press.

Hatheway v. Gannett Satellite Information Network, #86CV3650 (Circ. Ct. of Dane County, Wisconsin, 1989), aff'd. 459 N.W. 2d 873 (Ct. of Appeals of Wisconsin, 1990).

Hays, C. (1989, January 18). Gay group wins phone listing in Yellow Pages. *New York Times*, p. 13.

Hentoff, N. (1990a, July 21). Stanford and the thought police. *Washington Post*, p. A19.

Hentoff, N. (1990b, February 13). Tuning out Andy Rooney. *Washington Post*, A21.

Hudnut v. American Booksellers Association, 475 U. S. 1001 (1986).

in re Jack Baker, 41 FCC 2d 727 (1973).

in re Brent Buell, 97 FCC 2d 55 (1984).

in re Georgetown University, 66 FCC 2d 944 (1977).

in re Mae A. Junod, 50 FCC 2d 121 (1974).

in re James Robison Evangelistic Association, 85 FCC 2d 642 (1981).

in re Daniel H. Smith, 44 FCC 2d 773 (1974).

in the matter of Pacifica Foundation, 2 FCC Rcd. 2698 (1987).

Inosencio v. Johnson, 547 F. Supp. 130 (1982), aff'd sub nom. Brown vs. Johnson, 743 F. 2d 408 (1984).

Jacobs, J. & Tedford, W. (1980). Factors affecting the self-esteem of the homosexual individual. *Journal of Homosexuality*, *5*, 373-382.

Jones, A. (1988, June 16). Publisher is dismissed over ad ban. *New York Times*, p. 21.

Kane, R. (1989, October 13). Newspaper can refuse ads. *Washington Blade*, p. 18.

Karst, K. (1980). The freedom of intimate association. *Yale Law Journal*, *89*, 624-692.

Kastor, E. (1989, November 16). Bernstein rejects medal in arts controversy. *Washington Post*, pp. A1, A23.

Kelman, H. (1958). Compliance, identification and internalization. *Journal of Conflict Resolution*, *2*, 51-60.

Kristie v. Oklahoma City, 572 F. Supp. 88 (1983).

L. v. D., 630 S.W. 2d 240 (1982).

Lachenauer, K. (1990, July 28). A debate devalued. *Washington Post*, p. A17.

Lieblich, A. & Friedman, G. (1985). Attitudes toward male and female homosexuals and sex role stereotypes in Israeli and American students. *Sex Roles, 12*, 561-570.

Lopatka, K. (1984). The emerging law of wrongful discharge. *Business Lawyer, 40*, 1-32.

Loring v. Bellsouth Advertising and Publishing Company, 339 S.E. 2d 372 (1986).

M.P. v. S.P., 404 A. 2d 1257 (1979).

MacDonald, A.P., & Games, R.G. (1974). Some characteristics of those who hold positive and negative attitudes toward homosexuals. *Journal of Homosexuality, 1*, 9-27.

Madsen v. Erwin, 481 N.E. 2d 1160 (1984).

Manual Enterprises v. Day, 289 F. 2d 455 (1960), rev'd, 370 U.S. 478 (1962).

Masters, K. (1990a, June 20). Trial set for Mapplethorpe obscenity case. *Washington Post*, p. D2.

Masters, K. (1990b, June 30). Under pressure from critics, arts agency rejects 4 grants. *Washington Post*, p. A1.

Matthews v. Marsh, 755 F. 2d 182 (1985).

McConnell v. Anderson, 316 F. Supp. 809 (1970), rev'd, F. 2d 193 (1971).

McDonald, G. (1982). Individual differences in the coming out process for gay men: Implications for theoretical models. *Journal of Homosexuality, 8*, 47-60.

McDonald, S. (1984, June 26). Los Angeles lesbians relish restaurant victory as court opens door to private booths. *Advocate*, p. 10.

Meredith Corp. v. FCC, 809 F. 2d 863 (1987).

Middleton, K.R. & Chamberlin, B.F. (1988). *The law of public communication*. White Plains, NY: Longman.

Miscellaneous news notes. (1986, October). *Lesbian/Gay Notes*, p. 59-60.

Mishkin v. New York, 383 U.S. 502 (1966).

Mississippi Gay Alliance v. Goudelock, 536 F. 2d 1073 (1976).

Mohr, R. (1988). *Gays/justice: Moral, social and legal ideas*. New York: Columbia University Press.

Mohr, R. (1987). Mr. Justice Douglas at Sodom. *Columbia Human Rights Law Review, 18*, p. 43-110.

Morricoli v. Schwartz, 361 N.E. 2d 74 (1977).

Munson v. Gaylord Broadcasting Company, 491 So. 2d 780 (1986).

Near v. Minnesota, 283 U. S. 697 (1931).

New York v. St. Mark's Baths, 130 Misc. 2d 911 (1986).

New York v. Uplinger, 447 N.E. 2d 62 (1983), cert. dism. as improv. granted, 467 U. S. 246 (1984).

Newsbriefs (1986, December 23). *Advocate*, p. 26.

Newsbriefs (1987, January 20). *Advocate*, p. 26.

Newsfront (1987, November 24). *Advocate*, p. 24.

Newsfront (1988, March 29). *Advocate*, p. 21.

Office of the Attorney General of California (1986, April 30). 69 Op. Atty. Gen. Cal. 80.

Olivieri v. Ward, 637 F. Supp. 851, aff'd as modified, 801 F. 2d 602 (1986).

111 Wines and Liquors v. Division of Alcoholic Beverage Control, 235 A. 2d 12 (1967).

Other discrimination law notes. (1986, December). *Lesbian/Gay Law Notes*, p. 73.

Out on campus. (1988a, February 16). *Advocate*, p. 23.

Out on campus. (1988b, August 30). *Advocate*, p. 32.

Out on campus. (1987a, May 12). *Advocate*, pp. 21-27.

Out on campus. (1987b, August 4). *Advocate*, p. 21.

Paruohlnl, A. (1990, November 4). Victory, but no relief. *Los Angeles Times*, p. 4.

Pawlisch v. Barry, 376 N.W. 2d 368 (1985).

Pember, D. (1987). *Mass media law*. Dubuque, IA: Wm. C. Brown.

People v. Onofre, 415 N.E. 2d 936 (1980).

People for Better Education v. Station KAKM, 58 FCC 2d 1220 (1976).

Pittsburgh Press v. Pittsburgh Human Relations Commission, 413 U.S. 376 (1973).

Polenz, T. (1984, May 14). An inside look at the GSA. *Dartmouth Review*, p. 9.

Pope v. Illinois, 481 U. S. 497 (1987).

Raggi, R. (1977). An independent right to freedom of association. *Harvard Civil Rights-Civil Liberties Law Review*, *12*, 1-30.

Rand, C., Graham, D., & Rawlings, E. (1982). Psychological health and factors the court seeks to control in lesbian mother custody cases. *Journal of Homosexuality*, *8*, 27-39.

Red Lion Broadcasting v. FCC, 395 U.S. 367 (1969).

Reynolds, W. (1980). The Immigration and Nationality Act and the rights of homosexual aliens. *Journal of Homosexuality*, *5*, 79-87.

Richard, P. (1989, August 30). Artists cancel exhibitions at Corcoran. *Washington Post*, pp. A1, A9.

Richards, D. (1977). Unnatural acts and the constitutional right to privacy: A moral theory. *Fordham Law Review*, *45*, 1281-1348.

Richards, D. (1986). Constitutional privacy and homosexual love. *New York University Review of Law and Social Change*, *14*, 895-905.

Rivera, R. (1979). Our straight-laced judges: The legal position of homosexual persons in the United States. *Hastings Law Journal*, *30*, 799-955.

Rivera, R. (1981). Recent developments in sexual preference law. *Drake Law Review*, *30*, 311-346.

Rivera, R. (1985). Queer law: Sexual orientation law in the mid-eighties, part I. *University of Dayton Law Review*, *10*, 459-540.

Rivera, R. (1986). Queer law: Sexual orientation law in the mid-eighties, part II. *University of Dayton Law Review*, *11*, 275-398.

Robertson v. Anderson, #4-83-420 (U.S. Dist. Ct., Minn., 1985).

Rolan v. Kulwitsky, 200 Cal. Rptr. 217 (1984).

Rowan, F. (1984). *Broadcast fairness: Doctrine, practice, prospects*. New York: Longman.

258   *GAY PEOPLE, SEX, AND THE MEDIA*

Rowland v. Mad River School District, 730 F. 2d 444 (1984), cert. den., 470 U.S. 1009 (1985), reh. den., 471 U.S. 1062 (1985).
San Francisco Arts and Athletics, Inc. v. United States Olympic Committee, 483 U.S. 522 (1987).
Scarlett v. Scarlett, 390 A. 2d 1331 (1978).
Schuster v. Schuster, 1 Family Law Reporter 2004 (1974).
Shade, C. (1984, July 10). 2 men win right to dance together at Disneyland. *Advocate*, p. 6.
Shelton v. Tucker, 364 U.S. 479 (1960).
Siegel, P. (1981). Androgyny, sex role rigidity, and homophobia. In J.W. Cheesbro (Ed.), *Gayspeak: Gay male and lesbian communication* (pp. 142-152, 336-339). New York: Pilgrim Press.
Siegel, P. (1985). Laws against doing it and laws against saying it: The upshot of *Uplinger v. New York*. *Free Speech Yearbook, 24*, pp. 94-104.
Siegel, P. (1987). Protecting political speech: *Brandenburg v. Ohio* updated. In T. Tedford, J. Makay, and D. Jamison, (Eds.), *Perspectives on freedom of speech* (pp. 136-153, 285-87). Carbondale: Southern Illinois University Press.
Singer v. Hara, 522 P. 2d 1187 (1974).
Singer v. U.S. Civil Service Commission, 530 F. 2d 247 (1976), vacated, 429 U.S. 1034 (1977).
Sinn v. Daily Nebraskan, 638 F. Supp. 143 (1986), aff'd., 829 F. 2d 662 (1987).
Sipple v. Chronicle Publishing Company, 201 Cal. Rptr. 665 (1985).
Sipple v. Des Moines Register and Tribune Company, 147 Cal. Rptr. 59 (1978).
Society for Individual Rights v. PT&T, 71 Cal. PUC 662 (1970).
Solmitz v. Maine School Administrative District, 495 A. 2d 812 (1985).
State, ex rel., v. Brown, 313 N.E. 2d 842 (1974).
State v. Phipps, 389 N.E. 2d 1128 (1979).
Stein v. Trager, 36 Misc. 227 (1962).
Stoumen v. Reilly, 234 P. 2d 969 (1951).
Student Coalition for Gay Rights v. Austin Peay State University, 477 F. Supp. 1267 (1979).
Student Services for Lesbians/Gays v. Texas Tech University, 635 F. Supp. 776 (1986).
Susoeff, S. (1985). Assessing children's best interests when a parent is gay: Toward a rational custody standard. *UCLA Law Review, 32*, 852-903.
Syracuse Peace Council. 2 F.C.C. Rcd. 5043 (1987).
Taylor, S. (1988, January 12). Supreme Court roundup. *New York Times*, p. 6.
Telecommunication Research Action Center and Media Access Project v. FCC, 801 F. 2d 517, pet. for reh. den., 806 F. 2d 1115 (1986).
Tinker v. Community School District, 399 U.S. 503 (1969).
Toward a Gayer Bicentennial Committee v. Rhode Island Bicentennial Foundation, 417 F. Supp. 632 (1976).
U.S. v. City of Philadelphia, 798 F. 2d 81 (1986).
Vallerga v. Department of Alcoholic Beverage Control, 347 P. 2d 909 (1959).

Van Ooteghem v. Gray, 628 F. 2d 488 (1980), aff'd en banc, 654 F. 2d 304 (1982).

Vandervelden, M. (1987a, May 12). FCC seeks to prosecute L.A. radio station for broadcasting allegedly indecent gay play. *Advocate*, p. 16.

Vandervelden, M. (1987b, May 12). Gay man loses Dallas Council bid, wins free TV time. *Advocate*, p. 16.

Wallace v. Jaffree, 472 U.S. 38 (1985).

Webster v. Doe, 486 U.S. 592 (1988).

Weinberger, L. & Millham, J. (1979). Attitudinal homophobia and support of traditional sex roles. *Journal of Homosexuality, 4*, 237-245.

Weintraub, J. (1990, June 2). Iowa press turns down NEA grant. *Washington Post*, p. C9.

Westheimer, K. (1985, December 14). Fingers do the walking. *Gay Community News*, p. 2.

Whitney v. California, 274 U.S. 357 (1927).

Wood v. Davison, 351 F. Supp. 543 (1972).

Woodruff v. Woodruff, 260 S.E. 2d 775 (1979).

Woodward, C.V. (1986, October 15). Freedom of speech, not selectively (guest editorial). *New York Times*, p. 27.

Yale professors backing sophomore. (1986, September 29). *New York Times*, p. 15.

Zauderer v. Office of Disciplinary Council, 471 U.S. 626 (1985).

Zurcher v. Stanford Daily, 436 U.S. 547 (1978).

Gays, Lesbians, and the Media: A Selected Bibliography

Fred Fejes, PhD

Florida Atlantic University

SUMMARY. The focus of this selected bibliography is on print, aural, and visual resources dealing with gay males, lesbians, and the mass media. Listings were selected on the basis of their perceived value to scholarly researchers and interested members of the more general public. Individual news stories, reviews of specific films or television programs, and coverage of gay males and lesbians in the theatre and arts are not included. While references to popular music were sought, only a few items were located and are included. There were two major obstacles confronted when compiling this bibliography. First, much of the media of the gay and lesbian communities in the United States is not indexed. Second, very few libraries subscribe to many of the more popular and important print resources (e.g., *Advocate, Gay Community News*) on the topics of focus. Even more inaccessible are regional publications and literature that focus on erotica but often include valuable items on the gay and lesbian communities as well.

Fred Fejes is a 1982 graduate of the Institute of Communication Research at the University of Illinois and has taught at the University of Illinois and Wayne State University. He is currently Associate Professor in the Department of Communication at Florida Atlantic University.

Comments and inquiries may be addressed to him in care of Department of Communication, Florida Atlantic University, Boca Raton, FL 33486.

The following indices were consulted for this bibliography:

> *Alternative Press Index 1969-1983*
> *Business Index 1979-1986*
> *Communication Abstracts 1978-1986*
> *Film Literature Index 1980-1984*
> *Humanities Index 1980-1986*
> *International Index to Film Periodicals 1980-1985*
> *MLA International Bibliography 1981-1985*
> *Public Affairs Information Service 1980-1986*
> *Readers' Guide to Periodical Literature 1980-1986*
> *Resources in Education (ERIC) 1980-1986*
> *Social Sciences Index 1980-1986*
> *Sociological Abstracts 1980-1986*

In addition use was made of William Parker's superb and comprehensive three-volume bibliography on homosexuality (*Homosexuality: A Selective Bibliography of over 3,000 Items*. Metuchen, NJ, and London: Scarecrow Press, 1985; *Homosexuality Bibliography, Second Supplement 1976-1982*. Metuchen, NJ, and London: Scarecrow Press, 1985; *Homosexuality Bibliography: Supplement. 1970-1975*. Metuchen, NJ, and London: Scarecrow Press, 1977). This work is an invaluable tool for anyone doing research on the gay and lesbian community in the United States. Also consulted was Martin Weinberg and Alan Bell's *Homosexuality: An Annotated Bibliography*. New York: Harper and Row, 1972.

Items were selected on the basis of their perceived general value. This bibliography is weighted towards the print and visual media. As a rule individual news stories, reviews of individual movies or TV shows, and items dealing with gays in the theater and arts were not included. Although the topic, gays and popular music, was included in the search, few items were located.

One major obstacle in compiling this bibliography, and an obstacle confronting anyone doing research on the gay and lesbian community in the United States, is the fact that much of our own media is not indexed. Only the *Alternative Press Index* has included gay publications, among them the *Advocate* and the *Gay Community*

News. Unfortunately, many of the articles appearing in other gay publications about gays and the media are only included in this bibliography if contained in one of the above bibliographies. One would hope that in the future publishers of gay media would make a greater effort to have their publications included in the major indices.

Another obstacle confronting the researcher is that very few libraries, even major research and archival libraries subscribe to gay publications like the *Advocate, Christopher Street,* and *Gay Community News.* Publications that are more regional in scope or whose major focus is erotica but which nonetheless contain numerous valuable articles about the gay and lesbian community are even more inaccessible. It may take a concerted effort on the part of the local community to get the local library to subscribe at least to gay and lesbian publications, but it is well worth it.

These above issues represent more than just a problem to a scholarly researcher. The larger issue is one of demanding that our community and its experience and history, as contained in the pages of our media, be recognized by the larger systems of knowledge production in our society. Equally important is the need of keeping an account and record of our experience as a community that can be accessible to those in the future.

BIBLIOGRAPHY

A

A gay news chronology: January 1969-May 1975: Index and abstracts of articles from the New York Times. (1975). New York: Arno Press.

Advertising directed to gays. (1982, May 25). *San Francisco Chronicle*, p. 15.

Albert, E. (1986). Acquired Immune Deficiency Syndrome: The victim and the press. In T. McCormick (Ed.), *Studies in communication* (Vol. 3) (pp. 135-158). Greenwich, CT: Jai Press.

Alfred, R. (1982, January 2). Lesbian bites dog, more at 11: Gays in the news. *Advocate*, p. 31.

AIDS in sweep time. (1985 September-October). *Channels of Communication*, p. 6.

Aitken, W. (1975). Bertolucci's gay images. *Jump Cut, 16,* 23.

Anderson, S. (1979, December 13). The gay press proliferates: And so do its problems. *Advocate,* pp. 19-20.

Atwell, L. (1966, March, April). Homosexual themes in the cinema. *Tangents,* pp. 4-10; pp. 4-9.

Atwell, L. (1982, Winter). 'Word is Out' and 'Gay USA.' *Film Quarterly, 32,* 50-57.

B

Battling for objectivity. (1984, June 9). *Editor and Publisher*, p. 20.

Becker, E. (1981). Lesbians and film. *Jump Cut, 24/25,* 17.

Bearchell, C. (1982). Trading in secrets: The making of a TV documentary (On homosexuality in Canada). In E. Jackson & Persky, S. (Eds.), *Flaunting it! A decade of gay journalism from the Body Politic* (pp. 111-121). Toronto: Pink Triangle Press.

Biskind, P., & Ehrenreich, B. (1980). Machismo and Hollywood's working class. *Socialist Review, 50,* 109-130.

Block, A. (1985, November 26). An Early Frost: The story behind NBC's AIDS drama. *Advocate,* pp. 42-49.

Body Politic acquitted for third time. (1982, December). *Body Politic,* p. 11.

Braudy, S. (1979, December). The 'Cruising' controversy: Gay activists protest media violence. *Ms.,* p. 34.

Britton, A. (1977). Fox and his friends. *Jump Cut, 16,* 22.

Bronski, M. (1984). *Culture clash: The making of gay sensibility.* Boston: South End Press.

Byron, S. (1972, September 21). Gay news and the *New York Times*: An indelicate balance. *Village Voice,* pp. 1, 24, 26.

C

Censorship kills gay magazine in Brazil. (1982, May 22). *Gay Community News*, p. 1.

Charbonneau, C., & Winer, L. (1981). Lesbians in nice films. *Jump Cut, 24/25,* 25.

Chauncey, D.E. (1980). *Pro-gay media: An annotated media-graphy of non-print materials, 1969-1979.* (ERIC Document Reproduction Service No. Ed 201 914.)

Chesebro, J.W. (Ed.). (1981). *Gayspeak: Gay male and lesbian communication.* New York: The Pilgrim Press.

Circulation of magazines for gay males grows in size and publishers seek national advertisers. (1976, July 13). *New York Times*, p. 55.

Clarens, C. (1982, May/June). Masculine/feminine, feminine/masculine. *Film Comment*, pp. 18-19.

Cody, B. (1968, August). How the movies got gay . . . and gayer . . . and gayer. *Los Angeles Advocate*, pp. 16-19.

Cohn, S.F., & Gallagher, J.E. (1984). Gay movement and legal change: Some aspects of the dynamics of a social problem. *Social Problems, 32(1)*, 72-86.

Collins, M. (1967). A history of homosexuality in the movies. *Drum, 27*, 12-21, 30-32.

Connor, E. (1981). Film in drag: Transvestism on the screen. *Films in Review, 32*, 398-405.

Conrad, P. (1981, December 4). Conspicuous liberation. *Times Literary Supplement*, p. 1423.

Coon, E.A. (1957). Homosexuality in the news. *Archives of Criminal Psychodynamics, 2(4)*, 843-865.

Copely, U. (Ed.). (1975). *Directory of homosexual organizations and publications annotated.* Hollywood, CA: Homosexual Information Center.

Corzine, H.J. (1977). The gay press. (Doctoral dissertation, Washington University, 1977). *Dissertation Abstracts International, 38*, 7606A.

Crew, L. (1975, May). Protest and community: Gay male journalism now. *Margins*, pp. 14-21.

D

Dace, T. (1986, January 2). The Color Purple: Removing lavender from the movie. *Advocate*, p. 54.

Dallas TV explores local gay world. (1971, October 13). *Advocate*, p. 2.

DeStefano, G. (1985, September 17). Does G.Q. hate gay men? *Advocate*, p. 26.

Destefano, G. (1986, December 9). *The New York Times* vs. gay America. *Advocate*, p. 42.

DeVere, J. (1976, December). Gay images: Television and film. *Mandate*. pp. 10-11.

Dey, W. (1979, February 26). The boys in the band play on (trial of publishers of *Body Politic*, a gay journal). *Maclean's*, p. 26.

Director of gay film touring U.S. colleges with complications. (1976, June 2). *Variety*, p. 7.

Does it take men to sell women: The homosexual in advertising. (1964, June 26). *Printers Ink*, p. 52.

Drew, P. (1986, June 7). Alternative market: Low ratings, high profit (gay radio). *Billboard*, p. 19.

Durham, C.A. (1982). 'La Cage aux Folles': The inversion of laughter. *Jump Cut*, 27, 4.

Dvosin, A. (1975, May). Faggot culture quarterlies. *Margins*, pp. 21-23.

Dyer, R. (1977). Homosexuality and film noir. *Jump Cut*, 16, 18.

Dyer, R. (1985). Male gay porn: Coming to terms. *Jump Cut*, 30, 27-29.

Dyer, R. (1983, Spring). Review essay: Vito Russo and *The celluloid closet. Visual Communication*, pp. 52-56.

Dyer, R. (1983, Spring). Seen to be believed: Some problems in the representation of gay people as typical. *Visual Communication*, pp. 2-19.

Dyer, R. (Ed.). (1977, revised edition 1984). *Gays and film*. London: British Film Institute; New York: Zoetrope.

E

Editorial: Gay liberation. (1981). *Jump Cut*, 24/25, 58.

Edwards, D. (1980, February 7). Gay and the art of motion picture making. *Advocate*, pp. 28-32.

Ehrenstein, D. (1980). Within the pleasure principle or irresponsible homosexual propaganda. *Wide Angle*, 4(1), 62-65.

Eisenstark, D. (1981). Editorial: Lesbian feminism. *Jump Cut*, 24/25, 59-60.

F

Faber, C. (1983, September 14). Taking the wraps off gay media. *Advocate*, p. 45.

Farber, S. (1981, September). From sissies to studs. *American Film*, p. 72.

Farber, S. (1981, September). Hollywood comes out of the closet. *Saturday Review*, p. 48.

Fain, N. (1983, September 29). Rating crisis coverage (AIDS/Media). *Advocate*, p. 24.

Fain, N. (1983, September 16). The gay press association. *Advocate*, p. 27.

F.C.C. ruling appealed: Pacifica question obscenity charge. (1987, June 9). *Advocate*, p. 15.

F.C.C. seeks to prosecute L.A. radio station for broadcasting allegedly indecent gay play. (1987, May 26). *Advocate*, p. 16.

Fleming, M. (1983). Looking for what isn't there. *Jump Cut, 28*, 59-61.

Fisher, H. (1978). *Gay semiotics: A photographic study of visual coding among homosexual men.* Berkley, CA: NFS Press.

French ultra-rightists break up gay film fest. (1978, February 8). *Variety*, p. 1.

G

Galligan, D. (1982, April 15). Making public, making love. *Advocate*, p. 30.

Garfield, K. (1986, January 18). 'Desert Hearts': A lesbian love story heats up the silver screen. *Advocate*, p. 43.

Garfield, K. (1981, October 15). The filming of 'Partners.' *Advocate*, p. 45.

Garfield, K. (1987, January 20). The Front Runner makes it to the screen. *Advocate*, pp. 52-54.

Gay film seized in campus fuss. (1972, April 12). *Advocate*, p. 8.

Gay journalists caucus forms at District of Columbia convention. (1973, July 4). *Advocate*, p. 18.

Gay press association formed. (1981, February 19). *Advocate*, p. 9.

Gay-themed features hot B.O. stuff: Mainstream more accepting. (1986, April 9). *Variety*, p. 5.

Gay/Lesbian Task Force, Council of Social Education Work (1984). *Annotated filmography of selected films with lesbian/gay content*. (ERIC Document Reproduction Service No. ED 250 230.)

Gays: A major force in the market place. (1979, September 3). *Business Week*, p. 118.

Gays protest 'Marcus Welby' TV show. (1973, March 14). *Advocate*, pp. 1,21.

Gay, straights, film and the left. (1977). *Jump Cut*, *16*, 27.

Gays zap CBS network center. (1974, April 10). *Advocate*, p. 1.

Gays zap Dr. David Reubin on Chicago TV Show. (1971, March 1). *Advocate*, p. 1.

Gelman, D. (1975, October 20). Gays and the press. *Newsweek*, p. 93.

Gerson, P. (1977, August). Homosexuality on television. *Christopher Street*, pp. 47-49.

Gever, M., & Magnan, N. (1986). The same difference: On lesbian representation. *Exposure*, *24/2*, 27-35.

Gitlin, T. (1983, October 15). When the right talks, TV listens. *The Nation*, p. 333.

Gladue, B.A. (1984, December 7). Values, research questions and the news media (News coverage of AIDS research). *Science*, p. 1142.

Goldstein, R. (1982, December 7). Gay new wave (recent gay movies). *Village Voice*, pp. 48-48.

Gooch, B. (1985, July 23). The demise of the gay model. *Advocate*, p. 45.

Gould, R.E. (1973, October). Homosexuality on television. *Medical Aspects of Human Sexuality*, *7*, 116-127.

Graham, A. (1980, Fall). 'Outrageous' and 'Boys in the Band': The possibilities and limitations of coming out. *Film Criticism*, pp. 36-42.

Grenier, R. (1984, September). Movies: From Eton to Havana. *Commentary*, pp. 61-64.

Greyson, J. (1985). Home video. *Jump Cut*, *30*, 36-38.

Gross, L. (1976, February 22). Television under pressure: Are a handful of activists serving or wrecking the medium? *TV Guide*, pp. 4-7.

Guthmann, E. (1986, January 7). Delicious Dynasty: The behind the scenes story of a television phenomenon. *Advocate*, p. 43.

Guthmann, E. (1982). The celluloid closet. *Cineaste, 12*(2), 2.

Guthmann, E. (1980). The cruising controversy. *Cineaste, 10*(2), 2.

H

Hachem, S. (1987, December 17). Inside the tinseled closet. *Advocate*, pp. 42-49.

Haddad-Garcia, G. (1980, December). Box office gaps. *In Touch for Men*, pp. 68-72.

Hall, R. (1985, December 24). The gay arts in 1985. *Advocate*, p. 52.

Hayles, N.K., & Dohrmann, K. (1980). The shadow of violence. *Journal of Popular Film, 8/2*, 2-8.

Hodges, B. (Ed.). (1975). Special Issue: Lesbian feminist writing and publishing. *Margins: A Review of Little Magazines and Small Press Books*. August.

Hohn, G. (1976). 'Dog Day' aftertaste. *Jump Cut, 10*, 2.

Holley, S. (1987, April 28). Annual AGLA awards: Tony show honors gay portrayals in media. *Advocate*, p. 36.

Holley, S. (1981, November 26). Gays in entertainment. *Advocate*, p. 5.

Horne, L. & Ramirez, H. (1984). Conference report: The UCLA gay and lesbian media conference. *Jump Cut, 29*, 66-68.

Howard, D., & Escoffier, J. (1978). Word is Out: An interview with the Mariposa film group, *Cineaste, 8/4*, 8.

Hulser, K. (1985, May). Gay old time (gay history film). *American Film*, p. 65.

J

Jack Paar apologizes for anti-gay remarks on TV. (1973, February 28). *Advocate*, p. 6.

Jahr, C. (1975, June 30). Gay movies for straight people. *Village Voice*, pp. 12-13.

Jay, K. (1975, August). A look at lesbian magazines. *Margins*, pp. 19-21.

K

Kilday, G. (1986, March/April). Hollywood's homosexuals. *Film Comment*, p. 40.
King, K. (1986). The situation of lesbianism as feminism's magical sign: Contests for meaning and the U.S. women's movement, 1968-1972. *Communication, 9/1*, 65-91.
Kleinhaus, C. (1977). Gays and film. *Jump Cut, 16*, 13.
Kleinhaus, C. (1985). Sexual representation. *Jump Cut, 30*, 23-43.
Kriedle, B. (1983, November 24). Monitor the media and talk back effectively. *Advocate*, p. 38.
Kroll, J. (1986, October). William Hurt and the curse of the spider man. *Esquire*, pp. 105-111.

L

Laermer, R. (1987, January 6, 1987). Lesbian lives and AIDS crisis dominate gay imagery on the tube. *Advocate*, p. 62.
Laermer, R. (1985, February 2). The televised gay: How we are pictured on the tube. *Advocate*, p. 21.
Landers, P. (1984, March 6). Lesbians and soap opera life. *Advocate*, p. 34.
LaValley, A. (1985, April). The great escape. *American Film*, pp. 29-34.
LaValley, A. (1984, September). Out of the closet and onto the screen. *American Film*, pp. 57-64.
Lesbian and Gay Media Advocates. (1982). *Talk back: The gay person's guide to media action*. Boston: Alyson Publications.
Lesbians zap Dick Cavett show. (1974, January 2). *Advocate*, p. 5.
Levine, R. (1984, October). Family affair (gays on TV). *Esquire*, p. 225.
Levine, R. (1981, May 30). How the gay lobby has changed television. *TV Guide*, pp. 2-6 (Part 2: 1981, June 6, pp. 49-54.)
Los Angeles Times breaks silence on homosexuality. (1972, February 16). *Advocate*, p. 6.

M

McDonald, B. (1985). *Cruising the movies: A sexual guide to "oldies" on TV*. New York: Gay Presses of New York.

MacBean, J.R. (1984). Between kitsch and fascism: Notes on Fassbinder, Pasolini and homosexual politics. *Cineaste, 13*(4), 12-19.

McHenry, F.A. (1941). A note of homosexuality, crime and the newspapers. *Journal of Criminal Psychopathology, 2(4)*, 533-548.

Marvin, J. (1974, August). The gay heroes of the movies. *Queens' Quarterly*, pp. 17-19, 42-46.

Marvin, J. (1973, August). The gay villains in the movies. *Queens' Quarterly*, pp. 13-17, 40-41.

Marvin, J. (1972, December). Homosexuality on television. *Queens' Quarterly*, pp. 13-15.

Marvin, J. (1972 October 25). Those TV fags — Friend or foe. *Advocate*, p. 28.

Maynor, J.S. (1980, November 15). Acid test for the fairness doctrine (Clash between gay rights groups and fundamentalist ministers.) *TV Guide*, pp. 16-20.

Medhurst, A. (1984, July/August). 'Victim': Text as context. *Screen*, pp. 22-35.

Mellen, J. (1973). Lesbianism in the movies. In J. Mellen (Ed.), *Women and their sexuality in the new film* (pp. 74-105). New York: Horizon Press.

Metromedia: Gay programming gains. (1974, March 13). *Advocate*, p. 19.

Montgomery, C. (1982, March 4). Making Love: Good politics but will it play. *Advocate*, p. 33.

Montgomery, K. (1981). Gay activists and the networks. *Journal of Communication, 31*, 49-57.

Montgomery, K. (1979). Gay activists and the networks: A case study of special interest pressure on television. (Doctoral dissertation, University of California at Los Angeles.) *Dissertation Abstracts International, 40*, 5236A.

Moore, G. (1977, May-June). Television turns vicarious — gays going down the tube? *Queens' Quarterly*, pp. 23-25.

Murphy, M. (1980, November 15). I felt a lot of rage (Billy Crystal plays gay character in TV's 'Soap'). *TV Guide*, pp. 30-34.

Myth, male fantasy and simulacra in *Mad Max* and *The Road Warrior*. (1985). *Journal of Popular Film and Television*, *13*(2), 80-91.

N

Nelson, J. (1985). Homosexuality in Hollywood films: A contemporary paradox. *Critical Studies in Mass Communication*, *2*(1), 54-64.

Nichols, W. (1983, September 10). Good and not so good TV coverage. *Gay Community News*, p. 6.

Nichols, W. (1983, August 18). Gay news, straight media. *Gay Community News*, p. 14.

Nicholson, J. (1982, March/April). Coming out at the *New York Post*. *Columbia Journalism Review*, p. 26-29.

O

Olson, R. (1979). Gay film work, affecting but evasive. *Jump Cut*, *20*, p. 9-12.

O'Loughlin, R. (1982, April 15). On the radio: The airways are cracking with messages of gay liberation. *Advocate*, pp. 50-52.

O'Loughlin, R. (1984, February 2). Getting the news for gay news radio. *Advocate*, p. 39.

O'Neil, S. (1984). The role of the mass media and other socialization agents in the identity formation of gay males. In S. Thomas (Ed.), *Studies in communication. Vol. 1: Studies in mass communication and technology* (pp. 201-206). Norwood, NJ: Ablex.

Orr, C. (1980, Spring). Ideology and narrative strategy in Bertolucci's 'The Conformist.' *Film Criticism*, p. 41.

P

Packman, D. (1977). Jack Smith's 'Flaming Creatures.' *Film Culture*, *63*, 51-56.

Pally, M. (1987, January 6). Independent gay cinema fills screens with more sophisticated realities. *Advocate*, p. 58.

Pally, M. (1983, December 6). Who's legit. *Village Voice*, p. 56.

Pally, M. (March/April 1986). Women in love. *Film Comment*, p. 35.

Park, J.C. (1979). An annotated bibliography of gay and lesbian communication studies. (ERIC Document Reproduction Service No ED 169 604).

Pearce, F. (1973). How to be immoral and ill, pathetic and dangerous, all at the same time: Mass media and the homosexual. In S. Cohen & J. Young (Eds.), *The manufacture of news* (pp. 103-117). Beverly Hills, CA: Sage.

Perigard, M. (1983, November 26). Misogyny on the tube. *Gay Community News*, p. 17.

Perew, T. (1974, May 8). Gays on TV not the real thing. *Advocate*, pp. 32,39.

Pierson, R. (1982, July 22). Gay news: How good are the mainstream media. *Advocate*, p. 25.

Pierson, R. (1982, March/April). Uptight on gay news. *Columbia Journalism Review*, p. 25-33.

Printers refuse to print gay articles. (1972, February 7). *Gay*, p. 3.

Purdon, N. (1976, September/October). Gay cinema. *Cinema Papers*, p. 115.

R

Raskin, R. (1981, December). Protecting the aural majority (Suit charging gay man with disseminating material harmful to minors over radio). *The Progressive*, p. 17.

Reaching the gay market. (1984, March 26). *Advertising Age*, p. 4.

Rich, B. (1984, July/August). Bay of pix. *American Film*, pp. 57-9.

Rich, B. (1981). From repressive tolerance to erotic liberation. *Jump Cut*, 24/25, 44-50.

Richards, M. (1982, May/June). The gay deception. *Film Comment*, p. 15.

Rist, D.Y. (1986, April). Fear and loving and AIDS. *Film Comment*, pp. 44-50.

Roddick, N. (1982, September). Gay cinema. *Sight and Sound*, p. 80.

Rowland, C. (1986, April 1). A question of standards: Gay cable network vision or compromise. *Advocate*, pp. 49-50.

Russo, V. (1986, April). A state of being. *Film Comment*, pp. 32-34.

Russo, V. (1981, August). Gay filmography. *In Touch for Men*, pp. 76-83.

Russo, V. (1984, January 24). Gay films: Gay reality vs. political correctness. *Advocate*, p. 38.

Russo, V. (1984, September 4). Profile of an epidemic. *Advocate*, p. 36.

Russo, V. (1981, 2nd ed. 1987). *The celluloid closet: Homosexuality in the movies*. New York: Harper and Row.

S

Saslow, J.M. (1981, December 10). Gay presses: Getting the word out. *Advocate*, pp. 31-31.

Schickel, R. (1982, October 22). Gays to the fore, cautiously. *Time*, p. 78.

Shively, C. (1975). Getting it together journalism: A view of 'Fag Rag.' In K. Jay and A. Young (Eds.), *After you're out: Personal experiences of gay men and lesbian women* (pp. 236-47). New York: Links Books.

Siebenand, P.A. (1975). The beginnings of gay cinema in Los Angeles: The industry and audience. (Doctoral dissertation, University of Southern California.) *Dissertation Abstracts International, 36*, 5605A.

Sikov, E. (1982). Homosexuals, bandits and gangsters. *Cineaste, 11*(4), 30.

Simms, S.A. (1981). Gay images on television. In J.W. Chesebro (Ed.), *Gayspeak: Gay male and lesbian communication* (pp. 153-162). New York: The Pilgrim Press.

Slater, D., & Copely, U.E. (Eds.). (1982). *Directory of homosexual organizations and publications*. (6th ed.). Los Angeles: Homosexual Information Center.

Spiegelman, W. (1982). Progress of a genre: Gay journalism and its audience. *Salmagundi, 58/59*, 308-325.

Stabiner, K. (1982, May 2). The homosexual market (Advertising). *New York Times Magazine*, p. 34.

Starr, M. (1971, September 1, September 15, October 13). Homosexuality in the movies. *Advocate*, p. 20; pp. 18-19; pp. 17-18.

Straayer, C. (1984). Lesbian/feminist audience. *Jump Cut, 29,* 40-44.

St. Joan, J. (1976). A survey of lesbian publications. In G. Vida (Ed.), *Our right to love: A lesbian resource book* (pp. 246-249). Englewood Cliffs, NJ: Prentice Hall.

Sutherland, A.T. (1978-1979). Setting up of nighthawks. *Sight and Sound, 48, 50-52.*

T

Tartaglia, J. (1979, Summer/Fall). The gay sensibility in American avant-garde film. *Millennium*, pp. 53-58.

Tavernier-Courbin, J. (1984). "La cage aux folles" as comedy of manners: From the play to the film. *Thalia, 7*(2), 44-50.

Thomas, S. (1986). Gender and social class coding in popular photographic erotica. *Communication Quarterly, 34/2,* 103-114.

Thompson, M. (1982, January 1). RFD: A gay magazine for the heartland. *Advocate*, p. 21.

Tjetje, L., & Schuler, G. (1980, Spring/Summer). Setting 'Cruising' straight. *Union Seminary Quarterly Review*, pp. 211-216.

Treichler, P.A. (1987). AIDS, homophobia and biomedical discourse: An epidemic of signification. *Cultural Studies, 1*(3).

Tucker, S. (1982). Sex, death and free speech: The fight to stop Friedkin's *Cruising*. In E. Jackson & S. Persky, (Eds.), *Flaunting it! A decade of gay journalism from the body politic* (pp. 197-206). Toronto: Pink Triangle Press.

Turtell, S. (1979, February 8). Emerald City, New York's Cable TV show for gays. *Advocate*, pp. 40-41.

Tyler, P. (1972). *Screening the sexes: Homosexuality in the movies*. New York: Holt, Rinehart and Winston.

V

Vandervelden, M. (1987, January 20). Alliance for gay and lesbian artists. *Advocate*, p. 10.

Vida, G. (1976). The lesbian image in the media. In G. Vida (Ed.),

Our right to love: A lesbian resource book (pp. 240-245). Englewood Cliffs, NJ: Prentice Hall.

W

Warren, S. (1975, November 19). Director Sidney Lumet talks about 'Dog Day Afternoon.' *Advocate*, p. 43.

Watney, S. (1982, September/October). Hollywood's homosexual world. *Screen*, pp. 107-121.

Watney, S. (1987). *Policing desire: Pornography, AIDS and the media*. Minneapolis: University of Minnesota Press.

Watney, S. (1986, January/February). The rhetoric of AIDS. *Screen*, pp. 72-85.

Waugh, T. (1977). Films by gays for gays. *Jump Cut, 16*, 14.

Waugh, T. (1985). Men's pornography: Gay versus straight. *Jump Cut, 30*, 30-35.

Whitmore, G. (1975, December 31). Gay: A media fad. *Advocate*, pp. 20-21.

Williams, L. (1982). Personal best: Women in love. *Jump Cut, 27*, 1.

Winter, A.D. (1977). *The gay press: A history of the gay community and its publications*. Austin, TX: Privately printed.

Wolcott, J. (1981, September 30). Sidney Schorr: (T.V.'s) gay babysitter. *Village Voice*, p. 54.

Wood, R. (1980, May). 'Cruising' and gay life. *Canadian Forum*, p. 41.

Wood, R. (1983). The homosexual subtext: Raging bull. *Australian Journal of Screen Theory, 15/16*, 57-66.

Wood, R. (1983, June). Is there camp after cruising. *Films and Filming*, pp. 26-29.

Wood, R. (1978, January). Responsibilities of a gay film critic. *Film Comment*, pp. 12-17.

Y

Young, A. (1973, November 7). Heterosexual press oppresses gays. *Advocate*, pp. 37, 40.

Young, I. (1978, May 31). Gay presses (c. 1980 to present). *Advocate*, pp. 28-29.

Z

Zimmerman, B. (1981). Lesbian vampires. *Jump Cut*, *24/25*, 23-24.

Fear — Deception — Irrationality (mixed media photographic print with oils) *and* We Watch Television (multiple negative silver print)

Gary Borgstedt, MFA

Gary Borgstedt is an artist and graphic designer. His mixed-media photography deals with social issues, including a series on AIDS and politics currently being exhibited around the United States; it was published in the *Village Voice*.

Correspondence may be sent to Gary Borgstedt, 577 Castro Street #302, San Francisco, CA 94114.

religious right and in
in their attempts to use fear, deception & irrationali-
        create a public health policy in their own image.
            the efforts of these groups
                    le for elected of-
ficials to try to exploit the fear of AIDS. Until the

Self-Fusion
(photograph)

Robin Parker Garcia

Robin Parker Garcia has been taking photographs for ten years, mostly in black and white, which is preferred "because of the interaction between light and chance."

Correspondence may be sent to Robin Parker Garcia, 2212 V Street #5, Sacramento, CA 95818.

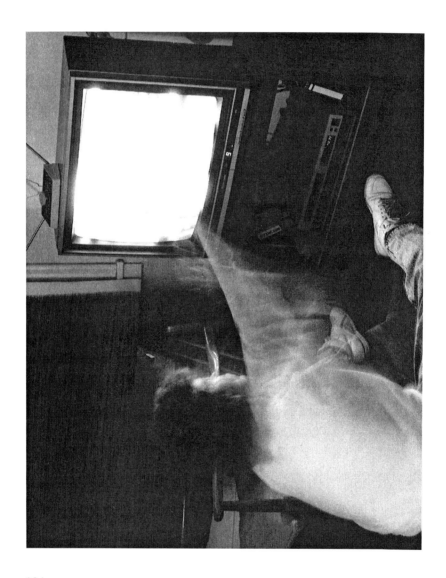